AMERICAN POETRY

1671-1928

AN ANTHOLOGY

AMERICAN POETRY

1671-1928

A COMPREHENSIVE
ANTHOLOGY

EDITED BY CONRAD AIKEN

THE MODERN LIBRARY · NEW YORK

Random House IS THE PUBLISHER OF

THE MODERN LIBRARY

BENNETT A. CERF · DONALD S. KLOPFER · ROBERT K. HAAS

Manufactured in the United States of America

Printed by Parkway Printing Company Bound by H. Wolff

PREFACE

AMERICAN poetry has been extensively anthologized; but so far as I am aware there has been no attempt hitherto to present in one volume a selection which shall represent the whole range of it, from its beginnings down to the present day. In a few text-books, it is true, one may find, along with prose selections also, a fairly adequate survey. But for some curious reason the notion of a compact and comprehensive anthology of the verse alone has not found expression. That such a thing should be useful goes without saying. That it should be difficult is obvious, too—almost as obvious as that the editor who undertakes it will inevitably make mistakes in judgment and will inevitably be reproached for them. At the very outset he faces the formidable question of proportion. How much space shall he give to "early" American poetry—the poetry of the seventeenth and eighteenth centuries? How much, in this regard, shall he allow himself to be weighed upon by purely historical considerations? Should the Connecticut wits—for example—be represented, simply on the ground that they existed, and that they enjoyed for a time a kind of popularity? Or should he frankly admit to himself that their work was almost wholly without æsthetic value, and ruthlessly exclude them?

The present editor has felt that the æsthetic judgment (whatever that may be, and however we may define it) is the only sound basis for procedure; and if now and then he has momentarily compromised with this principle, admitting here and there a poem merely because it has achieved an immense popularity, he has, on the whole, done this reluctantly and seldom. American poetry, if one takes it as a whole, is not yet a great or rich poetry, though it has shown not infrequently the elements of greatness and richness; it has been provincial, uneven, tentative, brilliant; but if one cannot as yet say that it takes a very high place in the poetry of the world, as the expression of a national soul or culture, one can at least say emphatically that the time has come for a firm revision of our critical attitude towards it. We are too much accustomed, I fear, to what one might term a high protective tariff in this matter. We are a little too willing to suspend or modify judgment, on the ground that too much was not to be expected of a pioneer people in a new continent. Insensibly, we have got into the habit of accepting the second-best; and by closing our eyes to the best,—by which I mean the best poetry of the world,—have found it not too difficult to persuade ourselves of the excellence of the native product.

It is time, I think, to give up this rather childish habit, and to regard American poetry as severely as we would regard Greek or Chinese or English poetry. For if American poetry is not yet great, it has at least reached that point at which one may say that it is mature. It has a history of nearly three hundred years. In sheer quantity, if one keep in mind all the minor poets and poetasters of the eighteenth and nineteenth centuries, it is enormous: few people, unless we except librarians, can have any idea of it. And if we admit cheerfully enough that the first two thirds of its history is pretty barren, nevertheless one can also say with some assurance that it now comprises names of which no country need be ashamed, and that it is beginning to wear the dignity that goes with a tradition.

In view of this, it has been the present editor's intention to be somewhat severer with his material than his predecessors have been, in order that the process of clarification of this tradition might take a step forward. He has been rather hard on certain national favorites; it will be thought by some that he has been too drastic with Longfellow and Holmes and Whittier and Lowell and Lanier; that he has been too generous with Poe and Whitman and Dickinson; and that he has perhaps erred in proportion by giving to the poetry of the last twenty years so much more space than has been given to that of any preceding era. To such an objection he can only reply that in his opinion the poetry which begins, roughly, with Emily Dickinson, has been the richest which America has produced; and that our so-called classics have been very seriously overestimated. If he can disturb prevailing notions about these things, and set in motion a revaluation of American poetry, which will find perhaps a higher place for comparatively unknown poets like Anne Bradstreet or Thomas Chivers or Trumbull Stickney than for Longfellow or Lowell or Bryant,—not, be it understood, in point of range, but in point of sheer excellence or intensity,—he will consider that he has been of some small service to American criticism. He has tried to eliminate, as far as possible, those things which embody the faults which so cursed American poetry in the nineteenth century—excessive sentimentality, sententiousness, easy dactylic exoticism—in order that the present movement in American poetry towards severer outline, both in idea and expression, might be more visible. If he has at all succeeded in this, he will have made one degree easier the ultimate compilation of a first-rate anthology by his successors.

CONRAD AIKEN.

ACKNOWLEDGMENTS

My thanks are due to the following for permission to reprint poems contained herein:

A. & C. Boni, Inc., for *Songs* by E. E. Cummings, from *Tulips & Chimneys.*

Cameron, Blake & Co. for *Day and Dark* by George Cabot Lodge, from *Poems.*

The Century Co. for *Ecce in Deserto* by Henry Augustin Beers, from *Collected Poems,* and for *Chanson of the Bells of Oseney* by Cale Young Rice, from *Wraiths and Realities.*

Copeland & Day for *The Happiest Heart* by John Vance Cheney, from *Out of the Silence,* and for *Clover* by John Banister Tabb, from *Lyrics.*

H. D. for *Not Honey,* from *Hymen.*

The Dial Press for poems by Marianne Moore, from *Observations.*

Funk & Wagnalls Co. for *Indirection* by Richard Realf, from *Poems.*

Harcourt, Brace & Co. for *Gone* by Carl Sandburg, from *Selected Poems; Nun Snow* by Alfred Kreymborg; *Long Feud* by Louis Untermeyer, from *Burning Bush;* and *You, Andrew Marvell* by Archibald MacLeish.

Harper & Bros. for poems by Edna St. Vincent Millay.

Henry Holt & Co. for poems by Robert Frost, from *A Boy's Will, North of Boston, Mountain Interval,* and *New Hampshire.*

Houghton Mifflin Co. for selections from Oliver Wendell Holmes, James Russell Lowell, Henry David Thoreau, Julia Ward Howe, Henry Wadsworth Longfellow, Ralph Waldo Emerson, Walt Whitman, Edward Rowland Sill, John Townsend Trowbridge, Thomas Bailey Aldrich, John Burroughs, William Vaughn Moody, Anna Hempstead Branch, Amy Lowell, H. D., John Gould Fletcher, and Archibald MacLeish.

A. A. Knopf, Inc., for *War is Kind* by Stephen Crane; poems by Elinor Wylie, from *Trivial Breath* and *Nets to Catch the Wind;* poems by Adelaide Crapsey, from *Verse;* poems by Wallace Stevens, from *Harmonium;* poems by T. S. Eliot, from *Poems;* and poems by John Crowe Ransom, from *Chills and Fever* and *Two Gentlemen in Bonds.*

Little, Brown & Co. for poems by Emily Dickinson, from *Poems: First Series, Poems: Second Series, Poems: Third Series* and *The Single Hound;* poems by Helen Hunt Jackson, from *Collected Poems;* and for *Hic Jacet* by Louise Chandler Moulton, from *Collected Poems.*

Horace Liveright for *They Went Forth to Battle* by Shaemas O'Sheel, from *Jealous of Dead Leaves;* poems by "H.D." from *A Sea Garden;* and poems by Ezra Pound, from *Personæ.*

Agnes Thompson Long for *Wild Honey* by Maurice Thompson.

The Macmillan Co. for poems by Trumbull Stickney, from *Poems;* poems by Edwin Arlington Robinson, from *Poems;* poems by Edgar Lee Masters, from *The Spoon River Anthology;* and poems by Vachel Lindsay, from *The Congo and Other Poems.*

Edwin Markham for *The Man with the Hoe,* from *Collected Poems.*

Princeton University Press for *L'Envoi* by Herman Melville, from *John Marr and Other Poems.*

Chas. Scribner's Sons for *Opposition* by Sidney Lanier, from *Collected Poems;* poems by George Santayana, from *Poems;* and *The Hermit of Carmel; For a Dead Lady* by Edwin Arlington Robinson, from *The Town Down the River;* and for *Earth* by John Hall Wheelock.

Stone & Kimball for *Odes* by George Santayana, from *Sonnets and Other Verses.*

The Viking Press for *The Image of Delight* by William Ellery Leonard, from *The Vaunt of Man.*

The Whitaker & Ray-Wiggin Co. for *At the Grave of Walker* by Joaquin Miller, from *Complete Poems.*

CONRAD AIKEN.

CONTENTS

Anne Bradstreet

THE FLESH AND THE SPIRIT

IN secret place where once I stood,
Close by the banks of lacrym flood,
I heard two sisters reason on
Things that are past and things to come.
One Flesh was called, who had her eye
On worldly wealth and vanity;
The other Spirit, who did rear
Her thoughts unto a higher sphere.
"Sister," quoth Flesh, "what livest thou on—
Nothing but meditation?
Doth contemplation feed thee, so
Regardlessly to let earth go?
Can speculation satisfy
Notion without reality?
Dost dream of things beyond the moon,
And dost thou hope to dwell there soon?
Hast treasures there laid up in store
That all in the world thou countest poor?
Art fancy sick, or turned a sot,
To catch at shadows which are not?
Come, come, I'll show unto thy sense
Industry hath its recompense.
What canst desire but thou mayst see
True substance in variety?
Dost honor like? Acquire the same,
As some to their immortal fame,
And trophies to thy name erect
Which wearing time shall ne'er deject.
For riches dost thou long full sore?
Behold enough of precious store;

Earth hath more silver, pearls, and gold
Than eyes can see or hands can hold.
Affectest thou pleasure? Take thy fill;
Earth hath enough of what you will.
Then let not go what thou mayst find
For things unknown, only in mind."

Spirit

"Be still, thou unregenerate part;
Disturb no more my settled heart,
For I have vowed, and so will do,
Thee as a foe still to pursue,
And combat with thee will and must
Until I see thee laid in the dust.
Sisters we are, yea, twins we be,
Yet deadly feud 'twixt thee and me;
For from one father are we not.
Thou by old Adam was begot,
But my arise is from above,
Whence my dear Father I do love.
Thou speakest me fair, but hatest me sore;
Thy flattering shows I'll trust no more.
How oft thy slave hast thou me made
When I believed what thou hast said,
And never had more cause of woe
Than when I did what thou bad'st do.
I'll stop mine ears at these thy charms,
And count them for my deadly harms.
Thy sinful pleasures I do hate,
Thy riches are to me no bait,
Thine honors do nor will I love,
For my ambition lies above.
My greatest honor it shall be
When I am victor over thee,
And triumph shall, with laurel head,
When thou my captive shalt be led.
How I do live thou needst not scoff,
For I have meat thou knowst not of:

The hidden manna I do eat,
The word of life it is my meat.
My thoughts do yield me more content
Than can thy hours in pleasure spent.
Nor are they shadows which I catch,
Nor fancies vain at which I snatch,
But reach at things that are so high
Beyond thy dull capacity.
Eternal substance I do see,
With which enrichéd I would be;
Mine eye doth pierce the heavens, and see
What is invisible to thee.
My garments are not silk or gold,
Nor such like trash which earth doth hold,
But royal robes I shall have on,
More glorious than the glistering sun.
My crown not diamonds, pearls, and gold,
But such as angels' heads enfold.
The city where I hope to dwell
There's none on earth can parallel:
The stately walls, both high and strong,
Are made of precious jasper stone;
The gates of pearl both rich and clear,
And angels are for porters there;
The streets thereof transparent gold,
Such as no eye did e'er behold;
A crystal river there doth run,
Which doth proceed from the Lamb's throne;
Of life there are the waters sure,
Which shall remain for ever pure;
Of sun or moon they have no need,
For glory doth from God proceed—
No candle there, nor yet torch-light,
For there shall be no darksome night.
From sickness and infirmity
For evermore they shall be free,
Nor withering age shall e'er come there,
But beauty shall be bright and clear.

This city pure is not for thee,
For things unclean there shall not be.
If I of Heaven may have my fill,
Take thou the world, and all that will."

CONTEMPLATIONS

SOME time now past in the Autumnal Tide,
When *Phœbus* wanted but one hour to bed,
The trees all richly clad, yet void of pride,
Were gilded o're by his rich golden head;
Their leaves & fruits seem'd painted, but was true
Of green, of red, of yellow, mixed hew;
Rapt were my sences at this delectable view.
I wist not what to wish; "yet sure," thought I,
"If so much excellence abide below,
How excellent is he that dwells on high,
Whose power and beauty by his works we know!
Sure he is goodness, wisdome, glory, light,
That hath this under-world so richly dight."
More Heaven then Earth was here, no winter & no night.

Then on a stately Oak I cast mine Eye,
Whose ruffling top the Clouds seem'd to aspire:
"How long since thou wast in thine Infancy?
Thy strength and stature, more thy years admire.
Hath hundred winters past since thou wast born,
Or thousand since thou brakest thy shell of horn?
If so, all these as nought Eternity doth scorn."

Then higher on the glistering Sun I gaz'd,
Whose beams was shaded by the leavie Tree.
The more I look'd the more I grew amaz'd,
And softly said: "What glory 's like to thee,
Soul of this world, this Universes Eye?
No wonder some made thee a Deity:
Had I not better known, alas. the same had I.

"Thou as a Bridegroom from thy Chamber rushes,
And as a strong man joyes to run a race;
The morn doth usher thee with smiles & blushes,
The Earth reflects her glances in thy face;
Birds, insects, Animals, with Vegative,
Thy heart from death and dulness doth revive,
And in the darksome womb of fruitful nature dive.

"Thy swift Annual and diurnal Course,
Thy daily streight and yearly oblique path,
Thy pleasing fervor and thy scorching force,
All mortals here the feeling knowledg hath.
Thy presence makes it day, thy absence night;
Quaternal Seasons caused by thy might.
Hail, Creature full of sweetness, beauty, & delight!

"Art thou so full of glory that no Eye
Hath strength thy shining Rayes once to behold?
And is thy splendid Throne erect so high
As to approach it can no earthly mould?
How full of glory, then, must thy Creator be
Who gave this bright light luster unto thee:
Admir'd, ador'd for ever be that Majesty!"

Silent, alone, where none or saw or heard,
In pathless paths I lead my wandring feet,
My humble Eyes to lofty Skyes I rear'd:
To sing some Song my mazed Muse thought meet;
My great Creator I would magnifie,
That nature had thus decked liberally;
But Ah, and Ah again, my imbecility!

I heard the merry grashopper then sing,
The black-clad Cricket bear a second part;
They kept one tune and plaid on the same string
Seeming to glory in their little Art.
Shall Creatures abject thus their voices raise,
And in their kind resound their makers praise,
Whilst I as mute can warble forth no higher layes?

When present times look back to Ages past,
And men in being fancy those are dead,
It makes things gone perpetually to last,
And calls back moneths and years that long since fled;
It makes a man more aged in conceit
Then was *Methuselah* or 's grand-sire great,
While of their persons & their acts his mind doth treat.

Sometimes in *Eden* fair he seems to be;
Sees glorious *Adam* there made Lord of all;
Fancyes the Apple dangle on the Tree,
That turn'd his Sovereign to a naked thral,
Who like a miscreant's driven from that place,
To get his bread with pain and sweat of face,
A penalty impos'd on his backsliding Race.

Here sits our Grandame in retired place,
And in her lap her bloody *Cain* new born;
The weeping Imp oft looks her in the face,
Bewails his unknown hap and fate forlorn:
His Mother sighs to think of Paradise,
And how she lost her bliss to be more wise,
Believing him that was and is Father of lyes.

Here *Cain* and *Abel* come to sacrifice;
Fruits of the Earth and Fatlings each do bring:
On *Abels* gift the fire descends from Skies,
But no such sign on false *Cain's* offering.
With sullen hateful looks he goes his wayes,
Hath thousand thoughts to end his brothers dayes,
Upon whose blood his future good he hopes to raise.

There *Abel* keeps his sheep, no ill he thinks;
His brother comes, then acts his fratricide:
The Virgin Earth of blood her first draught drinks,
But since that time she often hath been cloy'd.
The wretch, with gastly face and dreadful mind,
Thinks each he sees will serve him in his kind,
Though none on Earth but kindred near then could he find.

Who fancyes not his looks now at the Barr?
His face like death, his heart with horror fraught,
Nor Male-factor ever felt like warr
When deep dispair with wish of life hath fought.
Branded with guilt and crusht with treble woes,
A Vagabond to Land of *Nod* he goes;
A City builds, that wals might him secure from foes.

Who thinks not oft upon the Fathers ages?
Their long descent; how nephews sons they saw;
The starry observations of those Sages,
And how their precepts to their sons were law;
How Adam sigh'd to see his Progeny
Cloath'd all in his black sinfull Livery,
Who neither guilt nor yet the punishment could fly.

Our Life compare we with their length of dayes;
Who to the tenth of theirs doth now arrive?
And though thus short, we shorten many wayes,
Living so little while we are alive:
In eating, drinking, sleeping, vain delight,
So unawares comes on perpetual night,
And puts all pleasures vain unto eternal flight.

When I behold the heavens as in their prime,
And then the earth, though old, stil clad in green
The stones and trees insensible of time,
Nor age nor wrinkle on their front are seen;
If winter come and greeness then do fade,
A Spring returns and they more youthfull made;
But Man grows old, lies down, remains where once he's laid.

By birth more noble then those creatures all,
Yet seems by nature and by custome curs'd:
No sooner born but grief and care makes fall,
That state obliterate he had at first;
Nor youth nor strength nor wisdom spring again,
Nor habitations long their names retain,
But in oblivion to the final day remain.

Shall I, then, praise the heavens, the trees, the earth,
Because their beauty and their strength last longer?
Shall I wish there or never to had birth,
Because they 're bigger, & their bodyes stronger?
Nay, they shall darken, perish, fade, and dye,
And when unmade so ever shall they lye;
But man was made for endless immortality.

Under the cooling shadow of a stately Elm,
Close sate I by a goodly Rivers side,
Where gliding streams the Rocks did overwhelm;
A lonely place, with pleasures dignifi'd.
I once that lov'd the shady woods so well
Now thought the rivers did the trees excel;
And if the sun would ever shine, there would I dwell.

While on the stealing stream I fixt mine eye,
Which to the long'd for Ocean held its course,
I markt nor crooks nor rubs that there did lye
Could hinder ought, but still augment its force:
"Oh happy Flood," quoth I, "that holds thy race
Till thou arrive at thy beloved place,
Nor is it rocks or shoals that can obstruct thy pace.

"Nor is 't enough that thou alone may'st slide,
But hundred brooks in thy cleer waves do meet;
So hand in hand along with thee they glide
To *Thetis* house, where all imbrace and greet:
Thou Emblem true of what I count the best,
O could I lead my Rivolets to rest,
So may we press to that vast mansion ever blest!

"Ye Fish which in this liquid Region 'bide,
That for each season have your habitation,
Now salt, now fresh, where you think best to glide
To unknown coasts to give a visitation,
In Lakes and ponds you leave your numerous fry;
So nature taught, and yet you know not why,
You watry folk that know not your felicity.

"Look how the wantons frisk to tast the air,
Then to the colder bottome streight they dive;
Eftsoon to *Neptune*'s glassie Hall repair,
To see what trade they great ones there do drive,
Who forage o're the spacious sea-green field
And take the trembling prey before it yield,
Whose armour is their scales, their spreading fins
their shield."

While musing thus, with contemplation fed,
And thousand fancies buzzing in my brain,
The sweet-tongu'd Philomel percht ore my head,
And chanted forth a most melodious strain;
Which rapt me so with wonder and delight
I judg'd my hearing better then my sight,
And wisht me wings with her a while to take my flight.

"O merry Bird," said I, "that fears no snares,
That neither toyles nor hoards up in thy barn,
Feels no sad thoughts, nor cruciating cares
To gain more good or shun what might thee harm;
Thy cloaths ne're wear, thy meat is every where,
Thy bed a bough, thy drink the water cleer;
Reminds not what is past, nor whats to come dost fear.

"The dawning morn with songs thou dost prevent,
Sets hundred notes unto thy feathered crew,
So each one tunes his pretty instrument
And, warbling out the old, begin anew;
And thus they pass their youth in summer season,
Then follow thee into a better Region,
Where winter 's never felt by that sweet airy legion."

Man at the best a creature frail and vain,
In knowledg ignorant, in strength but weak,
Subject to sorrows, losses, sickness, pain,
Each storm his state, his mind, his body break;
From some of these he never finds cessation,
But day or night, within, without, vexation,
Troubles from foes from friends, from dearest, near'st
Relation.

And yet this sinfull creature, frail and vain,
This lump of wretchedness, of sin and sorrow,
This weather-beaten vessel wrackt with pain,
Joyes not in hope of an eternal morrow;
Nor all his losses, crosses, and vexation,
In weight, in frequency and long duration,
Can make him deeply groan for that divine Translation.

The Mariner that on smooth waves doth glide
Sings merrily and steers his Barque with ease,
As if he had command of wind and tide,
And now become great Master of the seas;
But suddenly a storm spoiles all the sport,
And makes him long for a more quiet port,
Which 'gainst all adverse winds may serve for fort.

So he that saileth in this world of pleasure,
Feeding on sweets, that never bit of th' sowre,
That 's full of friends, of honour, and of treasure,
Fond fool, he takes this earth ev'n for heav'ns bower.
But sad affliction comes & makes him see
Here's neither honour, wealth, nor safety:
Only above is found all with security.

O Time, the fatal wrack of mortal things,
That draws oblivions curtains over kings,
Their sumptuous monuments, men know them not,
Their names without a Record are forgot,
Their parts, their ports, their pomp's all laid in th' dust,
Nor wit nor gold nor buildings scape times rust:
But he whose name is grav'd in the white stone
Shall last and shine when all of these are gone.

A LETTER TO HER HUSBAND

PHŒBUS, make haste: the day 's too long; be gone;
The silent night 's the fittest time for moan
But stay this once, unto my suit give ear,
And tell my griefs in either Hemisphere;

And if the whirling of thy wheels don't drown'd
The woful accents of my doleful sound,
If in thy swift Carrier thou canst make stay,
I crave this boon, this Errand by the way:
Commend me to the man more lov'd then life;
Shew him the sorrows of his widdowed wife,
My dumpish thoughts, my groans, my brakish tears,
My sobs, my longing hopes, my doubting fears;
And if he love, how can he there abide?
My interest 's more then all the world beside.
He that can tell the starrs or Ocean sand,
Or all the grass that in the Meads do stand,
The leaves in th' woods, the hail or drops of rain,
Or in a corn-field number every grain,
Or every mote that in the sun-shine hops,
May count my sighs and number all my drops.
Tell him the countless steps that thou dost trace
That once a day thy Spouse thou mayst imbrace;
And when thou canst not treat by loving mouth,
Thy rayes afar salute her from the south.
But for one moneth I see no day, poor soul,
Like those far scituate under the pole,
Which day by day long wait for thy arise:
O how they joy when thou dost light the skyes.
O *Phœbus,* hadst thou but thus long from thine
Restrain'd the beams of thy beloved shine,
At thy return, if so thou could'st or durst,
Behold a Chaos blacker then the first.
Tell him here 's worse then a confused matter—
His little world 's a fathom under water;
Nought but the fervor of his ardent beams
Hath power to dry the torrent of these streams.
Tell him I would say more, but cannot well:
Oppressed minds abruptest tales do tell.
Now post with double speed, mark what I say;
By all our loves conjure him not to stay.

LONGING FOR HEAVEN

AS weary pilgrim now at rest
    Hugs with delight his silent nest,
His wasted limbes now lye full soft
    That myrie steps have troden oft,
Blesses himself to think upon
    his dangers past and travailes done;
The burning sun no more shall heat,
    Nor stormy raines on him shall beat;
The bryars and thornes no more shall scratch,
    nor hungry wolves at him shall catch;
He erring pathes no more shall tread,
    nor wild fruits eate in stead of bread;
For waters cold he doth not long,
    for thirst no more shall parch his tongue;
No rugged stones his feet shall gaule,
    nor stumps nor rocks cause him to fall;
All cares and feares he bids farwell,
    and meanes in safity now to dwell:
A pilgrim I on earth perplext,
    with sinns, with cares and sorrows vext,
By age and paines brought to decay,
    and my Clay house mouldring away,
Oh how I long to be at rest
    and soare on high among the blest!
This body shall in silence sleep,
    Mine eyes no more shall ever weep,
No fainting fits shall me assaile,
    nor grinding paines my body fraile,
With cares and fears ne'r cumbred be,
    Nor losses know nor sorrowes see.
What tho my flesh shall there consume?
    it is the bed Christ did perfume;
And when a few yeares shall be gone,
    this mortall shall be cloth'd upon:
A Corrupt Carcasse downe it lyes,
    a glorious body it shall rise;

In weaknes and dishonour sowne,
in power 't is rais'd by Christ alone.
Then soule and body shall unite,
and of their maker have the sight.
Such lasting joyes shall there behold
as eare ne'r heard nor tongue e'er told.
Lord, make me ready for that day:
then Come, deare bridgrome, Come away!

Thomas Godfrey

THE INVITATION

DAMON. Haste, Sylvia, haste, my charming maid!
Let 's leave these fashionable toys:
Let's seek the shelter of some shade,
And revel in ne'er fading joys.
See, *Spring* in liv'ry gay appears,
And winter's chilly blasts are fled;
Each grove its leafy honours rears,
And meads their lovely verdure spread.

Sylvia. Yes, Damon, glad I 'll quit the town:
It's gaieties now languid seem:
Then sweets to luxury unknown
We 'll taste, and sip th' untainted stream.
In *Summer*'s sultry noon-tide heat
I 'll lead thee to the shady grove,
There hush thy cares, or pleas'd repeat
Those vows that won my soul to love.

Damon. When o'er the mountain peeps the dawn,
And round her ruddy beauties play,
I'll wake my love to view the lawn,
Or hear the warblers hail the day.
But without thee the rising morn
In vain awakes the cooling breeze;
In vain does nature's face adorn—
Without my Sylvia nought can please.

Sylvia. At night, when universal gloom
Hides the bright prospects from our view,
When the gay groves give up their bloom
And verdant meads their lovely hue,
Tho' fleeting spectres round me move,
When in thy circling arms I 'm prest,
I 'll hush my rising fears with love,
And sink in slumber on thy Breast.

Damon. The new-blown rose, whilst on its leaves
Yet the bright scented dew-drop 's found,
Pleas'd on thy bosom whilst it heaves,
Shall shake its heav'nly fragrance round.
Then mingled sweets the sense shall raise,
Then mingled beauties catch the eye:
What pleasure on such charms to gaze,
What rapture 'mid such sweets to lie!

Sylvia. How sweet thy words! But, Damon, cease,
Nor strive to fix me ever here;
Too well you know these accents please,
That oft have fill'd my ravish'd ear.
Come, lead me to these promis'd joys
That dwelt so lately on thy tongue;
Direct me by thy well-known voice,
And calm my transports with thy song!

Philip Freneau

FROM "THE HOUSE OF NIGHT"

TREMBLING I write my dream, and recollect
A fearful vision at the midnight hour;
So late, death o'er me spreads his signal wings,
Painted with fancies of malignant power!

Such was the dream the sage Chaldean saw
Disclos'd to him that felt heaven's vengeful rod,
Such was the ghost, who through deep silence cry'd,
Shall mortal man—be juster than his God?

Let others draw from smiling skies their theme,
And tell of climes that boast unfading light,
I draw a darker scene, replete with gloom,
I sing the horrors of the *House of Night.*

Stranger, believe the truth experience tells,
Poetic dreams are of a finer cast
Than those which o'er the sober brain diffused,
Are but a repetition of some action past.

Fancy, I own thy power—when sunk in sleep
Thou play'st thy wild delusive part so well
You lift me into immortality,
Depict new heavens, or draw the scenes of hell.

By some sad means, when Reason holds no sway,
Lonely I rov'd at midnight o'er a plain
Where murmuring streams and mingling rivers flow
Far to their springs or seek the sea again.

Sweet vernal May! tho' then thy woods in bloom
Flourish'd, yet nought of this could Fancy see;
No wild pinks bless'd the meads, no green the fields,
And naked seem'd to stand each lifeless tree.

Dark was the sky, and not one friendly star
Shone from the zenith or horizon, clear;
Mist sate upon the woods, and darkness rode
In her black chariot with a wild career.

And from the woods the late-resounding note
Issued of the loquacious *Whip-poor-will;*
Hoarse, howling dogs and nightly roving wolves
Clamour'd from far-off clifts invisible.

Rude from the wide-extended *Chesapeke*
I heard the winds the dashing waves assail,
And saw from far, by picturing fancy form'd,
The black ship travelling through the noisy gale.

At last, by chance and guardian fancy led,
I reach'd a noble dome rais'd fair and high,
And saw the light from upper windows flame,
Presage of mirth and hospitality.

And by that light around the dome appear'd
A mournful garden of autumnal hue;
Its lately pleasing flowers all drooping stood
Amidst high weeds that in rank plenty grew.

The Primrose there, the violet darkly blue,
Daisies and fair Narcissus ceas'd to rise;
Gay spotted pinks their charming bloom withdrew,
And Polyanthus quench'd its thousand dyes.

No pleasant fruit or blossom gaily smil'd;
Nought but unhappy plants and trees were seen:
The yew, the myrtle, and the church-yard elm,
The cypress with its melancholy green.

There cedars dark, the osier, and the pine,
Shorn tamarisks, and weeping willows grew,
The poplar tall, the lotos, and the lime;
And pyracantha did her leaves renew.

The poppy there, companion to repose,
Display'd her blossoms that began to fall;
And here the purple amaranthus rose,
With mint strong-scented, for the funeral.

And here and there, with laurel shrubs between,
A tombstone lay, inscrib'd with strains of woe;
And stanzas sad, throughout the dismal green,
Lamented for the dead that slept below.

Peace to this awful dome!—when strait I heard
The voice of men in a secluded room;
Much did they talk of death and much of life,
Of coffins, shrouds, and horrors of a tomb. . . .

Then up three winding stairs my feet were brought
To a high chamber, hung with mourning sad;
The unsnuff'd candles glar'd with visage dim,
'Midst grief in ecstasy of woe run mad.

A wide-leaf'd table stood on either side,
Well fraught with phials, half their liquids spent;
And from a couch behind the curtain's veil
I heard a hollow voice of loud lament.

Turning to view the object whence it came,
My frighted eyes a horrid form survey'd
(*Fancy, I own thy power*): Death on the couch,
With fleshless limbs, at rueful length, was laid.

And o'er his head flew jealousies and cares,
Ghosts, imps, and half the black Tartarian crew,
Arch-angels damn'd; nor was their Prince remote,
Borne on the vaporous wings of Stygian dew.

Around his bed, by the dull flambeaux' glare,
I saw pale phantoms: Rage to madness vext,
Wan, wasting grief, and ever-musing care,
Distressful pain, and poverty perplext.

Sad was his countenance—if we can call
That *countenance* where only bones were seen—
And eyes sunk in their sockets, dark and low,
And teeth that only show'd themselves to grin.

Reft was his scull of hair, and no fresh bloom
Of chearful mirth sate on his visage hoar:
Sometimes he rais'd his head, while deep-drawn groans
Were mixt with words that did his fate deplore.

Oft did he wish to see the daylight spring;
And often toward the window lean'd to hear,
Fore-runner of the scarlet-mantled morn,
The early note of wakeful *Chanticleer*. . . .

Then with a hollow voice thus went he on:
"Get up and search, and bring, when found, to me
Some cordial, potion, or some pleasant draught,
Sweet, slumb'rous poppy or the mild Bohea.

"But hark, my pitying friend!—and if you can,
Deceive the grim physician at the door—
Bring half the mountain springs—ah, hither bring
The cold rock-water from the shady bower;

"For till this night such thirst did ne'er invade,
A thirst provok'd by heav'n's avenging hand:
Hence bear me, friends, to quaff and quaff again
The cool wave bubbling from the yellow sand.

"To these dark walls with stately step I came,
Prepar'd your drugs and doses to defy;
Smit with the love of never-dying fame,
I came, alas! to conquer—not to die!"

Glad, from his side I sprang and fetch'd the draught,
Which down his greedy throat he quickly swills;
Then on a second errand sent me strait,
To search in some dark corner for his pills.

Quoth he, "These pills have long compounded been
Of dead men's bones and bitter roots, I trow;
But that I may to wonted health return
Throughout my lank veins shall their substance go."

So down they went.—He rais'd his fainting head,
And oft in feeble tone essay'd to talk:
Quoth he, "Since remedies have small avail,
Assist unhappy Death once more to walk."

Then, slowly rising from his loathsome bed,
On wasted legs the meagre monster stood,
Gap'd wide, and foam'd, and hungry seem'd to ask,
Tho' sick, an endless quantity of food.

Said he, "The sweet melodious flute prepare,
The anthem, and the organ's solemn sound,
Such as may strike my soul with ecstacy,
Such as may from yon' lofty walls rebound.

"Sweet music can the fiercest pains assuage:
She bids the soul to heav'n's blest mansions rise;
She calms despair, controuls infernal rage;
And deepest anguish, when it hears her, dies.

"And see, the mizzling, misty midnight reigns,
And no soft dews are on my eye-lids sent:
Here, stranger, lend thy hand, assist me, pray,
To walk a circuit of no large extent."

On my prest shoulders leaning, round he went,
And could have made the boldest spectre flee.
I led him up stairs, and I led him down,
But not one moment's rest from pain got he. . . .

Up rush'd a band, with compasses and scales
To measure his slim carcase, long and lean.
"Be sure," said he, "to frame my coffin strong,
You, master workman, and your men, I mean;

"For if the Devil, so late my trusty friend,
Should get one hint where I am laid, from you,
Not with my soul content, he 'd seek to find
That mouldering mass of bones, my body, too!

"Of hardest ebon let the plank be found,
With clamps and ponderous bars secur'd around,
That if the box by Satan should be storm'd
It may be able for resistance found."

"Yes," said the master workman, "noble Death,
Your coffin shall be strong—that leave to me;
But who shall these your funeral dues discharge?
Nor friends nor pence you have, that I can see."

To this said Death, "You might have ask'd me, too,
Base caitiff, who are my executors,
Where my estate, and who the men that shall
Partake my substance and be call'd my heirs.

"Know, then, that hell is my inheritance;
The devil himself my funeral dues must pay:
Go—since you must be paid—go ask of him,
For he has gold, as fabling poets say."

Strait they retir'd—when thus he gave me charge,
Pointing from the light window to the west:
"Go three miles o'er the plain, and you shall see
A burying-yard of sinners dead, unblest.

"Amid the graves a spiry building stands,
Whose solemn knell resounding through the gloom
Shall call thee o'er the circumjacent lands
To the dull mansion destin'd for my tomb.

"There, since 't is dark, I 'll plant a glimmering light
Just snatch'd from hell, by whose reflected beams
Thou shalt behold a tomb-stone, full eight feet,
Fast by a grave replete with ghosts and dreams.

"And on that stone engrave this epitaph,
Since Death, it seems, must die like mortal men;
Yes, on that stone engrave this epitaph,
Though all hell's furies aim to snatch the pen:—

"Death in this tomb his weary bones hath laid,
Sick of dominion o'er the human kind:
Behold what devastations he hath made;
Survey the millions by his arm confin'd.

"Six thousand years has sovereign sway been mine;
None but myself can real glory claim:
Great Regent of the world I reign'd alone,
And princes trembled when my mandate came.

"Vast and unmatch'd throughout the world, my fame
Takes place of gods, and asks no mortal date—
No, by myself and by the heavens I swear
Not Alexander's name is half so great.

"Nor swords nor darts my prowess could withstand;
All quit their arms and bow'd to my decree:
Even mighty Julius *died beneath my hand,*
For slaves and Cesars were the same to me.

"Traveller, wouldst thou his noblest trophies seek,
Search in no narrow spot obscure for those;
The sea profound, the surface of all land,
Is moulded with the myriads of his foes." . . .

O'er a dark field I held my dubious way,
Where Jack-a-lanthorn walk'd his lonely round;
Beneath my feet substantial darkness lay,
And screams were heard from the distemper'd ground.

Nor look'd I back, till to a far-off wood,
Trembling with fear, my weary feet had sped:
Dark was the night, but at the inchanted dome
I saw the infernal windows flaming red.

And from within the howls of Death I heard,
Cursing the dismal night that gave him birth,
Damning his ancient sire and mother sin,
Who at the gates of hell, accursed, brought him forth.

(For fancy gave to my enraptur'd soul
An eagle's eye, with keenest glance to see;
And bade those distant sounds distinctly roll,
Which, waking, never had affected me.)

Oft his pale breast with cruel hand he smote,
And, tearing from his limbs a winding-sheet,
Roar'd to the black skies, while the woods around,
As wicked as himself, his words repeat.

Thrice tow'rd the skies his meagre arms he rear'd,
Invok'd all hell and thunders on his head,
Bid light'nings fly, earth yawn, and tempests roar,
And the sea wrap him in its oozy bed.

"My life for one cool draught! O, fetch your springs!
Can one unfeeling to my woes be found?
No friendly visage comes to my relief,
But ghosts impend and spectres hover round.

"Though humbled now, dishearten'd, and distrest,
Yet, when admitted to the peaceful ground,
With heroes, kings, and conquerors I shall rest,
Shall sleep as safely and perhaps as sound."

Dim burnt the lamp; and now the phantom Death
Gave his last groans in horror and despair:
"All hell demands me hence!" he said, and threw
The red lamp hissing through the midnight air.

Trembling, across the plain my course I held,
And found the grave-yard, loitering through the gloom,
And in the midst a hell-red, wandering light,
Walking in fiery circles round the tomb. . . .

At distance far, approaching to the tomb,
By lamps and lanthorns guided through the shade,
A coal-black chariot hurried through the gloom,
Spectres attending, in black weeds array'd,

Whose woeful forms yet chill my soul with dread:
Each wore a vest in Stygian chambers wove,
Death's kindred all—Death's horses they bestrode,
And gallop'd fiercely, as the chariot drove.

Each horrid face a grizly mask conceal'd;
Their busy eyes shot terror to my soul
As now and then, by the pale lanthorn's glare,
I saw them for their parted friend condole.

Before the herse Death's chaplain seem'd to go,
Who strove to comfort, what he could, the dead;
Talk'd much of *Satan* and the land of woe,
And many a chapter from the scriptures read.

At last he rais'd the swelling anthem high;
In dismal numbers seem'd he to complain:
The captive tribes that by *Euphrates* wept,
Their song was jovial to his dreary strain.

That done, they plac'd the carcase in the tomb,
To dust and dull oblivion now resign'd;
Then turn'd the chariot tow'rd the House of Night,
Which soon flew off and left no trace behind.

THE INDIAN BURYING GROUND

IN spite of all the learned have said,
  I still my old opinion keep:
The *posture* that *we* give the dead
  Points out the soul's eternal sleep.

Not so the ancients of these lands:
  The Indian, when from life released,
Again is seated with his friends,
  And shares again the joyous feast.

His imaged birds and painted bowl,
  And venison for a journey dressed,
Bespeak the nature of the soul—
  ACTIVITY that knows no rest.

His bow for action ready bent,
  And arrows with a head of stone,
Can only mean that life is spent,
  And not the old ideas gone.

Thou, stranger, that shalt come this way,
No fraud upon the dead commit:
Observe the swelling turf, and say,
"They do not *lie,* but here they *sit.*"

Here still a lofty rock remains,
On which the curious eye may trace
(Now wasted, half, by wearing rains)
The fancies of a ruder race.

Here still an aged elm aspires,
Beneath whose far-projecting shade
(And which the shepherd still admires)
The children of the forest played.

There oft a restless Indian queen,
Pale *Shebah,* with her braided hair,
And many a barbarous form is seen,
To chide the man that lingers there.

By midnight moons, o'er moistening dews,
In habit for the chase arrayed,
The hunter still the deer pursues,
The hunter and the deer a shade.

And long shall timorous fancy see
The painted chief and pointed spear,
And Reason's self shall bow the knee
To shadows and delusions here.

SONG OF THYRSIS

THE turtle on yon withered bough,
That lately mourned her murdered mate,
Has found another comrade now—
Such changes all await!
Again her drooping plume is drest,
Again she's willing to be blest
And takes her lover to her nest.

If nature has decreed it so
With all above, and all below,
Let us like them forget our woe,
And not be killed with sorrow.
If I should quit your arms to-night
And chance to die before 't was light,
I would advise you—and you might—
Love again to-morrow.

Richard Henry Dana

THE LITTLE BEACH-BIRD

THOU little bird, thou dweller by the sea,
Why takest thou its melancholy voice,
And with that boding cry
Why o'er the waves dost fly?
O, rather, bird, with me
Through the fair land rejoice!

Thy flitting form comes ghostly dim and pale,
As driven by a beating storm at sea;
Thy cry is weak and scared,
As if thy mates had shared
The doom of us. Thy wail,—
What doth it bring to me?

Thou call'st along the sand, and haunt'st the surge
Restless and sad; as if, in strange accord
With the motion and the roar
Of waves that drive to shore,
One spirit did ye urge—
The Mystery—the Word.

Of thousands, thou, both sepulcher and pall,
Old Ocean! A requiem o'er the dead,
From out thy gloomy cells,
A tale of mourning tells,—

Tells of man's woe and fall,
  His sinless glory fled.

Then turn thee, little bird, and take thy flight
  Where the complaining sea shall sadness bring
    Thy spirit nevermore.
    Come, quit with me the shore,
For gladness and the light,
  Where birds of summer sing.

William Cullen Bryant

TO A WATERFOWL

WHITHER, midst falling dew,
  While glow the heavens with the last steps of day,
Far, through their rosy depths, dost thou pursue
  Thy solitary way?

  Vainly the fowler's eye
Might mark thy distant flight to do thee wrong,
As, darkly painted on the crimson sky,
  Thy figure floats along.

  Seek'st thou the plashy brink
Of weedy lake, or marge of river wide,
Or where the rocking billows rise and sink
  On the chafed ocean-side?

  There is a Power whose care
Teaches thy way along that pathless coast,—
The desert and illimitable air,—
  Lone wandering, but not lost.

  All day thy wings have fanned
At that far height, the cold, thin atmosphere,
Yet stoop not, weary, to the welcome land,
  Though the dark night is near.

And soon that toil shall end;
Soon shalt thou find a summer home, and rest,
And scream among thy fellows; reeds shall bend
Soon, o'er thy sheltered nest.

Thou'rt gone, the abyss of heaven
Hath swallowed up thy form; yet, on my heart
Deeply hath sunk the lesson thou hast given,
And shall not soon depart.

He who, from zone to zone,
Guides through the boundless sky thy certain flight,
In the long way that I must tread alone,
Will lead my steps aright.

THANATOPSIS

To him who in the love of nature holds
Communion with her visible forms, she speaks
A various language; for his gayer hours
She has a voice of gladness, and a smile
And eloquence of beauty, and she glides
Into his darker musings, with a mild
And healing sympathy, that steals away
Their sharpness, ere he is aware. When thoughts
Of the last bitter hour come like a blight
Over thy spirit, and sad images
Of the stern agony, and shroud, and pall,
And breathless darkness, and the narrow house,
Make thee to shudder and grow sick at heart;—
Go forth, under the open sky, and list
To Nature's teachings, while from all around—
Earth and her waters, and the depths of air—
Comes a still voice:—

Yet a few days, and thee
The all-beholding sun shall see no more
In all his course; nor yet in the cold ground,

Where thy pale form was laid, with many tears,
Nor in the embrace of ocean, shall exist
Thy image. Earth, that nourished thee, shall claim
Thy growth, to be resolved to earth again,
And, lost each human trace, surrendering up
Thine individual being, shalt thou go
To mix forever with the elements,
To be a brother to the insensible rock
And to the sluggish clod, which the rude swain
Turns with his share, and treads upon. The oak
Shall send his roots abroad and pierce thy mold.

Yet not to thine eternal resting-place
Shalt thou retire alone, nor couldst thou wish
Couch more magnificent. Thou shalt lie down
With patriarchs of the infant world—with kings,
The powerful of the earth—the wise, the good,
Fair forms, and hoary seers of ages past,
All in one mighty sepulcher. The hills,
Rock-ribbed and ancient as the sun,—the vales
Stretching in pensive quietness between;
The venerable woods—rivers that move
In majesty, and the complaining brooks
That make the meadows green; and, poured round all,
Old Ocean's gray and melancholy waste,—
Are but the solemn decorations all
Of the great tomb of man. The golden sun,
The planets, all the infinite host of heaven,
Are shining on the sad abodes of death
Through the still lapse of ages. All that tread
The globe are but a handful to the tribes
That slumber in its bosom.—Take the wings
Of morning, pierce the Barcan wilderness,
Or lose thyself in the continuous woods
Where rolls the Oregon, and hears no sound
Save his own dashings—yet the dead are there:
And millions in those solitudes, since first
The flight of years began, have laid them down
In their last sleep—the dead reign there alone.

So shalt thou rest, and what if thou withdraw
In silence from the living, and no friend
Take note of thy departure? All that breathe
Will share thy destiny. The gay will laugh
When thou art gone, the solemn brood of care
Plod on, and each one as before will chase
His favorite phantom; yet all these shall leave
Their mirth and their employments, and shall come
And make their bed with thee. As the long train
Of ages glides away, the sons of men—
The youth in life's fresh spring, and he who goes
In the full strength of years, matron and maid,
The speechless babe, and the gray-headed man—
Shall one by one be gathered to thy side,
By those who in their turn shall follow them.

So live, that when thy summons comes to join
The innumerable caravan, which moves
To that mysterious realm, where each shall take
His chamber in the silent halls of death,
Thou go not, like the quarry-slave at night,
Scourged to his dungeon, but, sustained and soothed
By an unfaltering trust, approach thy grave
Like one who wraps the drapery of his couch
About him, and lies down to pleasant dreams.

"OH FAIREST OF THE RURAL MAIDS"

OH fairest of the rural maids!
Thy birth was in the forest shades;
Green boughs, and glimpses of the sky,
Were all that met thine infant eye.

Thy sports, thy wanderings, when a child,
Were ever in the sylvan wild;
And all the beauty of the place
Is in thy heart and on thy face.

The twilight of the trees and rocks
Is in the light shade of thy locks;
Thy step is as the wind, that weaves
Its playful way among the leaves.

Thine eyes are springs, in whose serene
And silent waters heaven is seen;
Their lashes are the herbs that look
On their young figures in the brook.

The forest depths, by foot unpressed,
Are not more sinless than thy breast;
The holy peace, that fills the air
Of those calm solitudes, is there.

TO THE FRINGED GENTIAN

THOU blossom bright with autumn dew,
And colored with the heaven's own blue,
That openest when the quiet light
Succeeds the keen and frosty night.

Thou comest not when violets lean
O'er wandering brooks and springs unseen,
Or columbines, in purple dressed,
Nod o'er the ground-bird's hidden nest.

Thou waitest late and com'st alone,
When woods are bare and birds are flown,
And frosts and shortening days portend
The aged year is near his end.

Then doth thy sweet and quiet eye
Look through its fringes to the sky,
Blue—blue—as if that sky let fall
A flower from its cerulean wall.

I would that thus, when I shall see
The hour of death draw near to me,
Hope, blossoming within my heart,
May look to heaven as I depart.

Edgar Allan Poe

SONNET—TO SCIENCE

SCIENCE, true daughter of Old Time thou art!
Who alterest all things with thy peering eyes.
Why preyest thou thus upon the poet's heart,
Vulture, whose wings are dull realities?
How should he love thee, or how deem thee wise,
Who wouldst not leave him in his wandering
To seek for treasure in the jewelled skies,
Albeit he soared with an undaunted wing?
Hast thou not dragged Diana from her car,
And driven the Hamadryad from the wood
To seek a shelter in some happier star?
Hast thou not torn the Naiad from her flood,
The Elfin from the green grass, and from me
The summer dream beneath the tamarind tree?

SONG FROM "AL AARAAF"

NEATH blue-bell or streamer,
Or tufted wild spray
That keeps from the dreamer
The moonbeam away,
Bright beings that ponder,
With half-closing eyes,
On the stars which your wonder
Hath drawn from the skies,
'Till they glance thro' the shade and
Come down to your brow

Like eyes of the maiden
  Who calls on you now,—
Arise from your dreaming
  In violet bowers,
To duty beseeming
  These star-litten hours,
And shake from your tresses
  Encumber'd with dew
The breath of those kisses
  That cumber them too
(Oh, how, without you, Love,
  Could angels be blest?)—
Those kisses of true love
  That lull'd ye to rest!
Up! shake from your wing
  Each hindering thing:
The dew of the night—
  It would weigh down your flight;
And true-love caresses—
  O, leave them apart;
They are light on the tresses,
  But lead on the heart.
Ligeia! Ligeia!
  My beautiful one!
Whose harshest idea
  Will to melody run,
O, is it thy will
  On the breezes to toss?
Or, capriciously still,
  Like the lone Albatross,
Incumbent on night
  (As she on the air)
To keep watch with delight
  On the harmony there?
Ligeia, wherever
  Thy image may be,
No magic shall sever
  Thy music from thee!
Thou hast bound many eyes

In a dreamy sleep;
But the strains still arise
Which *thy* vigilance keep:
The sound of the rain
Which leaps down to the flower,
And dances again
In the rhythm of the shower,
The murmur that springs
From the growing of grass,
Are the music of things—
But are modell'd, alas!
Away, then, my dearest,
O, hie thee away
To springs that lie clearest
Beneath the moon-ray;
To lone lake that smiles,
In its dream of deep rest,
At the many star-isles
That enjewel its breast.
Where wild flowers, creeping,
Have mingled their shade,
On its margin is sleeping
Full many a maid;
Some have left the cool glade, and
Have slept with the bee:
Arouse them, my maiden,
On the moorland and lea;
Go, breathe on their slumber,
All softly in ear,
The musical number
They slumber'd to hear;
For what can awaken
An angel so soon,
Whose sleep hath been taken
Beneath the cold moon,
As the spell which no slumber
Of witchery may test,
The rhythmical number
Which lull'd him to rest?

TO HELEN

HELEN, thy beauty is to me
  Like those Nicean barks of yore,
That gently, o'er a perfumed sea,
  That weary, way-worn wanderer bore
  To his own native shore.

On desperate seas long wont to roam,
  Thy hyacinth hair, thy classic face,
Thy Naiad airs have brought me home
  To the glory that was Greece
  And the grandeur that was Rome.

Lo, in yon brilliant window-niche
  How statue-like I see thee stand,
The agate lamp within thy hand!
  Ah, Psyche, from the regions which
  Are Holy Land!

ISRAFEL

IN Heaven a spirit doth dwell
  "Whose heart-strings are a lute":
None sing so wildly well
As the angel Israfel,
And the giddy stars (so legends tell),
Ceasing their hymns, attend the spell

  Of his voice, all mute.
Tottering above
  In her highest noon,
  The enamoured moon
Blushes with love,
  While, to listen, the red levin
  (With the rapid Pleiades, even,
  Which were seven)
  Pauses in Heaven.

And they say (the starry choir
  And the other listening things)
That Israfeli's fire
Is owing to that lyre
  By which he sits and sings—
The trembling living wire
  Of those unusual strings.

But the skies that angel trod,
  Where deep thoughts are a duty,
Where Love 's a grown-up God,
  Where the Houri glances are
Imbued with all the beauty
  Which we worship in a star.

Therefore thou art not wrong,
  Israfeli, who despisest
An unimpassioned song:
To thee the laurels belong,
  Best bard because the wisest;
Merrily live, and long!

The ecstasies above
  With thy burning measures suit—
Thy grief, thy joy, thy hate, thy love,
  With the fervour of thy lute:
  Well may the stars be mute!
Yes, Heaven is thine; but this
  Is a world of sweets and sours:
  Our flowers are merely—flowers,
And the shadow of thy perfect bliss
  Is the sunshine of ours.

If I could dwell
Where Israfel
  Hath dwelt, and he where I,
He might not sing so wildly well
  A mortal melody,
While a bolder note than this might swell
  From my lyre within the sky.

THE CITY IN THE SEA

LO, Death has reared himself a throne
In a strange city lying alone
Far down within the dim West,
Where the good and the bad and the worst and the best
Have gone to their eternal rest.
There shrines and palaces and towers
(Time-eaten towers that tremble not!)
Resemble nothing that is ours.
Around, by lifting winds forgot,
Resignedly beneath the sky
The melancholy waters lie.
No rays from the holy heaven come down
On the long night-time of that town;
But light from out the lurid sea
Streams up the turrets silently—
Gleams up the pinnacles far and free—
Up domes—up spires—up kingly halls—
Up fanes—up Babylon-like walls—
Up shadowy long-forgotten bowers
Of sculptured ivy and stone flowers—
Up many and many a marvellous shrine
Whose wreathèd friezes intertwine
The viol, the violet, and the vine.
Resignedly beneath the sky
The melancholy waters lie.
So blend the turrets and shadows there
That all seem pendulous in air,
While from a proud tower in the town
Death looks gigantically down.
There open fanes and gaping graves
Yawn level with the luminous waves;
But not the riches there that lie
In each idol's diamond eye,
Not the gaily-jewelled dead
Tempt the waters from their bed:
For no ripples curl, alas,
Along that wilderness of glass;

No swellings tell that winds may be
Upon some far-off happier sea;
No heavings hint that winds have been
On scenes less hideously serene.
But, lo, a stir is in the air!
The wave—there is a movement there,
As if the towers had thrust aside,
In slightly sinking, the dull tide,
As if their tops had feebly given
A void within the filmy Heaven!
The waves have now a redder glow;
The hours are breathing faint and low;
And when, amid no earthly moans,
Down, down that town shall settle hence,
Hell, rising from a thousand thrones,
Shall do it reverence.

THE SLEEPER

AT midnight, in the month of June,
I stand beneath the mystic moon.
An opiate vapour, dewy, dim,
Exhales from out her golden rim,
And softly dripping, drop by drop,
Upon the quiet mountain top,
Steals drowsily and musically
Into the universal valley.
The rosemary nods upon the grave;
The lily lolls upon the wave;
Wrapping the fog about its breast,
The ruin moulders into rest;
Looking like Lethe, see, the lake
A conscious slumber seems to take,
And would not, for the world, awake.
All Beauty sleeps! And, lo, where lies
Irene, with her Destinies!
Oh, lady bright, can it be right—
This window open to the night?

The wanton airs, from the tree-top,
Laughingly through the lattice drop—
The bodiless airs, a wizard rout,
Flit through thy chamber in and out,
And wave the curtain canopy
So fitfully—so fearfully—
Above the closed and fringèd lid
'Neath which thy slumb'ring soul lies hid,
That, o'er the floor and down the wall,
Like ghosts the shadows rise and fall!
Oh, lady dear, hast thou no fear?
Why and what art thou dreaming here?
Sure thou art come o'er far-off seas,
A wonder to these garden trees!
Strange is thy pallor! strange thy dress!
Strange, above all, thy length of tress,
  And this all solemn silentness!
  The lady sleeps! Oh, may her sleep,
Which is enduring, so be deep!
Heaven have her in its sacred keep!
This chamber changed for one more holy,
This bed for one more melancholy,
I pray to God that she may lie
Forever with unopened eye,
While the pale sheeted ghosts go by!
  My love, she sleeps! Oh, may her sleep,
As it is lasting, so be deep!
Soft may the worms about her creep!
Far in the forest, dim and old,
For her may some tall vault unfold—
Some vault that oft hath flung its black
And wingèd panels fluttering back,
Triumphant, o'er the crested palls,
Of her grand family funerals—
Some sepulchre, remote, alone,
Against whose portal she hath thrown,
In childhood, many an idle stone—
Some tomb from out whose sounding door
She ne'er shall force an echo more,

Thrilling to think, poor child of sin,
It was the dead who groaned within.

TO ONE IN PARADISE

THOU wast all that to me, love,
For which my soul did pine—
A green isle in the sea, love,
A fountain and a shrine,
All wreathed with fairy fruits and flowers,
And all the flowers were mine.

Ah, dream too bright to last!
Ah, starry Hope, that didst arise
But to be overcast!
A voice from out the Future cries,
"On! on!"—but o'er the Past
(Dim gulf!) my spirit hovering lies
Mute, motionless, aghast!

For, alas, alas, with me
The light of Life is o'er!
"No more—no more—no more—"
(Such language holds the solemn sea
To the sands upon the shore)
Shall bloom the thunder-blasted tree,
Or the stricken eagle soar!

And all my days are trances,
And all my nightly dreams
Are where thy grey eye glances,
And where thy footstep gleams—
In what ethereal dances,
By what eternal streams.

THE HAUNTED PALACE

IN the greenest of our valleys
  By good angels tenanted,
Once a fair and stately palace—
  Radiant palace—reared its head.
In the monarch Thought's dominion,
  It stood there;
Never seraph spread a pinion
  Over fabric half so fair!

Banners yellow, glorious, golden,
  On its roof did float and flow
(This—all this—was in the olden
  Time long ago);
And every gentle air that dallied,
  In that sweet day,
Along the ramparts plumed and pallid,
  A wingèd odor went away.

Wanderers in that happy valley,
  Through two luminous windows, saw
Spirits moving musically,
  To a lute's well-tunèd law,
Round about a throne where, sitting
  (Porphyrogene!)
In state his glory well befitting,
  The ruler of the realm was seen.

And all with pearl and ruby glowing
  Was the fair palace door,
Through which came flowing, flowing, flowing,
  And sparkling evermore,
A troop of Echoes, whose sweet duty
  Was but to sing,
In voices of surpassing beauty,
  The wit and wisdom of their king.

But evil things, in robes of sorrow,
  Assailed the monarch's high estate.
(Ah, let us mourn! for never morrow
  Shall dawn upon him desolate!)
And round about his home the glory
  That blushed and bloomed
Is but a dim-remembered story
  Of the old time entombed.

And travellers now, within that valley,
  Through the red-litten windows see
Vast forms, that move fantastically
  To a discordant melody;
While, like a ghastly rapid river,
  Through the pale door
A hideous throng rush out forever
  And laugh—but smile no more.

THE CONQUEROR WORM

LO, 'tis a gala night
  Within the lonesome latter years;
An angel throng, bewinged, bedight
  In veils, and drowned in tears,
Sit in a theater, to see
  A play of hopes and fears,
While the orchestra breathes fitfully
  The music of the spheres.

Mimes, in the form of God on high,
  Mutter and mumble low,
And hither and thither fly—
  Mere puppets they, who come and go
At bidding of vast formless things
  That shift the scenery to and fro,
Flapping from out their Condor wings
  Invisible wo!

That motley drama, oh, be sure
It shall not be forgot!
With its Phantom chased for evermore
By a crowd that seize it not,
Through a circle that ever returneth in
To the self-same spot,
And much of Madness, and more of Sin,
And Horror the soul of the plot.

But see, amid the mimic rout
A crawling shape intrude!
A blood-red thing that writhes from out
The scenic solitude!
It writhes! it writhes! with mortal pangs
The mimes become its food,
And seraphs sob at vermin fangs
In human gore imbued.

Out, out are the lights—out all!
And over each quivering form
The curtain, a funeral pall,
Comes down with the rush of a storm;
While the angels, all pallid and wan,
Uprising, unveiling, affirm
That the play is the tragedy "Man,"
And its hero the Conqueror Worm.

THE RAVEN

ONCE upon a midnight dreary, while I pondered, weak and weary,
Over many a quaint and curious volume of forgotten lore,
While I nodded, nearly napping, suddenly there came a tapping,
As of some one gently rapping, rapping at my chamber door.
"'T is some visitor," I muttered, "tapping at my chamber door—
Only this and nothing more."

Ah, distinctly I remember it was in the bleak December,
And each separate dying ember wrought its ghost upon the floor.
Eagerly I wished the morrow; vainly I had sought to borrow
From my books surcease of sorrow—sorrow for the lost Lenore,
For the rare and radiant maiden whom the angels name Lenore—
Nameless *here* for evermore

And the silken, sad, uncertain rustling of each purple curtain
Thrilled me—filled me with fantastic terrors never felt before;
So that now, to still the beating of my heart, I stood repeating,
" 'T is some visitor entreating entrance at my chamber door—
Some late visitor entreating entrance at my chamber door—
This it is and nothing more."

Presently my soul grew stronger: hesitating then no longer,
"Sir," said I, "or Madam, truly your forgiveness I implore;
But the fact is I was napping, and so gently you came rapping,
And so faintly you came tapping, tapping at my chamber door,
That I scarce was sure I heard you"—here I opened wide the door—
Darkness there and nothing more.

Deep into that darkness, peering, long I stood there, wondering, fearing,
Doubting, dreaming dreams no mortal ever dared to dream before;
But the silence was unbroken, and the stillness gave no token,
And the only word there spoken was the whispered word "Lenore!"
This I whispered, and an echo murmured back the word "Lenore!"
Merely this and nothing more.

Back into the chamber turning, all my soul within me
burning,
Soon again I heard a tapping, somewhat louder than before.
"Surely," said I, "surely that is something at my window
lattice;
Let me see, then, what thereat is, and this mystery explore,—
Let my heart be still a moment and this mystery explore—
'T is the wind and nothing more."

Open here I flung the shutter, when, with many a flirt and
flutter,
In there stepped a stately Raven of the saintly days of yore.
Not the least obeisance made he, not a minute stopped or
stayed he,
But with mien of lord or lady perched above my chamber
door—
Perched upon a bust of Pallas just above my chamber door—
Perched and sat, and nothing more.

Then, this ebony bird beguiling my sad fancy into smiling
By the grave and stern decorum of the countenance it wore,
"Though thy crest be shorn and shaven, thou," I said, "art
sure no craven,
Ghastly, grim, and ancient Raven, wandering from the
Nightly shore:
Tell me what thy lordly name is on the Night's Plutonian
shore!"
Quoth the Raven, "Nevermore."

Much I marvelled this ungainly fowl to hear discourse so
plainly,
Though its answer little meaning, little revelancy, bore;
For we cannot help agreeing that no living human being
Ever yet was blessed with seeing bird above his chamber
door—
Bird or beast upon the sculptured bust above his chambered
door—
With such name as "Nevermore."

But the Raven, sitting lonely on the placid bust, spoke only
That one word, as if his soul in that one word he did outpour.
Nothing farther then he uttered, not a feather then he fluttered;
Till I scarcely more than muttered, "Other friends have flown before;
On the morrow *he* will leave me, as my Hopes have flown before."
Then the bird said, "Nevermore."

Startled at the stillness broken by reply so aptly spoken,
"Doubtless," said I, "what it utters is its only stock and store,
Caught from some unhappy master whom unmerciful Disaster
Followed fast and followed faster till his songs one burden bore,
Till the dirges of his Hope that melancholy burden bore
Of 'Never—nevermore.'"

But the Raven still beguiling my sad fancy into smiling,
Straight I wheeled a cushioned seat in front of bird and bust and door;
Then, upon the velvet sinking, I betook myself to linking
Fancy unto fancy, thinking what this ominous bird of yore,
What this grim, ungainly, ghastly, gaunt, and ominous bird of yore,
Meant in croaking "Nevermore."

This I sat engaged in guessing, but no syllable expressing
To the fowl whose fiery eyes now burned into my bosom's core;
This and more I sat divining, with my head at ease reclining
On the cushion's velvet lining that the lamp-light gloated o'er,
But whose velvet violet lining, with the lamp-light gloating o'er,
She shall press, ah, nevermore!

Then, methought, the air grew denser, perfumed from an
unseen censer
Swung by seraphim whose footfalls tinkled on the tufted floor.
"Wretch!" I cried, "thy God hath lent thee, by these angels
he hath sent thee,
Respite—respite and nepenthe from thy memories of Lenore!
Quaff, oh quaff this kind nepenthe, and forget this lost
Lenore!"
Quoth the Raven, "Nevermore."

"Prophet!" said I, "thing of evil! prophet still, if bird or devil!
Whether Tempter sent, or whether tempest tossed thee here
ashore,
Desolate yet all undaunted, on this desert land enchanted—
On this home by Horror haunted—tell me truly, I implore,
Is there—*is* there balm in Gilead?—tell me—tell me, I
implore!"
Quoth the Raven, "Nevermore."

"Prophet!" said I, "thing of evil! prophet still, if bird or devil!
By that Heaven that bends above us—by that God we both
adore—
Tell this soul with sorrow laden if, within the distant Aidenn,
It shall clasp a sainted maiden whom the angels name
Lenore—
Clasp a rare and radiant maiden whom the angels name
Lenore."
Quoth the Raven, "Nevermore."

"Be that word our sign of parting, bird or fiend!" I shrieked,
upstarting;
"Get thee back into the tempest and the Night's Plutonian
shore!
Leave no black plume as a token of that lie thy soul hath
spoken!
Leave my loneliness unbroken!—quit the bust above my
door!
Take thy beak from out my heart, and take thy form from
off my door!"
Quoth the Raven, "Nevermore."

And the Raven, never flitting, still is sitting, *still* is sitting
On the pallid bust of Pallas just above my chamber door;
And his eyes have all the seeming of a demon's that is
dreaming,
And the lamp-light o'er him streaming throws his shadow
on the floor;
And my soul from out that shadow that lies floating on the
floor

Shall be lifted—nevermore!

ULALUME

THE skies they were ashen and sober,
The leaves they were crispèd and sere—
The leaves they were withering and sere;
It was night in the lonesome October
Of my most immemorial year;
It was hard by the dim lake of Auber,
In the misty mid region of Weir—
It was down by the dank tarn of Auber,
In the ghoul-haunted woodland of Weir.

Here once, through an alley Titanic
Of cypress, I roamed with my Soul—
Of cypress, with Psyche, my Soul.
These were days when my heart was volcanic
As the scoriac rivers that roll—
As the lavas that restlessly roll
Their sulphurous currents down Yaanek,
In the ultimate climes of the pole—
That groan as they roll down Mount Yaanek,
In the realms of the boreal pole.

Our talk had been serious and sober,
But our thoughts they were palsied and sere—
Our memories were treacherous and sere,—
For we knew not the month was October,

And we marked not the night of the year
(Ah, night of all nights in the year!)—
We noted not the dim lake of Auber
(Though once we had journeyed down here)—
Remembered not the dank tarn of Auber,
Nor the ghoul-haunted woodland of Weir.

And now, as the night was senescent
And star-dials pointed to morn—
As the star-dials hinted of morn,—
At the end of our path a liquescent
And nebulous lustre was born,
Out of which a miraculous crescent
Arose with a duplicate horn—
Astarte's bediamonded crescent
Distinct with its duplicate horn.

And I said: "She is warmer than Dian:
She rolls through an ether of sighs—
She revels in a region of sighs;
She has seen that the tears are not dry on
These cheeks, where the worm never dies,
And has come past the stars of the Lion
To point us the path to the skies—
To the Lethean peace of the skies,—
Come up, in despite of the Lion,
To shine on us with her bright eyes—
Come up through the lair of the Lion,
With love in her luminous eyes."

But Psyche, uplifting her finger,
Said: "Sadly this star I mistrust—
Her pallor I strangely mistrust:—
Oh, hasten!—oh, let us not linger!
Oh, fly! let us fly!—for we must."
In terror she spoke, letting sink her
Wings until they trailed in the dust—
In agony sobbed, letting sink her
Plumes till they trailed in the dust—
Till they sorrowfully trailed in the dust.

I replied: "This is nothing but dreaming:
  Let us on by this tremulous light!
  Let us bathe in this crystalline light!
Its Sibyllic splendor is beaming
  With Hope and in Beauty to-night—
  See! it flickers up the sky through the night!
Ah, we safely may trust to its gleaming,
  And be sure it will lead us aright—
We safely may trust to a gleaming
  That cannot but guide us aright,
  Since it flickers up to Heaven through the night."

Thus I pacified Psyche, and kissed her,
  And tempted her out of her gloom—
  And conquered her scruples and gloom;
And we passed to the end of the vista,
  But were stopped by the door of a tomb—
  By the door of a legended tomb;
And I said: "What is written, sweet sister,
  On the door of this legended tomb?"
  She replied: "Ulalume—Ulalume—
  'T is the vault of thy lost Ulalume!"

Then my heart it grew ashen and sober
  As the leaves that were crispèd and sere—
  As the leaves that were withering and sere;
And I cried: "It was surely October
  On *this* very night of last year
  That I journeyed—I journeyed down here,—
  That I brought a dread burden down here:
  On this night of all nights in the year,
  Ah, what demon has tempted me here?
Well I know, now, this dim lake of Auber—
  This misty mid region of Weir,—
Well I know, now, this dank tarn of Auber—
  This ghoul-haunted woodland of Weir."

ANNABEL LEE

IT was many and many a year ago,
In a kingdom by the sea,
That a maiden there lived whom you may know
By the name of ANNABEL LEE;
And this maiden she lived with no other thought
Than to love and be loved by me.

I was a child and *she* was a child,
In this kingdom by the sea;
But we loved with a love that was more than love—
I and my ANNABEL LEE—
With a love that the wingèd seraphs of heaven
Coveted her and me.

And this was the reason that, long ago,
In this kingdom by the sea,
A wind blew out of a cloud, chilling
My beautiful ANNABEL LEE;
So that her high-born kinsmen came
And bore her away from me,
To shut her up in a sepulchre
In this kingdom by the sea.

The angels, not half so happy in heaven,
Went envying her and me—
Yes! that was the reason (as all men know,
In this kingdom by the sea)
That the wind came out of the cloud by night,
Chilling and killing my ANNABEL LEE.

But our love it was stronger by far than the love
Of those who were older than we—
Of many far wiser than we;
And neither the angels in heaven above,
Nor the demons down under the sea,
Can ever dissever my soul from the soul
Of the beautiful ANNABEL LEE:

For the moon never beams without bringing me dreams
  Of the beautiful ANNABEL LEE;
And the stars never rise but I feel the bright eyes
  Of the beautiful ANNABEL LEE;
And so, all the night-tide, I lie down by the side
Of my darling—my darling—my life and my bride,
  In the sepulchre there by the sea,
  In her tomb by the sounding sea.

ELDORADO

GAILY bedight,
  A gallant knight,
In sunshine and in shadow,
  Had journeyed long,
  Singing a song,
In search of Eldorado.

  But he grew old—
  This knight so bold,—
And o'er his heart a shadow
  Fell as he found
  No spot of ground
That looked like Eldorado.

  And, as his strength
  Failed him at length,
He met a pilgrim shadow.
  "Shadow," said he,
  "Where can it be—
This land of Eldorado?"
  "Over the Mountains
  Of the Moon,
Down the Valley of the Shadow,
  Ride, boldly ride,"
  The shade replied,
"If you seek for Eldorado!"

ROMANCE

ROMANCE, who loves to nod and sing,
With drowsy head and folded wing,
Among the green leaves as they shake
Far down within some shadowy lake,
To me a painted paroquet
Hath been—a most familiar bird—
Taught me my alphabet to say—
To lisp my very earliest word
While in the wild wood I did lie,
A child—with a most knowing eye.

Of late, eternal Condor years
So shake the very Heaven on high
With tumult as they thunder by,
I have no time for idle cares
Through gazing on the unquiet sky.
And when an hour with calmer wings
Its down upon my spirit flings—
That little time with lyre and rhyme
To while away—forbidden things!
My heart would feel to be a crime
Unless it trembled with the strings.

A DREAM WITHIN A DREAM

TAKE this kiss upon the brow!
And, in parting from you now,
Thus much let me avow—
You are not wrong, who deem
That my days have been a dream;
Yet if hope has flown away
In a night, or in a day,
In a vision, or in none,
Is it therefore the less *gone?*
All that we see or seem
Is but a dream within a dream.

I stand amid the roar
Of a surf-tormented shore,
And I hold within my hand
Grains of the golden sand—
How few! yet how they creep
Through my fingers to the deep,
While I weep—while I weep!
O God! can I not grasp
Them with a tighter clasp?
O God! can I not save
One from the pitiless wave?
Is *all* that we see or seem
But a dream within a dream?

LENORE

AH, broken is the golden bowl! the spirit flown forever!
Let the bell toll!—a saintly soul floats on the Stygian river,
And, Guy De Vere, hast *thou* no tear?—weep now or never more!
See! on yon drear and rigid bier low lies thy love, Lenore!
Come! let the burial rite be read—the funeral song be sung!—
An anthem for the queenliest dead that ever died so young—
A dirge for her the doubly dead in that she died so young.

"Wretches! ye loved her for her wealth and hated her for her pride,
"And when she fell in feeble health, ye blessed her—that she died!
"How *shall* the ritual, then, be read?—the requiem how be sung
"By you—by yours, the evil eye,—by yours, the slanderous tongue
"That did to death the innocence that died, and died so young?"

Peccavimus; but rave not thus! and let a Sabbath song
Go up to God so solemnly the dead may feel no wrong!

The sweet Lenore hath "gone before," with Hope, that flew beside,
Leaving thee wild for the dear child that should have been thy bride—
For her, the fair and *debonair,* that now so lowly lies,
The life upon her yellow hair but not within her eyes—
The life still there, upon her hair—the death upon her eyes.

"Avaunt! to-night my heart is light. No dirge will I upraise.
"But waft the angel on her flight with a pæan of old days!
"Let *no* bell toll!—lest her sweet soul, amid its hallowed mirth,
"Should catch the note, as it doth float up from the damnèd Earth.
"To friends above, from fiends below, the indignant ghost is riven—
"From Hell unto a high estate far up within the Heaven—
"From grief and groan, to a golden throne, beside the King of Heaven."

DREAM-LAND

BY a route obscure and lonely,
Haunted by ill angels only,
Where an Eidolon, named NIGHT,
On a black thone reigns upright,
I have reached these lands but newly
From an ultimate dim Thule—
From a wild weird clime that lieth, sublime,
Out of SPACE—out of TIME.

Bottomless vales and boundless floods,
And chasms, and caves, and Titan woods,
With forms that no man can discover
For the tears that drip all over;
Mountains toppling evermore
Into seas without a shore;
Seas that restlessly aspire,
Surging, unto skies of fire;

Lakes that endlessly outspread
Their lone waters—lone and dead,—
Their still waters—still and chilly
With the snows of the lolling lily.

By the lakes that thus outspread
Their lone waters, lone and dead,—
Their sad waters, sad and chilly
With the snows of the lolling lily,—
By the mountains—near the river
Murmuring lowly, murmuring ever,—
By the grey woods,—by the swamp
Where the toad and the newt encamp,—
By the dismal tarns and pools
  Where dwell the Ghouls,—
By each spot the most unholy—
In each nook most melancholy,—
There the traveller meets, aghast,
Sheeted Memories of the Past—
Shrouded forms that start and sigh
As they pass the wanderer by
White-robed forms of friends long given,
In agony, to the Earth—and Heaven.

For the heart whose woes are legion
'Tis a peaceful, soothing region—
For the spirit that walks in shadow
'Tis—oh 'tis an Eldorado!
But the traveller, travelling through it,
May not—dare not openly view it;
Never its mysteries are exposed
To the weak human eye unclosed;
So wills its King, who hath forbid
The uplifting of the fringèd lid;
And thus the sad Soul that here passes
Beholds it but through darkened glasses.

By a route obscure and lonely,
Haunted by ill angels only,

Where an Eidolon, named NIGHT,
On a black throne reigns upright,
I have wandered home but newly
From this ultimate dim Thule.

FOR ANNIE

THANK Heaven! the crisis—
The danger is past,
And the lingering illness
Is over at last—
And the fever called "Living"
Is conquered at last.

Sadly, I know
I am shorn of my strength,
And no muscle I move
As I lie at full length—
But no matter!—I feel
I am better at length.

And I rest so composedly
Now, in my bed,
That any beholder
Might fancy me dead—
Might start at beholding me,
Thinking me dead.

The moaning and groaning,
The sighing and sobbing,
Are quieted now,
With that horrible throbbing
At heart:—ah that horrible,
Horrible throbbing!

The sickness—the nausea—
The pitiless pain—
Have ceased with the fever

That maddened my brain—
With the fever called "Living"
That burned in my brain.

And oh! of all tortures
That torture the worst
Has abated—the terrible
Torture of thirst
For the napthaline river
Of Passion accurst:—
I have drank of a water
That quenches all thirst:—

Of a water that flows,
With a lullaby sound,
From a spring but a very few
Feet under ground—
From a cavern not very far
Down under ground.

And ah! let it never
Be foolishly said
That my room it is gloomy
And narrow my bed;
For a man never slept
In a different bed—
And, to sleep, you must slumber
In just such a bed.

My tantalized spirit
Here blandly reposes,
Forgetting, or never
Regretting, its roses—
Its old agitations
Of myrtles and roses:

For now, while so quietly
Lying, it fancies
A holier odor
About it, of pansies—

A rosemary odor,
  Commingled with pansies—
With rue and the beautiful
  Puritan pansies.

And so it lies happily,
  Bathing in many
A dream of the truth
  And the beauty of Annie—
Drowned in a bath
  Of the tresses of Annie.

She tenderly kissed me,
  She fondly caressed,
And then I fell gently
  To sleep on her breast—
Deeply to sleep
  From the heaven of her breast.

When the light was extinguished,
  She covered me warm,
And she prayed to the angels
  To keep me from harm—
To the queen of the angels
  To shield me from harm.

And I lie so composedly,
  Now, in my bed,
(Knowing her love)
  That you fancy me dead—
And I rest so contentedly,
  Now, in my bed,
(With her love at my breast)
  That you fancy me dead—
That you shudder to look at me,
  Thinking me dead:—

But my heart it is brighter
  Than all of the many

Stars of the sky,
For it sparkles with Annie—
It glows with the light
Of the love of my Annie—
With the thought of the light
Of the eyes of my Annie.

Edward Coate Pinkney

A SERENADE

LOOK out upon the stars, my love,
And shame them with thine eyes,
On which, than on the lights above,
There hang more destinies.
Night's beauty is the harmony
Of blending shades and light;
Then, lady, up,—look out, and be
A sister to the night!

Sleep not! thine image wakes for aye
Within my watching breast:
Sleep not! from her soft sleep should fly
Who robs all hearts of rest.
Nay, lady, from thy slumbers break,
And make this darkness gay
With looks, whose brightness well might make
Of darker nights a day.

VOTIVE SONG

I BURN no incense, hang no wreath,
On this thine early tomb:
Such cannot cheer the place of death,
But only mock its gloom.
Here odorous smoke and breathing flower
No grateful influence shed;

They lose their perfume and their power,
  When offered to the dead.

And if, as is the Afghan's creed,
  The spirit may return,
A disembodied sense to feed,
  On fragrance, near its urn,—
It is enough that she, whom thou
  Didst love in living years,
Sits desolate beside it now,
  And fall these heavy tears.

T. H. Chivers

AVALON

DEATH'S pale cold orb has turned to an eclipse
    My Son of Love!
The worms are feeding on thy lily-lips,
  My milk-white Dove!
Pale purple tinges thy soft finger-tips!
While nectar thy pure soul in glory sips,
As Death's cold frost mine own forever nips!
    Where thou art lying
    Beside the beautiful undying
In the valley of the pausing of the Moon,
Oh! Avalon! my son! my son!

Wake up, oh! Avalon! my son! my son!
  And come from Death!
Heave off the clod that lies so heavy on
  Thy breast beneath
In that cold grave, my more than Precious One!
And come to me! for I am here alone—
With none to comfort me!—my hopes are gone
    Where thou art lying
    Beside the beautiful undying

In the Valley of the pausing of the Moon,
Oh! Avalon! my son! my son!

Forever more must I, on this damp sod,
  Renew and keep
My Covenant of Sorrows with my God,
  And weep, weep, weep!
Writhing in pain beneath Death's iron rod!
Till I shall go to that Divine Abode—
Treading the path that thy dear feet have trod—
    Where thou art lying
    Beside the beautiful undying
In the Valley of the pausing of the Moon,
Oh! Avalon! my son! my son!

Oh! precious Saviour! gracious heavenly Lord!
  Refresh my soul!
Here, with the healings of thy heavenly Word,
  Make my heart whole!
My little Lambs are scattered now abroad
In Death's dark Valley, where they bleat unheard!
Dear Shepherd! give their Shepherd his reward
    Where they are lying
    Beside the beautiful undying
In the Valley of the pausing of the Moon,
With Avalon! my son! my son!

For thou didst tread with fire-ensandaled feet,
  Star-crowned, forgiven,
The burning diapason of the stars so sweet,
  To God in Heaven!
And, walking on the sapphire-paven street,
Didst take upon the highest Sill thy seat—
Waiting in glory there my soul to meet,
    When I am lying
    Beside the beautiful undying
In the Valley of the pausing of the Moon,
Oh! Avalon! my son! my son!

Thou wert my Micro-Uranos below—
  My Little Heaven!
My Micro-Cosmos in this world of wo,
  From morn till even!
A living Lyre of God who charmed me so
With thy sweet songs, that I did seem to go
Out of this world where thou art shining now,
    But without lying
    Beside the beautiful undying
In the Valley of the pausing of the Moon,
Oh! Avalon! my son! my son!

Thou wert my son of Melody alway,
  Oh! Child Divine!
Whose golden radiance filled the world with Day!
  For thou didst shine
A lustrous Diadem of Song for aye,
Whose Divertisements, through Heaven's Holyday,
Now ravish Angel's ears—as well they may—
    While I am crying
    Beside the beautiful undying
In the Valley of the pausing of the Moon,
Oh! Avalon! my son! my son!

Thy soul did soar up to the Gates of God,
  Oh! Lark-like Child!
And through Heaven's Bowers of Bliss, by Angels trod,
  Poured Wood-notes wild!
In emulation of that Bird, which stood,
In solemn silence, listening to thy flood
Of golden Melody deluge the wood
    Where thou art lying
    Beside the beautiful undying
In the Valley of the pausing of the Moon,
Oh! Avalon! my son! my son!

The redolent quintessence of thy tongue,
  Oh! Avalon!
Embowered by Angels Heaven's sweet Bowers among—
  Many in one—

Is gathered from the choicest of the throng,
In an Æonian Hymn forever young,
Thou Philomelian Eclecticist of Song!
While I am sighing
Beside the beautiful undying
In the Valley of the pausing of the Moon,
For Avalon! my son! my son!

Thou wert like Taleisin, "full of eyes,"
Bardling of Love!
My beautiful Divine Eumenides!
My gentle Dove!
Thou silver Swan of Golden Elegies!
Whose Mendelssohnian Songs now fill the skies!
While I am weeping where my Lily lies!
Where thou art lying
Beside the beautiful undying
In the Valley of the pausing of the Moon,
Oh! Avalon! my son! my son!

Kindling the high-uplifted stars at even
With thy sweet song,
The Angels, on the Sapphire Sills of Heaven,
In Rapturous throng,
Melted to milder meekness, with the Seven
Bright Lamps of God to glory given,
Leant down to hear thy voice roll up the leven,
Where thou art lying
Beside the beautiful undying
In the Valley of the pausing of the Moon,
Oh! Avalon! my son! my son!

Can any thing that Christ has ever said,
Make my heart whole?
Can less than bringing back the early dead,
Restore my soul?
No! this alone can make my Heavenly bread—
Christ's Bread of Life brought down from Heaven,
instead

Of this sad Song, on which my soul has fed,
Where thou art lying
Beside the beautiful undying
In the Valley of the pausing of the Moon,
Oh! Avalon! my son! my son!

Have I not need to weep from Morn till Ever
Far bitterer tears
Than cruel Earth, the unforgiven,
Through his long years—
Inquisitorial Hell, or strictest Heaven,
Wrung from Christ's bleeding heart when riven?
Thus from one grief unto another driven,
Where thou art lying
Beside the beautiful undying
In the Valley of the pausing of the Moon,
Oh! Avalon! my son! my son!

John Greenleaf Whittier

THE ETERNAL GOODNESS

O FRIENDS! with whom my feet have trod
The quiet aisles of prayer,
Glad witness to your zeal for God
And love of man I bear.

I trace your lines of argument;
Your logic linked and strong
I weigh as one who dreads dissent,
And fears a doubt as wrong.

But still my human hands are weak
To hold your iron creeds:
Against the words ye bid me speak
My heart within me pleads.

Who fathoms the Eternal Thought?
  Who talks of scheme and plan?
The Lord is God! He needeth not
  The poor device of man.

I walk with bare, hushed feet the ground
  Ye tread with boldness shod;
I dare not fix with mete and bound
  The love and power of God.

Ye praise His justice; even such
  His pitying love I deem:
Ye seek a king; I fain would touch
  The robe that hath no seam.

Ye see the curse which overbroods
  A world of pain and loss;
I hear our Lord's beatitudes
  And prayer upon the cross.

More than your schoolmen teach, within
  Myself, alas! I know:
Too dark ye cannot paint the sin,
  Too small the merit show.

I bow my forehead to the dust,
  I veil mine eyes for shame,
And urge, in trembling self-distrust,
  A prayer without a claim.

I see the wrong that round me lies,
  I feel the guilt within;
I hear, with groan and travail-cries,
  The world confess its sin.

Yet, in the maddening maze of things,
  And tossed by storm and flood,
To one fixed trust my spirit clings;
  I know that God is good!

Not mine to look where cherubim
  And seraphs may not see,
But nothing can be good in Him
  Which evil is in me.

The wrong that pains my soul below
  I dare not throne above,
I know not of His hate,—I know
  His goodness and His love.

I dimly guess from blessings known
  Of greater out of sight,
And, with the chastened Psalmist, own
  His judgments too are right.

I long for household voices gone,
  For vanished smiles I long,
But God hath led my dear ones on,
  And He can do no wrong.

I know not what the future hath
  Of marvel or surprise,
Assured alone that life and death
  His mercy underlies.

And if my heart and flesh are weak
  To bear an untried pain,
The bruisëd reed He will not break,
  But strengthen and sustain.

No offering of my own I have,
  Nor works my faith to prove;
I can but give the gifts He gave,
  And plead His love for love.

And so beside the Silent Sea
  I wait the muffled oar;
No harm from Him can come to me
  On ocean or on shore.

I know not where His islands lift
  Their fronded palms in air;
I only know I cannot drift
  Beyond His love and care.

O brothers! if my faith is vain,
  If hopes like these betray,
Pray for me that my feet may gain
  The sure and safer way.

And Thou, O Lord! by whom are seen
  Thy creatures as they be,
Forgive me if too close I lean
  My human heart on Thee!

ICHABOD

SO fallen, so lost! the light withdrawn
    Which once he wore!
The glory from his gray hairs gone
    Forevermore!

Revile him not—the Tempter hath
    A snare for all;
And pitying tears, not scorn and wrath,
    Befit his fall.

Oh dumb be passion's stormy rage
    When he who might
Have lighted up and led his age
    Falls back in night.

Scorn? would the angels laugh to mark
    A bright soul driven,
Fiend-goaded, down the endless dark,
    From hope and heaven?

Let not the land once proud of him
Insult him now,
Nor brand with deeper shame his dim,
Dishonored brow.

But let its humbled sons, instead,
From sea to lake,
A long lament as for the dead
In sadness make.

Of all we loved and honored, nought
Save power remains—
A fallen angel's pride of thought,
Still strong in chains.

All else is gone; from those great eyes
The soul has fled:
When faith is lost, when honor dies,
The man is dead.

Then pay the reverence of old days
To his dead fame;
Walk backward, with averted gaze,
And hide the shame.

MY PLAYMATE

THE pines were dark on Ramoth hill,
Their song was soft and low;
The blossoms in the sweet May wind
Were falling like the snow.

The blossoms drifted at our feet,
The orchard birds sang clear;
The sweetest and the saddest day
It seemed of all the year.

For, more to me than birds or flowers,
  My playmate left her home,
And took with her the laughing spring,
  The music and the bloom.

She kissed the lips of kith and kin,
  She laid her hand in mine:
What more could ask the bashful boy.
  Who fed her father's kine?

She left us in the bloom of May:
  The constant years told o'er
Their seasons with as sweet May morns,
  But she came back no more.

I walk, with noiseless feet, the round
  Of uneventful years;
Still o'er and o'er I sow the spring
  And reap the autumn ears.

She lives where all the golden year
  Her summer roses blow;
The dusky children of the sun
  Before her come and go.

There haply with her jewelled hands
  She smooths her silken gown—
No more the homespun lap wherein
  I shook the walnuts down.

The wild grapes wait us by the brook,
  The brown nuts on the hill,
And still the May-day flowers make sweet
  The woods of Follymill.

The lilies blossom in the pond,
  The bird builds in the tree,
The dark pines sing on Ramoth hill
  The slow song of the sea.

I wonder if she thinks of them,
  And how the old time seems;
If ever the pines of Ramoth wood
  Are sounding in her dreams.

I see her face, I hear her voice:
  Does she remember mine?
And what to her is now the boy
  Who fed her father's kine?

What cares she that the orioles build
  For other eyes than ours;
That other hands with nuts are filled,
  And other laps with flowers?

O playmate in the golden time,
  Our mossy seat is green,
Its fringing violets blossom yet,
  The old trees o'er it lean.

The winds so sweet with birch and fern
  A sweeter memory blow;
And there in spring the veeries sing
  The song of long ago.

And still the pines of Ramoth wood
  Are moaning like the sea—
The moaning of the sea of change
  Between myself and thee!

Oliver Wendell Holmes

THE LAST LEAF

I SAW him once before,
As he passed by the door,
        And again
The pavement stones resound,
As he totters o'er the ground
        With his cane.

They say that in his prime,
Ere the pruning-knife of Time
Cut him down,
Not a better man was found
By the Crier on his round
Through the town.

But now he walks the streets,
And he looks at all he meets
Sad and wan,
And he shakes his feeble head,
That it seems as if he said,
"They are gone."

The mossy marbles rest
On the lips that he has prest
In their bloom,
And the names he loved to hear
Have been carved for many a year
On the tomb.

My grandmama has said,—
Poor old lady, she is dead
Long ago,—
That he had a Roman nose,
And his cheek was like a rose
In the snow;

But now his nose is thin,
And it rests upon his chin
Like a staff,
And a crook is in his back,
And a melancholy crack
In his laugh.

I know it is a sin
For me to sit and grin
At him here;
But the old three-cornerd hat,
And the breeches, and all that,
Are so queer!

And if I should live to be
The last leaf upon the tree,
In the spring,
Let them smile, as I do now,
At the old forsaken bough
Where I cling.

James Russell Lowell

HEBE

I SAW the twinkle of white feet,
I saw the flash of robes descending;
Before her ran an influence fleet,
That bow'd my heart like barley bending.

As, in bare fields, the searching bees
Pilot to blooms beyond our finding,
It led me on,—by sweet degrees,
Joy's simple honey-cells unbinding.

Those graces were that seem'd grim fates;
With nearer love the sky lean'd o'er me;
The long-sought secret's golden gates
On musical hinges swung before me.

I saw the brimm'd bowl in her grasp
Thrilling with godhood; like a lover,
I sprang the proffer'd life to clasp:
The beaker fell, the luck was over.

The earth has drunk the vintage up;
What boots it patch the goblet's splinters?
Can Summer fill the icy cup
Whose treacherous crystal is but Winter's?

O spendthrift haste! Await the gods;
Their nectar crowns the lips of Patience.
Haste scatters on unthankful sods
The immortal gift in vain libations.

Coy Hebe flies from those that woo,
And shuns the hands would seize upon her;
Follow thy life, and she will sue
To pour for thee the cup of honour!

AUSPEX

MY heart, I cannot still it,
Nest that had song-birds in it;
And when the last shall go,
The dreary days to fill it,
Instead of lark or linnet,
Shall whirl dead leaves and snow.

Had they been swallows only,
Without the passion stronger
That skyward longs and sings,—
Woe 's me, I shall be lonely
When I can feel no longer
The impatience of their wings!

A moment, sweet delusion,
Like birds the brown leaves hover;
But it will not be long
Before their wild confusion
Fall wavering down to cover
The poet and his song.

ST. MICHAEL THE WEIGHER

STOOD the tall Archangel weighing
All man's dreaming, doing, saying,
All the failure and the pain,
All the triumph and the gain,

In the unimagined years,
Full of hopes, more full of tears,
Since old Adam's hopeless eyes
Backward searched for Paradise,
And, instead, the flame-blade saw
Of inexorable Law.
Waking, I beheld him there,
With his fire-gold, flickering hair,
In his blinding armor stand,
And the scales were in his hand:
Mighty were they, and full well
They could poise both heaven and hell.

"Angel," asked I humbly then,
"Weighest thou the souls of men?
That thine office is, I know."
"Nay," he answered me, "not so;
But I weigh the hope of Man
Since the power of choice began,
In the world, of good or ill."
Then I waited and was still.

In one scale I saw him place
All the glories of our race,
Cups that lit Belshazzar's feast,
Gems, the lightning of the East,
Kublai's sceptre, Cæsar's sword,
Many a poet's golden word,
Many a skill of science, vain
To make men as gods again.

In the other scale he threw
Things regardless, outcast, few,
Martyr-ash, arena sand,
Of St. Francis' cord a strand,
Beechen cups of men whose need
Fasted that the poor might feed,
Disillusions and despairs
Of young saints with grief-grayed hairs,
Broken hearts that brake for Man.

Marvel through my pulses ran
Seeing then the beam divine
Swiftly on this hand decline,
While Earth's splendor and renown
Mounted light as thistle-down.

Maria White Lowell

AN OPIUM FANTASY

SOFT hangs the opiate in the brain,
And lulling soothes the edge of pain,
Till harshest sound, far off or near,
Sings floating in its mellow sphere.

What wakes me from my heavy dream?
Or am I still asleep?
Those long and soft vibrations seem
A slumberous charm to keep.

The graceful play, a moment stopt,
Distance again unrolls,
Like silver balls, that, softly dropt,
Ring into golden bowls.

I question of the poppies red,
The fairy flaunting band,
While I, a weed with drooping head,
Within their phalanx stand:—

"Some airy one, with scarlet cap,
The name unfold to me
Of this new minstrel who can lap
Sleep in his melody!"

Bright grew their scarlet-kerchief'd heads,
As freshening winds had blown,
And from their gently-swaying beds
They sang in undertone:—

"Oh he is but a little owl,
The smallest of his kin,
Who sits beneath the midnight's cowl
And makes this airy din."

"Deceitful tongues of fiery tints!
Far more than this ye know,
That he is your enchanted prince
Doom'd as an owl to go;—

"Nor his fond play for years hath stopt,
But nightly he unrolls
His silver balls, that, softly dropt,
Ring into golden bowls."

Ralph Waldo Emerson

THE RHODORA:

ON BEING ASKED, WHENCE IS THE FLOWER?

IN May, when sea-winds pierced our solitudes,
I found the fresh Rhodora in the woods,
Spreading its leafless blooms in a damp nook,
To please the desert and the sluggish brook.
The purple petals, fallen in the pool,
Made the black water with their beauty gay;
Here might the red-bird come his plumes to cool,
And court the flower that cheapens his array.
Rhodora! if the sages ask thee why
This charm is wasted on the earth and sky,
Tell them, dear, that if eyes were made for seeing,
Then Beauty is its own excuse for being:
Why thou wert there, O rival of the rose!
I never thought to ask, I never knew;
But, in my simple ignorance, suppose
The self-same Power that brought me there brought you.

COMPENSATION

WHY should I keep holiday
When other men have none?
Why but because, when these are gay,
I sit and mourn alone?

And why, when mirth unseals all tongues,
Should mine alone be dumb?
Ah! late I spoke to silent throngs,
And now their hour is come.

GIVE ALL TO LOVE

GIVE all to love;
Obey thy heart;
Friends, kindred, days,
Estate, good-fame,
Plans, credit, and the Muse,—
Nothing refuse.

'Tis a brave master;
Let it have scope:
Follow it utterly,
Hope beyond hope:
High and more high
It dives into noon,
With wing unspent,
Untold intent;
But it is a god,
Knows its own path,
And the outlets of the sky.

It was never for the mean;
It requireth courage stout,
Souls above doubt,
Valor unbending;

It will reward,—
They shall return
More than they were,
And ever ascending

Leave all for love;
Yet, hear me, yet,
One word more thy heart behoved,
One pulse more of firm endeavor,—
Keep thee to-day
To-morrow, forever,
Free as an Arab
Of thy beloved.

Cling with life to the maid;
But when the surprise,
First vague shadow of surmise
Flits across her bosom young
Of a joy apart from thee,
Free be she, fancy-free;
Nor thou detain her vesture's hem,
Nor the palest rose she flung
From her summer diadem.

Though thou loved her as thyself,
As a self of purer clay,
Though her parting dims the day,
Stealing grace from all alive;
Heartily know,
When half-gods go,
The gods arrive.

BACCHUS

BRING me wine, but wine which never grew
In the belly of the grape,
Or grew on vine whose tap-roots, reaching through
Under the Andes to the Cape,
Suffer no savor of the earth to scape.

Let its grapes the morn salute
From a nocturnal root,
Which feels the acrid juice
Of Styx and Erebus;
And turns the woe of Night,
By its own craft, to a more rich delight.

We buy ashes for bread;
We buy diluted wine;
Give me of the true,—
Whose ample leaves and tendrils curled
Among the silver hills of heaven,
Draw everlasting dew;
Wine of wine,
Blood of the world,
Form of forms, and mould of statures,
That I intoxicated,
And by the draught assimilated,
May float at pleasure through all natures;
The bird-language rightly spell,
And that which roses say so well.

Wine that is shed
Like the torrents of the sun
Up the horizon walls,
Or like the Atlantic streams, which run
When the South Sea calls.

Water and bread,
Food which needs no transmuting,
Rainbow-flowering, wisdom-fruiting,
Wine which is already man,
Food which teach and reason can.

Wine which Music is,—
Music and wine are one,—
That I, drinking this,
Shall hear far Chaos talk with me;
Kings unborn shall walk with me;

And the poor grass shall plot and plan
What it will do when it is man.
Quickened so, will I unlock
Every crypt of every rock.

I thank the joyful juice
For all I know;—
Winds of remembering
Of the ancient being blow,
And seeming-solid walls of use
Open and flow.

Pour, Bacchus! the remembering wine;
Retrieve the loss of me and mine!
Vine for vine be antidote,
And the grape requite the lote!
Haste to cure the old despair,—
Reason in Nature's lotus drenched,
The memory of ages quenched;
Give them again to shine;
Let wine repair what this undid;
And where the infection slid,
A dazzling memory revive;
Refresh the faded tints,
Recut the aged prints,
And write my old adventures with the pen
Which on the first day drew,
Upon the tablets blue,
The dancing Pleiads and eternal men.

BRAHMA

IF the red slayer think he slays,
  Or if the slain think he is slain,
They know not well the subtle ways
  I keep, and pass, and turn again.

Far or forgot to me is near;
  Shadow and sunlight are the same;
The vanquished gods to me appear;
  And one to me are shame and fame.

They reckon ill who leave me out;
  When me they fly, I am the wings;
I am the doubter and the doubt,
  And I the hymn the Brahmin sings.

The strong gods pine for my abode,
  And pine in vain the sacred Seven;
But thou, meek lover of the good!
  Find me, and turn thy back on heaven.

MEROPS

WHAT care I, so they stand the same,—
  Things of the heavenly mind,—
How long the power to give them name
  Tarries yet behind?

Thus far to-day your favors reach,
  O fair, appeasing presences!
Ye taught my lips a single speech,
  And a thousand silences.

Space grants beyond his fated road
  No inch to the god of day;
And copious language still bestowed
  One word, no more, to say.

URIEL

IT fell in the ancient periods
  Which the brooding soul surveys,
Or ever the wild Time coined itself
  Into calendar months and days.

This was the lapse of Uriel,
Which in Paradise befell.
Once, among the Pleiads walking,
Seyd overhead the young gods talking;
And the treason, too long pent,
To his ears was evident.
The young deities discussed
Laws of form, and metre just,
Orb, quintessence, and sunbeams,
What subsisteth, and what seems.
One, with low tones that decide,
And doubt and reverend use defied,
With a look that solved the sphere,
And stirred the devils everywhere,
Gave his sentiment divine
Against the being of a line.
'Line in nature is not found;
Unit and universe are round;
In vain produced, all rays return;
Evil will bless, and ice will burn.'
As Uriel spoke with piercing eye,
A shudder ran around the sky;
The stern old war-gods shook their heads,
The seraphs frowned from myrtle-beds;
Seemed to the holy festival
The rash word boded ill to all;
The balance-beam of Fate was bent;
The bounds of good and ill were rent;
Strong Hades could not keep his own,
But all slid to confusion.

A sad self-knowledge, withering, fell
On the beauty of Uriel;
In heaven once eminent, the god
Withdrew, that hour, into his cloud;
Whether doomed to long gyration
In the sea of generation,
Or by knowledge grown too bright
To hit the nerve of feebler sight.

Straightway, a forgetting wind
Stole over the celestial kind,
And their lips the secret kept,
If in ashes and fire-seed slept.
But now and then, truth-speaking things
Shamed the angels' veiling wings;
And, shrilling from the solar course,
Or from fruit of chemic force,
Procession of a soul in matter,
Or the speeding change of water,
Or out of the good of evil born,
Came Uriel's voice of cherub scorn,
And a blush tinged the upper sky,
And the gods shook, they knew not why.

DAYS

DAUGHTERS of Time, the hypocritic Days,
Muffled and dumb like barefoot dervishes,
And marching single in an endless file,
Bring diadems and fagots in their hands.
To each they offer gifts after his will,
Bread, kingdoms, stars, and sky that holds them all
I, in my pleached garden, watched the pomp,
Forgot my morning wishes, hastily
Took a few herbs and apples, and the Day
Turned and departed silent. I, too late,
Under her solemn fillet saw the scorn.

CHARACTER

THE sun set, but set not his hope:
Stars rose; his faith was earlier up:
Fixed on the enormous galaxy,
Deeper and older seemed his eye;
And matched his sufferance sublime
The taciturnity of time.

He spoke, and words more soft than rain
Brought the Age of Gold again:
His action won such reverence sweet
As hid all measure of the feat.

Henry David Thoreau

INSPIRATION

IF with light head erect I sing,
Though all the Muses lend their force,
From my poor love of anything,
The verse is weak and shallow as its source.

But if with bended neck I grope
Listening behind me for my wit,
With faith superior to hope,
More anxious to keep back than forward it,—

Making my soul accomplice there
Unto the flame my heart hath lit,
Then will the verse forever wear,—
Time cannot bend the line which God has writ.

I hearing get, who had but ears,
And sight, who had but eyes before;
I moments live, who lived but years,
And truth discern, who knew but learning's lore.

Now chiefly is my natal hour,
And only now my prime of life;
Of manhood's strength it is the flower,
'T is peace's end, and war's beginning strife.

It comes in summer's broadest noon,
By a gray wall, or some chance place,
Unseasoning time, insulting June,
And vexing day with its presuming face.

I will not doubt the love untold
Which not my worth nor want hath bought,
Which wooed me young, and wooes me old,
And to this evening hath me brought.

SMOKE

LIGHT-WINGED Smoke! Icarian bird,
Melting thy pinions in thy upward flight,
Lark without song, and messenger of dawn,
Circling above the hamlets as thy nest;
Or else, departing dream, and shadowy form
Of midnight vision, gathering up thy skirts;
By night star-veiling, and by day
Darkening the light and blotting out the sun;
Go thou my incense upward from this hearth,
And ask the gods to pardon this clear flame.

Julia Ward Howe

THE BATTLE-HYMN OF THE REPUBLIC

MINE eyes have seen the glory of the coming of the Lord;
He is trampling out the vintage where the grapes of wrath are stored;
He hath loosed the fateful lightning of His terrible swift sword;
His truth is marching on.

I have seen Him in the watch-fires of a hundred circling camps;
They have builded Him an altar in the evening dews and damps;
I can read His righteous sentence by the dim and flaring lamps;
His day is marching on.

I have read a fiery gospel, writ in burnished rows of steel:
"As ye deal with my contemners, so with you my grace shall deal;
Let the Hero, born of woman, crush the serpent with his heel,
Since God is marching on."

He has sounded forth the trumpet that shall never call retreat;
He is sifting out the hearts of men before His judgment-seat:
Oh, be swift, my soul, to answer Him! be jubilant, my feet!
Our God is marching on.

In the beauty of the lilies Christ was born across the sea,
With a glory in His bosom that transfigures you and me:
As He died to make men holy, let us die to make men free,
While God is marching on.

Henry Wadsworth Longfellow

HYMN TO THE NIGHT

'Ασπασίη, τρίλλιστος

I HEARD the trailing garments of the Night
Sweep through her marble halls;
I saw her sable skirts all fringed with light
From the celestial walls.

I felt her presence, by its spell of might,
Stoop o'er me from above—
The calm, majestic presence of the Night,
As of the one I love.

I heard the sounds of sorrow and delight,
The manifold, soft chimes,
That fill the haunted chambers of the Night,
Like some old poet's rhymes.

From the cool cisterns of the midnight air
  My spirit drank repose;
The fountain of perpetual peace flows there,
  From those deep cisterns flows.

O holy Night! from thee I learn to bear
  What man has borne before;
Thou layest thy finger on the lips of Care,
  And they complain no more.

Peace! Peace! Orestes-like I breathe this prayer;
  Descend with broad-winged flight,
The welcome, the thrice-prayed for, the most fair,
  The best-beloved Night!

MY LOST YOUTH

OFTEN I think of the beautiful town
    That is seated by the sea,
Often in thought go up and down
The pleasant streets of that dear old town,
  And my youth comes back to me.
    And a verse of a Lapland song
    Is haunting my memory still:
  "A boy's will is the wind's will,
And the thoughts of youth are long, long thoughts."

I can see the shadowy lines of its trees,
  And catch, in sudden gleams,
The sheen of the far-surrounding seas,
And islands that were the Hesperides
  Of all my boyish dreams.
    And the burden of that old song,
    It murmurs and whispers still:
  "A boy's will is the wind's will,
And the thoughts of youth are long, long thoughts."

I remember the black wharves and the slips,
And the sea-tides tossing free,
And Spanish sailors with bearded lips,
And the beauty and mystery of the ships,
And the magic of the sea.
And the voice of that wayward song
Is singing and saying still:
"A boy's will is the wind's will,
And the thoughts of youth are long, long thoughts."

I remember the bulwarks by the shore,
And the fort upon the hill;
The sunrise gun, with its hollow roar,
The drum-beat repeated o'er and o'er,
And the bugle wild and shrill.
And the music of that old song
Throbs in my memory still:
"A boy's will is the wind's will,
And the thoughts of youth are long, long thoughts."

I remember the sea-fight far away,
How it thundered o'er the tide!
And the dead captains, as they lay
In their graves, o'erlooking the tranquil bay,
Where they in battle died.
And the sound of that mournful song
Goes through me with a thrill:
"A boy's will is the wind's will,
And the thoughts of youth are long, long thoughts."

I can see the breezy dome of groves,
The shadows of Deering's Woods;
And the friendships old and the early loves
Come back with a sabbath sound, as of doves
In quiet neighborhoods.
And the verse of that sweet old song,
It flutters and murmurs still:
"A boy's will is the wind's will,
And the thoughts of youth are long, long thoughts."

I remember the gleams and glooms that dart
  Across the school-boy's brain;
The song and the silence in the heart,
That in part are prophecies and in part
  Are longings wild and vain.
    And the voice of that fitful song
    Sings on, and is never still:
  "A boy's will is the wind's will,
And the thoughts of youth are long, long thoughts."

There are things of which I may not speak;
  There are dreams that cannot die;
There are thoughts that make the strong heart weak,
And bring a pallor into the cheek
  And a mist before the eye.
    And the words of that fatal song
    Come over me like a chill:
  "A boy's will is the wind's will,
And the thoughts of youth are long, long thoughts."

Strange to me now are the forms I meet
  When I visit the dear old town;
But the native air is pure and sweet,
And the trees that o'ershadow each well-known street,
  As they balance up and down,
    Are singing the beautiful song,
    Are sighing and whispering still:
  "A boy's will is the wind's will,
And the thoughts of youth are long, long thoughts."

And Deering's Woods are fresh and fair;
  And with joy that is almost pain
My heart goes back to wander there,
And among the dreams of the days that were
  I find my lost youth again.
    And the strange and beautiful song,
    The groves are repeating it still:
  "A boy's will is the wind's will,
And the thoughts of youth are long, long thoughts."

THE THREE SILENCES OF MOLINOS

TO JOHN GREENLEAF WHITTIER

THREE Silences there are: the first of speech,
The second of desire, the third of thought;
This is the lore a Spanish monk, distraught
With dreams and visions, was the first to teach.
These Silences, commingling each with each,
Made up the perfect Silence that he sought
And prayed for, and wherein at times he caught
Mysterious sounds from realms beyond our reach.
O thou, whose daily life anticipates
The life to come, and in whose thought and word
The spiritual world preponderates,
Hermit of Amesbury! thou too hast heard
Voices and melodies from beyond the gates,
And speakest only when thy soul is stirred!

THE SOUND OF THE SEA

THE sea awoke at midnight from its sleep,
And round the pebbly beaches far and wide
I heard the first wave of the rising tide
Rush onward with uninterrupted sweep;
A voice out of the silence of the deep,
A sound mysteriously multiplied
As of a cataract from the mountain's side,
Or roar of winds upon a wooded steep.
So comes to us at times, from the unknown
And inaccessible solitudes of being,
The rushing of the sea-tides of the soul;
And inspirations, that we deem our own,
Are some divine foreshadowing and foreseeing
Of things beyond our reason or control.

DIVINA COMMEDIA

I

OFT have I seen at some cathedral door
A laborer, pausing in the dust and heat,
Lay down his burden, and with reverent feet
Enter, and cross himself, and on the floor
Kneel to repeat his paternoster o'er;
Far off the noises of the world retreat;
The loud vociferations of the street
Become an undistinguishable roar.
So, as I enter here from day to day,
And leave my burden at this minster gate,
Kneeling in prayer, and not ashamed to pray,
The tumult of the time disconsolate
To inarticulate murmurs dies away,
While the eternal ages watch and wait.

II

How strange the sculptures that adorn these towers!
This crowd of statues, in whose folded sleeves
Birds build their nests; while canopied with leaves
Parvis and portal bloom like trellised bowers,
And the vast minster seems a cross of flowers!
But fiends and dragons on the gargoyled eaves
Watch the dead Christ between the living thieves,
And, underneath, the traitor Judas lowers!
Ah! from what agonies of heart and brain,
What exultations trampling on despair,
What tenderness, what tears, what hate of wrong,
What passionate outcry of a soul in pain,
Uprose this poem of the earth and air,
This mediæval miracle of song!

III

I enter, and I see thee in the gloom
Of the long aisles, O poet saturnine!

And strive to make my steps keep pace with thine.
The air is filled with some unknown perfume;
The congregation of the dead make room
For thee to pass; the votive tapers shine;
Like rooks that haunt Ravenna's groves of pine
The hovering echoes fly from tomb to tomb.
From the confessionals I hear arise
Rehearsals of forgotten tragedies,
And lamentations from the crypts below;
And then a voice celestial that begins
With the pathetic words, "Although your sins
As scarlet be," and ends with "as the snow."

IV

With snow-white veil and garments as of flame,
She stands before thee, who so long ago
Filled thy young heart with passion and the woe
From which thy song and all its splendors came;
And while with stern rebuke she speaks thy name,
The ice about thy heart melts as the snow
On mountain heights, and in swift overflow
Comes gushing from thy lips in sobs of shame.
Thou makest full confession; and a gleam,
As of the dawn on some dark forest cast,
Seems on thy lifted forehead to increase;
Lethe and Eunoë—the remembered dream
And the forgotten sorrow—bring at last
That perfect pardon which is perfect peace.

V

I lift mine eyes, and all the windows blaze
With forms of Saints and holy men who died,
Here martyred and hereafter glorified;
And the great Rose upon its leaves displays
Christ's Triumph, and the angelic roundelays,
With splendor upon splendor multiplied;
And Beatrice again at Dante's side
No more rebukes, but smiles her words of praise.

And then the organ sounds, and unseen choirs
  Sing the old Latin hymns of peace and love
  And benedictions of the Holy Ghost;
And the melodious bells among the spires
  O'er all the house-tops and through heaven above
  Proclaim the elevation of the Host!

VI

O star of morning and of liberty!
  O bringer of the light, whose splendor shines
  Above the darkness of the Apennines,
  Forerunner of the day that is to be!
The voices of the city and the sea,
  The voices of the mountains and the pines,
  Repeat thy song, till the familiar lines
  Are footpaths for the thought of Italy!
Thy flame is blown abroad from all the heights,
  Through all the nations, and a sound is heard,
  As of a mighty wind, and men devout,
Strangers of Rome, and the new proselytes,
  In their own language hear thy wondrous word,
  And many are amazed and many doubt.

Walt Whitman

THE LAST INVOCATION

AT the last, tenderly,
  From the walls of the powerful, fortressed house,
From the clasp of the knitted locks—from the keep of the
  well-closed doors,
Let me be wafted.

Let me glide noiselessly forth;
With the key of softness unlock the locks—with a whisper
Set ope the doors, O Soul!

Tenderly! be not impatient!
(Strong is your hold, O mortal flesh!
Strong is your hold, O love.)

OUT OF THE CRADLE ENDLESSLY ROCKING

OUT of the cradle endlessly rocking,
Out of the mocking-bird's throat, the musical shuttle,
Out of the Ninth-month midnight,
Over the sterile sands and the fields beyond, where the child leaving his bed wandered alone, bareheaded, barefoot,
Down from the showered halo,
Up from the mystic play of shadows twining and twisting as if they were alive,
Out from the patches of briers and blackberries,
From the memories of the bird that chanted to me,
From your memories, sad brother, from the fitful risings and fallings I heard,
From under that yellow half-moon late-risen and swollen as if with tears,
From those beginning notes of yearning and love there in the mist,
From the thousand responses of my heart never to cease,
From the myriad thence-aroused words,
From the word stronger and more delicious than any,
From such as now they start the scene revisiting,
As a flock, twittering, rising, or overhead passing,
Borne hither, ere all eludes me, hurriedly,
A man, yet by these tears a little boy again,
Throwing myself on the sand, confronting the waves,
I, chanter of pains and joys, uniter of here and hereafter,
Taking all hints to use them, but swiftly leaping beyond them,
A reminiscence sing.
Once Paumanok,
When the lilac-scent was in the air and Fifth-month grass was growing,
Up this seashore in some briers,
Two feathered guests from Alabama, two together,

And their nest, and four light-green eggs spotted with brown,
And every day the he-bird to and fro near at hand,
And every day the she-bird crouched on her nest, silent, with
bright eyes,
And every day I, a curious boy, never too close, never disturbing
them,
Cautiously peering, absorbing, translating.

Shine! shine! shine!
Pour down your warmth, great sun!
While we bask, we two together.

Two together!
Winds blow south, or winds blow north,
Day come white, or night come black,
Home, or rivers and mountains from home,
Singing all time, minding no time,
While we two keep together.

Till of a sudden,
Maybe killed, unknown to her mate,
One forenoon the she-bird crouched not on the nest,
Nor returned that afternoon, nor the next,
Nor ever appeared again.

And thenceforward all summer in the sound of the sea,
And at night under the full of the moon in calmer weather,
Over the hoarse surging of the sea,
Or flitting from brier to brier by day,
I saw, I heard at intervals the remaining one, the he-bird,
The solitary guest from Alabama.

Blow! blow! blow!
Blow up sea-winds along Paumanok's shore;
I wait and I wait till you blow my mate to me.

Yes, when the stars glistened,
All night long on the prong of a moss-scalloped stake,
Down almost amid the slapping waves,
Sat the lone singer, wonderful, causing tears.

He called on his mate,
He poured forth the meanings which I of all men know.

Yes, my brother, I know,—
The rest might not, but I have treasured every note,
For more than once dimly down to the beach gliding,
Silent, avoiding the moonbeams, blending myself with the
shadows,
Recalling now the obscure shapes, the echoes, the sounds and
sights after their sorts,
The white arms out in the breakers tirelessly tossing,
I, with bare feet, a child, the wind wafting my hair,
Listened long and long.

Listened to keep, to sing, now translating the notes,
Following you, my brother.

Soothe! soothe! soothe!
Close on its wave soothes the wave behind,
And again another behind embracing and lapping, every one
close,
But my love soothes not me, not me.

Low hangs the moon, it rose late,
It is lagging—O I think it is heavy with love, with love.

O madly the sea pushes upon the land,
With love, with love.

O night! do I not see my love fluttering out among the
breakers?
What is that little black thing I see there in the white?

Loud! loud! loud!
Loud I call to you, my love!

High and clear I shoot my voice over the waves,
Surely you must know who is here, is here,
You must know who I am, my love.

Low-hanging moon!
What is that dusky spot in your brown yellow?
O it is the shape, the shape of my mate!
O moon, do not keep her from me any longer.

Land! land! O land!
Whichever way I turn, O, I think you could give me my mate back again if you only would,
For I am almost sure I see her dimly whichever way I look.

O rising stars!
Perhaps the one I want so much will rise, will rise with some of you.

O throat! O trembling throat!
Sound clearer through the atmosphere!
Pierce the woods, the earth,
Somewhere listening to catch you must be the one I want.

Shake out carols!
Solitary here, the night's carols!
Carols of lonesome love! death's carols!
Carols under that lagging, yellow, waning moon!
O under that moon where she droops almost down into the sea!
O reckless despairing carols!

But soft! sink low!
Soft! let me just murmur,
And do you wait a moment, you husky-noised sea,
For somewhere I believe I heard my mate responding to me,
So faint, I must be still, be still to listen,
But not altogether still, for then she might not come immediately to me.

Hither, my love!
Here I am! here!
With this just-sustained note I announce myself to you,
This gentle call is for you, my love, for you.

Do not be decoyed elsewhere:
That is the whistle of the wind, it is not my voice,
That is the fluttering, the fluttering of the spray,
Those are the shadows of leaves.

O darkness! O in vain!
O I am very sick and sorrowful.
O brown halo in the sky near the moon, drooping upon the sea!
O troubled reflection in the sea!
O throat! O throbbing heart!
And I singing uselessly! uselessly all the night.

O past! O happy life! O songs of joy!
In the air, in the woods, over fields,
Loved! loved! loved! loved! loved!
But my mate no more, no more with me!
We two together no more.

The aria sinking,
All else continuing, the stars shining,
The winds blowing, the notes of the bird continuous echoing,
With angry moans the fierce old mother incessantly moaning,
On the sands of Paumanok's shore gray and rustling,
The yellow half-moon enlarged, sagging down, drooping, the
face of the sea almost touching,
The boy ecstatic, with his bare feet the waves, with his hair
the atmosphere dallying,
The love in the heart long pent, now loose, now at last tumultu-
ously bursting,
The aria's meaning, the ears, the soul, swiftly depositing,
The strange tears down the cheeks coursing,
The colloquy there, the trio, each uttering,
The undertone, the savage old mother incessantly crying,
To the boy's soul's questions sullenly timing, some drown'd
secret hissing,
To the outsetting bard.
Demon or bird! (said the boy's soul)
Is it indeed toward your mate you sing? or is it really to me?

For I, that was a child, my tongue's use sleeping, now I have
heard you,
Now in a moment I know what I am for, I awake,
And already a thousand singers, a thousand songs, clearer,
louder and more sorrowful than yours,
A thousand warbling echoes have started to life within me,
never to die.

O you singers solitary, singing by yourself, projecting me,
O solitary me listening, never more shall I cease perpetuating
you,
Never more shall I escape, never more the reverberations,
Never more the cries of unsatisfied love be absent from me,
Never again leave me to be the peaceful child I was before
what there in the night,
By the sea under the yellow and sagging moon,
The messenger there aroused, the fire, the sweet hell within,
The unknown want, the destiny of me.
O give me the clew! (it lurks in the night here somewhere)
O if I am to have so much, let me have more!

A word then, (for I will conquer it)
The word final, superior to all,
Subtle, sent up—what is it?—I listen;
Are you whispering it, and have been all the time, you sea-
waves?
Is that it from your liquid rims and wet sands?
Whereto answering, the sea,
Delaying not, hurrying not,
Whispered me through the night, and very plainly before
daybreak,
Lisped to me the low and delicious word death,
And again death, death, death, death,
Hissing melodious, neither like the bird nor like my aroused
child's heart,
But edging near as privately for me, rustling at my feet,
Creeping thence steadily up to my ears and laving me softly
all over,
Death, death, death, death. death.

Which I do not forget,
But fuse the song of my dusky demon and brother,
That he sang to me in the moonlight on Paumanok's gray beach,
With the thousand responsive songs at random,
My own songs awaked from that hour,
And with them the key, the word up from the waves,
The word of the sweetest song and all songs,
That strong and delicious word which, creeping to my feet,
(Or like some old crone rocking the cradle, swathed in sweet garments, bending aside)
The sea whispered me.

DEATH CAROL

(From "When Lilacs Last in the Door-Yard Bloomed")

COME, lovely and soothing Death,
Undulate round the world, serenely arriving, arriving,
In the day, in the night, to all, to each,
Sooner or later, delicate Death.

Praised be the fathomless universe,
For life and joy, and for objects and knowledge curious;
And for love, sweet love—But praise! praise! praise!
For the sure-enwinding arms of cool-enfolding Death.

Dark Mother, always gliding near, with soft feet,
Have none chanted for thee a chant of fullest welcome?
Then I chant it for thee—I glorify thee above all;
I bring thee a song that when thou must indeed come, come unfalteringly.

Approach, strong deliveress!
When it is so—when thou hast taken them, I joyously sing the dead,
Lost in the loving, floating ocean of thee,
Laved in the flood of thy bliss, O Death.

From me to thee glad serenades,
Dances for thee I propose, saluting thee—adornments and feastings for thee;
And the sights of the open landscape, and the high-spread sky, are fitting,
And life and the fields, and the huge and thoughtful night.

The night, in silence, under many a star;
The ocean shore, and the husky whispering wave, whose voice I know;
And the soul turning to thee, O vast and well-veiled Death,
And the body gratefully nestling close to thee.

Over the tree-tops I float thee a song!
Over the rising and sinking waves—over the myriad fields, and the prairies wide;
Over the dense-packed cities all, and the teeming wharves and ways,
I float this carol with joy, with joy to thee, O Death!

A NOISELESS, PATIENT SPIDER

A NOISELESS, patient spider,
I marked, where, on a little promontory, it stood isolated;
Marked how, to explore the vacant, vast surrounding,
It launched forth filament, filament, filament, out of itself;
Ever unreeling them—ever tirelessly speeding them.

And you, O my Soul, where you stand,
Surrounded, surrounded, in measureless oceans of space,
Ceaselessly musing, venturing, throwing,—seeking the spheres, to connect them;
Till the bridge you will need, be formed—till the ductile anchor hold;
Till the gossamer thread you fling, catch somewhere, O my Soul.

SONG OF MYSELF

1

I CELEBRATE myself, and sing myself,
And what I assume you shall assume,
For every atom belonging to me as good belongs to you.

I loafe and invite my soul,
I lean and loafe at my ease observing a spear of summer grass.

My tongue, every atom of my blood, form'd from this soil,
 this air,
Born here of parents born here from parents the same, and
 their parents the same,
I, now thirty-seven years old in perfect health begin,
Hoping to cease not till death.

Creeds and schools in abeyance,
Retiring back a while sufficed at what they are, but never
 forgotten,
I harbor for good or bad, I permit to speak at every hazard,
Nature without check with original energy.

2

Houses and rooms are full of perfumes, the shelves are crowded
 with perfumes,
I breathe the fragrance myself and know it and like it,
The distillation would intoxicate me also, but I shall not let it.

The atmosphere is not a perfume, it has no taste of the distilla-
 tion, it is odorless,
It is for my mouth forever, I am in love with it,
I will go to the bank by the wood and become undisguised
 and naked,
I am mad for it to be in contact with me.

The smoke of my own breath,
Echoes, ripples, buzz'd whispers, love-root, silk-thread, crotch
 and vine,

My respiration and inspiration, the beating of my heart, the
passing of blood and air through my lungs,
The sniff of green leaves and dry leaves, and of the shore
and dark-color'd sea-rocks, and of hay in the barn,
The sound of the belch'd words of my voice loos'd to the eddies
of the wind,
A few light kisses, a few embraces, a reaching around of arms,
The play of shine and shade on the trees as the supple boughs
wag,
The delight alone or in the rush of the streets, or along the
fields and hill-sides,
The feeling of health, the full-moon trill, the song of me
rising from bed and meeting the sun.

Have you reckon'd a thousand acres much? have you reckon'd
the earth much?
Have you practis'd so long to learn to read?
Have you felt so proud to get at the meaning of poems?

Stop this day and night with me and you shall possess the
origin of all poems,
You shall possess the good of the earth and sun, (there are
millions of suns left,)
You shall no longer take things at second or third hand, nor
look through the eyes of the dead, nor feed on the spectres
in books,
You shall not look through my eyes either, nor take things
from me,
You shall listen to all sides and filter them from your self.

3

I have heard what the talkers were talking, the talk of the
beginning and the end,
But I do not talk of the beginning or the end.

There was never any more inception than there is now,
Nor any more youth or age than there is now,
And will never be any more perfection than there is now,
Nor any more heaven or hell than there is now.

Urge and urge and urge,
Always the procreant urge of the world.
Out of the dimness opposite equals advance, always substance
and increase, always sex,
Always a knit of identity, always distinction, always a breed
of life.

To elaborate is no avail, learn'd and unlearn'd feel that it is so.

Sure as the most certain sure, plumb in the uprights, well
entretied, braced in the beams,
Stout as a horse, affectionate, haughty, electrical,
I and this mystery here we stand.

Clear and sweet is my soul, and clear and sweet is all that is
not my soul.

Lack one lacks both, and the unseen is proved by the seen,
Till that becomes unseen and receives proof in its turn.

Showing the best and dividing it from the worst age vexes age,
Knowing the perfect fitness and equanimity of things, while
they discuss I am silent, and go bathe and admire myself.

Welcome is every organ and attribute of me, and of any man
hearty and clean,
Not an inch nor a particle of an inch is vile, and none shall be
less familiar than the rest.

I am satisfied—I see, dance, laugh, sing;
As the hugging and loving bed-fellow sleeps at my side
through the night, and withdraws at the peep of the day
with stealthy tread,
Leaving me baskets cover'd with white towels swelling the
house with their plenty,
Shall I postpone my acceptation and realization and scream
at my eyes,
That they turn from gazing after and down the road,
And forthwith cipher and show me to a cent,
Exactly the value of one and exactly the value of two, and
which is ahead?

4

Trippers and askers surround me,
People I meet, the effect upon me of my early life or the ward
and city I live in, or the nation,
The latest dates, discoveries, inventions, societies, authors old
and new,
My dinner, dress, associates, looks, compliments, dues,
The real or fancied indifference of some man or woman I love,
The sickness of one of my folks or of myself, or ill-doing or
loss or lack of money, or depressions or exaltations,
Battles, the horrors of fratricidal war, the fever of doubtful
news, the fitful events;
These come to me days and nights and go from me again,
But they are not the Me myself.

Apart from the pulling and hauling stands what I am,
Stands amused, complacent, compassionating, idle, unitary,
Looks down, is erect, or bends an arm on an impalpable certain
rest,
Looking with side-curved head curious what will come next,
Both in and out of the game and watching and wondering
at it.

Backward I see in my own days where I sweated through
fog with linguists and contenders,
I have no mockings or arguments, I witness and wait.

5

I believe in you my soul, the other I am must not abase itself
to you,
And you must not be abased to the other.

Loafe with me on the grass, loose the stop from your throat,
Not words, not music or rhyme I want, not custom or lecture,
not even the best,
Only the lull I like, the hum of vour valvèd voice.

I mind how once we lay such a transparent summer morning,
How you settled your head athwart my hips and gently turn'd over upon me,
And parted the shirt from my bosom-bone, and plunged your tongue to my bare-stript heart,
And reach'd till you felt my beard, and reach'd till you held my feet.

Swiftly arose and spread around me the peace and knowledge that pass all the argument of the earth,
And I know that the hand of God is the promise of my own,
And I know that the spirit of God is the brother of my own,
And that all the men ever born are also my brothers, and the women my sisters and lovers,
And that a kelson of the creation is love,
And limitless are leaves stiff or drooping in the fields,
And brown ants in the little wells beneath them,
And mossy scabs of the worm fence, heap'd stones, elder, mullein and poke-weed.

6

A child said *What is the grass?* fetching it to me with full hands,
How could I answer the child? I do not know what it is any more than he.

I guess it must be the flag of my disposition, out of hopeful green stuff woven.

Or I guess it is the handkerchief of the Lord,
A scented gift and remembrancer designedly dropt,
Bearing the owner's name some way in the corners, that we may see and remark, and say *Whose?*

Or I guess the grass is itself a child, the produced babe of the vegetation.

Or I guess it is a uniform hieroglyphic,
And it means, Sprouting alike in broad zones and narrow zones,

Growing among black folks as among white,
Kanuck, Tuckahoe, Congressman, Cuff, I give them the same,
I receive them the same.

And now it seems to me the beautiful uncut hair of graves.

Tenderly will I use you curling grass,
It may be you transpire from the breasts of young men,
It may be if I had known them I would have loved them,
It may be you are from old people, or from offspring taken soon out of their mothers' laps,
And here you are the mothers' laps.

This grass is very dark to be from the white heads of old mothers,
Darker than the colorless beards of old men,
Dark to come from under the faint red roofs of mouths.

O I perceive after all so many uttering tongues,
And I perceive they do not come from the roofs of mouths for nothing.

I wish I could translate the hints about the dead young men and women,
And the hints about old men and mothers, and the offspring taken soon out of their laps.

What do you think has become of the young and old men?
And what do you think has become of the women and children?

They are alive and well somewhere,
The smallest sprout shows there is really no death,
And if ever there was it led forward life, and does not wait at the end to arrest it,
And ceas'd the moment life appear'd.

All goes onward and outward, nothing collapses,
And to die is different from what any one supposed, and luckier.

7

Has any one supposed it lucky to be born?
I hasten to inform him or her it is just as lucky to die, and
I know it.

I pass death with the dying and birth with the new-wash'd
babe, and am not contain'd between my hat and boots,
And peruse manifold objects, no two alike and every one good,
The earth good and the stars good, and their adjuncts all good.

I am not an earth nor an adjunct of an earth,
I am the mate and companion of people, all just as immortal
and fathomless as myself,
(They do not know how immortal, but I know.)

Every kind for itself and its own, for me mine male and
female,
For me those that have been boys and that love women,
For me the man that is proud and feels how it stings to be
slighted,
For me the sweet-heart and the old maid, for me mothers and
the mothers of mothers,
For me lips that have smiled, eyes that have shed tears,
For me children and the begetters of children.

Undrape! you are not guilty to me, nor stale nor discarded,
I see through the broadcloth and gingham whether or no,
And am around, tenacious, acquisitive, tireless, and cannot be
shaken away.

8

The little one sleeps in its cradle,
I lift the gauze and look a long time, and silently brush away
flies with my hand.

The youngster and the red-faced girl turn aside up the bushy
hill,
I peeringly view them from the top.

The suicide sprawls on the bloody floor of the bedroom,
I witness the corpse with its dabbled hair, I note where the
pistol has fallen.

The blab of the pave, tires of carts, sluff of boot-soles, talk of
the promenaders,
The heavy omnibus, the driver with his interrogating thumb,
the clank of the shod horses on the granite floor,
The snow-sleighs, clinking, shouted jokes, pelts of snow-balls,
The hurrahs for popular favorites, the fury of rous'd mobs,
The flap of the curtain'd litter, a sick man inside borne to the
hospital,
The meeting of enemies, the sudden oath, the blows and fall,
The excited crowd, the policeman with his star quickly work-
ing his passage to the centre of the crowd,
The impassive stones that receive and return so many echoes,
What groans of over-fed or half-starv'd who fall sunstruck or
in fits,
What exclamations of women taken suddenly who hurry home
and give birth to babes,
What living and buried speech is always vibrating here, what
howls restrain'd by decorum,
Arrests of criminals, slights, adulterous offers made, acceptances,
rejections with convex lips,
I mind them or the show or resonance of them—I come and
I depart.

9

The big doors of the country barn stand open and ready,
The dried grass of the harvest-time loads the slow-drawn
wagon,
The clear light plays on the brown gray and green intertinged,
The armfuls are pack'd to the sagging mow.

I am there, I help, I came stretch'd atop of the load,
I felt its soft jolts, one leg reclined on the other,
I jump from the cross-beams and seize the clover and timothy,
And roll head over heels and tangle my hair full of wisps.

10

Alone far in the wilds and mountains I hunt,
Wandering amazed at my own lightness and glee,
In the late afternoon choosing a safe spot to pass the night,
Kindling a fire and broiling the fresh-kill'd game,
Falling asleep on the gather'd leaves with my dog and gun
by my side.

The Yankee clipper is under her sky-sails, she cuts the sparkle
and scud,
My eyes settle the land, I bend at her prow or shout joyously
from the deck.

The boatmen and clam-diggers arose early and stopt for me,
I tuck'd my trowser-ends in my boots and went and had a
good time;
You should have been with us that dav round the chowder-
kettle.

I saw the marriage of the trapper in the open air in the far
west, the bride was a red girl,
Her father and his friends sat near cross-legged and dumbly
smoking, they had moccasins to their feet and large thick
blankets hanging from their shoulders,
On a bank lounged the trapper, he was drest mostly in skins,
his luxuriant beard and curls protected his neck, he held
his bride by the hand,
She had long eyelashes, her head was bare, her coarse straight
locks descended upon her voluptuous limbs and reach'd
to her feet.

The runaway slave came to my house and stopt outside,
I heard his motions crackling the twigs of the woodpile,
Through the swung half-door of the kitchen I saw him limpsy
and weak,
And went where he sat on a log and led him in and assured
him,
And brought water and fill'd a tub for his sweated body and
bruis'd feet,

And gave him a room that enter'd from my own, and gave
him some coarse clean clothes,
And remember perfectly well his revolving eyes and his awk-
wardness,
And remember putting plasters on the galls of his neck and
ankles;
He staid with me a week before he was recuperated and pass'd
north,
I had him sit next to me at table, my fire-lock lean'd in the
corner.

11

Twenty-eight young men bathe by the shore,
Twenty-eight young men and all so friendly;
Twenty-eight years of womanly life and all so lonesome.

She owns the fine house by the rise of the bank,
She hides handsome and richly drest aft the blinds of the
window.

Which of the young men does she like the best?
Ah the homeliest of them is beautiful to her.

Where are you off to, lady? for I see you,
You splash in the water there, yet stay stock still in your
room.

Dancing and laughing along the beach came the twenty-ninth
bather,
The rest did not see her, but she saw them and loved them.

The beards of the young men glisten'd with wet, it ran from
their long hair,
Little streams pass'd all over their bodies.

An unseen hand also pass'd over their bodies,
It descended tremblingly from their temples and ribs.

The young men float on their backs, their white bellies bulge
to the sun, they do not ask who seizes fast to them,

They do not know who puffs and declines with pendant and
bending arch,
They do not think whom they souse with spray.

12

The butcher-boy puts off his killing-clothes, or sharpens his
knife at the stall in the market,
I loiter enjoying his repartee and his shuffle and break-down.

Blacksmiths with grimed and hairy chests environ the anvil,
Each has his main-sledge, they are all out, there is a great heat
in the fire.

From the cinder-strew'd threshold I follow their movements,
The lithe sheer of their waists plays even with their massive
arms,
Overhand the hammers swing, overhand so slow, overhand so
sure,
They do not hasten, each man hits in his place.

13

The negro holds firmly the reins of his four horses, the block
swags underneath on its tied-over chain,
The negro that drives the long dray of the stone-yard, steady
and tall he stands pois'd on one leg on the string-piece,
His blue shirt exposes his ample neck and breast and loosens
over his hip-band,
His glance is calm and commanding, he tosses the slouch of
his hat away from his forehead,
The sun falls on his crispy hair and mustache, falls on the
black of his polish'd and perfect limbs.

I behold the picturesque giant and love him, and I do not
stop there,
I go with the team also.

In me the caresser of life wherever moving, backward as well
as forward sluing,

To niches aside and junior bending, not a person or object
missing,
Absorbing all to myself and for this song.

Oxen that rattle the yoke and chain or halt in the leafy shade,
what is that you express in your eyes?
It seems to me more than all the print I have read in my life.

My tread scares the wood-drake and wood-duck on my distant
and day-long ramble,
They rise together, they slowly circle around.

I believe in those wing'd purposes,
And acknowledge red, yellow, white, playing within me,
And consider green and violet and the tufted crown intentional,
And do not call the tortoise unworthy because she is not
something else,
And the jay in the woods never studied the gamut, yet trills
pretty well to me,
And the look of the bay mare shames silliness out of me.

14

The wild gander leads his flock through the cool night,
Ya-honk he says, and sounds it down to me like an invitation,
The pert may suppose it meaningless, but I listening close,
Find its purpose and place up there toward the wintry sky.

The sharp-hoof'd moose of the north, the cat on the house-
sill, the chickadee, the prairie-dog,
The litter of the grunting sow as they tug at her teats,
The brood of the turkey-hen and she with her half-spread
wings,
I see in them and myself the same old law.

The press of my foot to the earth springs a hundred affections,
They scorn the best I can do to relate them.

I am enamour'd of growing out-doors,
Of men that live among cattle or taste of the ocean or woods,

Of the builders and steerers of ships and the wielders of axes
and mauls, and the drivers of horses,
I can eat and sleep with them week in and week out.

What is commonest, cheapest, nearest, easiest, is Me,
Me going in for my chances, spending for vast returns,
Adorning myself to bestow myself on the first that will take
me,
Not asking the sky to come down to my good will,
Scattering it freely forever.

15

The pure contralto sings in the organ loft,
The carpenter dresses his plank, the tongue of his foreplane
whistles its wild ascending lisp,
The married and unmarried children ride home to their
Thanksgiving dinner,
The pilot seizes the king-pin, he heaves down with a strong
arm,
The mate stands braced in the whale-boat, lance and harpoon
are ready,
The duck-shooter walks by silent and cautious stretches,
The deacons are ordain'd with cross'd hands at the altar,
The spinning-girl retreats and advances to the hum of the big
wheel,
The farmer stops by the bars as he walks on a First-day loafe
and looks at the oats and rye,
The lunatic is carried at last to the asylum a confirm'd case,
(He will never sleep any more as he did in the cot in his
mother's bed-room;)
The jour printer with gray head and gaunt jaws works at his
case,
He turns his quid of tobacco while his eyes blurr with the
manuscript;
The malform'd limbs are tied to the surgeon's table,
What is removed drops horribly in a pail;
The quadroon girl is sold at the auction-stand, the drunkard
nods by the bar-room stove,

The machinist rolls up his sleeves, the policeman travels his beat, the gate-keeper marks who pass,
The young fellow drives the express wagon, (I love him, though I do not know him;)
The half-breed straps on his light boots to compete in the race,
The western turkey-shooting draws old and young, some lean on their rifles, some sit on logs,
Out from the crowds steps the marksman, takes his position, levels his piece;
The groups of newly-come immigrants cover the wharf or levee,
As the woolly-pates hoe in the sugar-field, the overseer views them from his saddle,
The bugle calls in the ball-room, the gentlemen run for their partners, the dancers bow to each other,
The youth lies awake in the cedar-roof'd garret and harks to the musical rain,
The Wolverine sets traps on the creek that helps fill the Huron,
The squaw wrapt in her yellow-hemm'd cloth is offering moccasins and bead-bags for sale,
The connoisseur peers along the exhibition-gallery with half-shut eyes bent sideways,
As the deck-hands make fast the steamboat the plank is thrown for the shore-going passengers,
The young sister holds out the skein while the elder sister winds it off in a ball, and stops now and then for the knots,
The one-year wife is recovering and happy having a week ago borne her first child,
The clean-hair'd Yankee girl works with her sewing-machine or in the factory or mill,
The paving-man leans on his two-handed rammer, the reporter's lead flies swiftly over the note-book, the sign-painter is lettering with blue and gold,
The canal boy trots on the tow-path, the book-keeper counts at his desk, the shoemaker waxes his thread,
The conductor beats time for the band and all the performers follow him,

The child is baptized, the convert is making his first professions,
The regatta is spread on the bay, the race is begun, (how the white sails sparkle!)
The drover watching his drove sings out to them that would stray,
The pedler sweats with his pack on his back, (the purchaser higgling about the odd cent;)
The bride unrumples her white dress, the minute-hand of the clock moves slowly,
The opium-eater reclines with rigid head and just-open'd lips,
The prostitute draggles her shawl, her bonnet bobs on her tipsy and pimpled neck,
The crowd laugh at her blackguard oaths, the men jeer and wink to each other,
(Miserable! I do not laugh at your oaths nor jeer you;)
The President holding a cabinet council is surrounded by the great Secretaries,
On the piazza walk three matrons stately and friendly with twined arms,
The crew of the fish-smack pack repeated layers of halibut in the hold,
The Missourian crosses the plains toting his wares and his cattle,
As the fare-collector goes through the train he gives notice by the jingling of loose change,
The floor-men are laying the floor, the tinners are tinning the roof, the masons are calling for mortar,
In single file each shouldering his hod pass onward the laborers;
Seasons pursuing each other the indescribable crowd is gather'd, it is the fourth of Seventh-month, (what salutes of cannon and small arms!)
Seasons pursuing each other the plougher ploughs, the mower mows, and the winter-grain falls in the ground;
Off on the lakes the pike-fisher watches and waits by the hole in the frozen surface,
The stumps stand thick round the clearing, the squatter strikes deep with his axe,

Flatboatmen make fast towards dusk near the cotton-wood or
pecan-trees,
Coon-seekers go through the regions of the Red river or through
those drain'd by the Tennessee, or through those of the
Arkansas,
Torches shine in the dark that hangs on the Chattahooche or
Altamahaw,
Patriarchs sit at supper with sons and grandsons and great-
grandsons around them,
In walls of adobe, in canvas tents, rest hunters and trappers
after their day's sport,
The city sleeps and the country sleeps,
The living sleep for their time, the dead sleep for their time,
The old husband sleeps by his wife and the young husband
sleeps by his wife;
And these tend inward to me, and I tend outward to them,
And such as it is to be of these more or less I am,
And of these one and all I weave the song of myself.

16

I am of old and young, of the foolish as much as the wise,
Regardless of others, ever regardful of others,
Maternal as well as paternal, a child as well as a man,
Stuff'd with the stuff that is coarse and stuff'd with the stuff
that is fine,
One of the Nation of many nations, the smallest the same and
the largest the same,
A Southerner soon as a Northerner, a planter nonchalant and
hospitable down by the Oconee I live,
A Yankee bound my own way ready for trade, my joints the
limberest joints on earth and the sternest joints on earth,
A Kentuckian walking the vale of the Elkhorn in my deer-
skin leggings, a Louisianian or Georgian,
A boatman over lakes or bays or along coasts, a Hoosier,
Badger, Buckeye;
At home on Kanadian snow-shoes or up in the bush, or with
fishermen off Newfoundland,
At home in the fleet of ice-boats, sailing with the rest and
tacking,

At home on the hills of Vermont or in the woods of Maine, or the Texan ranch,
Comrade of Californians, comrade of free North-Westerners, (loving their big proportions,)
Comrade of raftsmen and coalmen, comrade of all who shake hands and welcome to drink and meat,
A learner with the simplest, a teacher of the thoughtfullest,
A novice beginning yet experient of myriads of seasons,
Of every hue and caste am I, of every rank and religion,
A farmer, mechanic, artist, gentleman, sailor, quaker,
Prisoner, fancy-man, rowdy, lawyer, physician, priest.

I resist any thing better than my own diversity,
Breathe the air but leave plenty after me,
And am not stuck up, and am in my place.

(The moth and the fish-eggs are in their place,
The bright suns I see and the dark suns I cannot see are in their place,
The palpable is in its place and the impalpable is in its place.)

17

These are really the thoughts of all men in all ages and lands, they are not original with me,
If they are not yours as much as mine they are nothing, or next to nothing,
If they are not the riddle and the untying of the riddle they are nothing,
If they are not just as close as they are distant they are nothing.

This is the grass that grows wherever the land is and the water is,
This is the common air that bathes the globe.

18

With music strong I come, with my cornets and my drums,
I play not marches for accepted victors only, I play marches for conquer'd and slain persons.

Have you heard that it was good to gain the day?
I also say it is good to fall, battles are lost in the same spirit
in which they are won.

I beat and pound for the dead,
I blow through my embouchures my loudest and gayest for
them.

Vivas to those who have fail'd!
And to those whose war-vessels sank in the sea!
And to those themselves who sank in the sea!
And to all generals that lost engagements, and all overcome
heroes!
And the numberless unknown heroes equal to the greatest
heroes known!

19

This is the meal equally set, this the meat for natural hunger,
It is for the wicked just the same as the righteous, I make
appointments with all,
I will not have a single person slighted or left away,
The kept-woman, sponger, thief, are hereby invited,
The heavy-lipp'd slave is invited, the venerealee is invited;
There shall be no difference between them and the rest.

This is the press of a bashful hand, this the float and odor of
hair,
This is the touch of my lips to yours, this the murmur of
yearning,
This the far-off depth and height reflecting my own face,
This the thoughful merge of myself, and the outlet again.

Do you guess I have some intricate purpose?
Well I have, for the Fourth-month showers have, and the mica
on the side of a rock has.

Do you take it I would astonish?
Does the daylight astonish? does the early redstart twittering
through the woods?
Do I astonish more than they?

This hour I tell things in confidence,
I might not tell everybody, but I will tell you.

20

Who goes there? hankering, gross, mystical, nude;
How is it I extract strength from the beef I eat?

What is a man anyhow? what am I? what are you?

All I mark as my own you shall offset it with your own,
Else it were time lost listening to me.

I do not snivel that snivel the world over,
That months are vacuums and the ground but wallow and
filth.

Whimpering and truckling fold with powders for invalids,
conformity goes to the fourth-remov'd,
I wear my hat as I please indoors or out.

Why should I pray? why should I venerate and be cere-
monious?

Having pried through the strata, analyzed to a hair, counsel'd
with doctors and calculated close,
I find no sweeter fat than sticks to my own bones.

In all people I see myself, none more and not one a barley-
corn less,
And the good or bad I say of myself I say of them.

I know I am solid and sound,
To me the converging objects of the universe perpetually flow,
All are written to me, and I must get what the writing means.

I know I am deathless,
I know this orbit of mine cannot be swept by a carpenter's
compass,
I know I shall not pass like a child's carlacue cut with a
burnt stick at night.

I know I am august,
I do not trouble my spirit to vindicate itself or be understood,
I see that the elementary laws never apologize,
(I reckon I behave no prouder than the level I plant my house
by, after all.)

I exist as I am, that is enough,
If no other in the world be aware I sit content,
And if each and all be aware I sit content.

One world is aware and by the far largest to me, and that is
myself,
And whether I come to my own to-day or in ten thousand or
ten million years,
I can cheerfully take it now, or with equal cheerfulness I can
wait.

My foothold is tenon'd and mortis'd in granite,
I laugh at what you call dissolution,
And I know the amplitude of time.

21

I am the poet of the Body and I am the poet of the Soul,
The pleasures of heaven are with me and the pains of hell are
with me,
The first I graft and increase upon myself, the latter I translate into a new tongue.

I am the poet of the woman the same as the man,
And I say it is as great to be a woman as to be a man,
And I say there is nothing greater than the mother of men.

I chant the chant of dilation or pride,
We have had ducking and deprecating about enough,
I show that size is only development.

Have you outstript the rest? are you the President?
It is a trifle, they will more than arrive there every one, and
still pass on.

I am he that walks with the tender and growing night,
I call to the earth and sea half-held by the night.

Press close bare-bosom'd night—press close magnetic nourishing night!
Night of south winds—night of the large few stars!
Still nodding night—mad naked summer night.

Smile O voluptuous cool-breath'd earth!
Earth of the slumbering and liquid trees!
Earth of departed sunset—earth of the mountains misty-topt!
Earth of the vitreous pour of the full moon just tinged with blue!
Earth of shine and dark mottling the tide of the river!
Earth of the limpid gray of clouds brighter and clearer for my sake!
Far-swooping elbow'd earth—rich apple-blossom'd earth!
Smile, for your lover comes.

Prodigal, you have given me love—therefore I to you give love!
O unspeakable passionate love.

22

You sea! I resign myself to you also—I guess what you mean,
I behold from the beach your crooked inviting fingers,
I believe you refuse to go back without feeling of me,
We must have a turn together, I undress, hurry me out of sight of the land,
Cushion me soft, rock me in billowy drowse,
Dash me with amorous wet, I can repay you.

Sea of stretch'd ground-swells,
Sea breathing broad and convulsive breaths,
Sea of the brine of life and of unshovell'd yet always-ready graves,
Howler and scooper of storms, capricious and dainty sea,
I am integral with you, I too am of one phase and of all phases.

Partaker of influx and efflux, I, extoller of hate and conciliation,
Extoller of amies and those that sleep in each others' arms.

I am he attesting sympathy,
(Shall I make my list of things in the house and skip the house
that supports them?)

I am not the poet of goodness only, I do not decline to be the
poet of wickedness also.

What blurt is this about virtue and about vice?
Evil propels me and reform of evil propels me, I stand indif-
ferent,
My gait is no fault-finder's or rejector's gait,
I moisten the roots of all that has grown.

Did you fear some scrofula out of the unflagging pregnancy?
Did you guess the celestial laws are yet to be work'd over and
rectified?

I find one side a balance and the antipodal side a balance,
Soft doctrine as steady help as stable doctrine,
Thoughts and deeds of the present our rouse and early start.

This minute that comes to me over the past decillions,
There is no better than it and now.

What behaved well in the past or behaves well to-day is not
such a wonder,
The wonder is always and always how there can be a mean
man or an infidel.

23

Endless unfolding of words of ages!
And mine a word of the modern, the word En-Masse.

A word of the faith that never balks,
Here or henceforward it is all the same to me, I accept Time
absolutely.

It alone is without flaw, it alone rounds and completes all,
That mystic baffling wonder alone completes all.

I accept Reality and dare not question it,
Materialism first and last imbuing.

Hurrah for positive science! long live exact demonstration!
Fetch stonecrop mixt with cedar and branches of lilac,
This is the lexicographer, this the chemist, this made a grammar of the old cartouches,
These mariners put the ship through dangerous unknown seas,
This is the geologist, this works with the scalpel, and this is a mathematician.

Gentlemen, to you the first honors always!
Your facts are useful, and yet they are not my dwelling,
I but enter by them to an area of my dwelling.

Less the reminders of properties told my words,
And more the reminders they of life untold, and of freedom and extrication,
And make short account of neuters and geldings, and favor men and women fully equipt,
And beat the gong of revolt, and stop with fugitives and them that plot and conspire.

24

Walt Whitman, a kosmos, of Manhattan the son,
Turbulent, fleshy, sensual, eating, drinking and breeding,
No sentimentalist, no stander above men and women or apart from them,
No more modest than immodest.

Unscrew the locks from the doors!
Unscrew the doors themselves from their jambs!

Whoever degrades another degrades me,
And whatever is done or said returns at last to me.

Through me the afflatus surging and surging, through me the
current and index.

I speak the pass-word primeval, I give the sign of democracy,
By God! I will accept nothing which all cannot have their
counterpart of on the same terms.

Through me many long dumb voices,
Voices of the interminable generations of prisoners and slaves,
Voices of the diseas'd and despairing and of thieves and
dwarfs,
Voices of cycles of preparation and accretion,
And of the threads that connect the stars, and of wombs and
of the father-stuff,
And of the rights of them the others are down upon,
Of the deform'd, trivial, flat, foolish, despised,
Fog in the air, beetles rolling balls of dung.

Through me forbidden voices,
Voices of sexes and lusts, voices veil'd and I remove the veil,
Voices indecent by me clarified and transfigur'd.

I do not press my fingers across my mouth,
I keep as delicate around the bowels as around the head and
heart,
Copulation is no more rank to me than death is.

I believe in the flesh and the appetites,
Seeing, hearing, feeling, are miracles, and each part and tag of
me is a miracle.

Divine am I inside and out, and I make holy whatever I
touch or am touch'd from,
The scent of these arm-pits aroma finer than prayer,
This head more than churches, bibles, and all the creeds.

If I worship one thing more than another it shall be the spread
of my own body, or any part of it,
Translucent mould of me it shall be you!

Shaded ledges and rests it shall be you!
Firm masculine colter it shall be you!
Whatever goes to the tilth of me it shall be you!
You my rich blood! your milky stream pale strippings of my life!
Breast that presses against other breasts it shall be you!
My brain it shall be your occult convolutions!
Root of wash'd sweet-flag! timorous pond-snipe! nest of guarded duplicate eggs! it shall be you!
Mix'd tussled hay of head, beard, brawn, it shall be you!
Trickling sap of maple, fibre of manly wheat, it shall be you!
Sun so generous it shall be you!
Vapors lighting and shading my face it shall be you!
You sweaty brooks and dews it shall be you!
Winds whose soft-tickling genitals rub against me it shall be you!
Broad muscular fields, branches of live oak loving lounger in my winding paths, it shall be you!
Hands I have taken, face I have kiss'd, mortal I have ever touch'd, it shall be you.

I dote on myself, there is that lot of me and all so luscious,
Each moment and whatever happens thrills me with joy,
I cannot tell how my ankles bend, nor whence the cause of my faintest wish,
Nor the cause of the friendship I emit, nor the cause of the friendship I take again.

That I walk up my stoop, I pause to consider if it really be,
A morning-glory at my window satisfies me more than the metaphysics of books.

To behold the day-break!
The little light fades the immense and diaphanous shadows,
The air tastes good to my palate.

Hefts of the moving world at innocent gambols silently rising, freshly exuding,
Scooting obliquely high and low.

Something I cannot see puts upward libidinous prongs,
Seas of bright juice suffuse heaven.

The earth by the sky staid with, the daily close of their junction,
The heav'd challenge from the east that moment over my head,
The mocking taunt, See then whether you shall be master!

25

Dazzling and tremendous how quick the sun-rise would kill me,
If I could not now and always send sun-rise out of me.

We also ascend dazzling and tremendous as the sun,
We found our own O my soul in the calm and cool of the daybreak.

My voice goes after what my eyes cannot reach,
With the twirl of my tongue I encompass worlds and volumes of worlds.

Speech is the twin of my vision, it is unequal to measure itself,
It provokes me forever, it says sarcastically,
Walt you contain enough, why don't you let it out then?

Come now I will not be tantalized, you conceive too much of articulation,
Do you not know O speech how the buds beneath you are folded?
Waiting in gloom, protected by frost,
The dirt receding before my prophetical screams,
I underlying causes to balance them at last,
My knowledge my live parts, it keeping tally with the meaning of all things,
Happiness, (which whoever hears me let him or her set out in search of this day.)

My final merit I refuse you, I refuse putting from me what I really am,

Encompass worlds, but never try to encompass me,
I crowd your sleekest and best by simply looking toward you.

Writing and talk do not prove me,
I carry the plenum of proof and every thing else in my face,
With the hush of my lips I wholly confound the skeptic.

26

Now I will do nothing but listen,
To accrue what I hear into this song, to let sounds contribute toward it.

I hear bravuras of birds, bustle of growing wheat, gossip of flames, clack of sticks cooking my meals,
I hear the sound I love, the sound of the human voice,
I hear all sounds running together, combined, fused or following,
Sounds of the city and sounds out of the city, sounds of the day and night,
Talkative young ones to those that like them, the loud laugh of work-people at their meals,
The angry base of disjointed friendship, the faint tones of the sick,
The judge with hands tight to the desk, his pallid lips pronouncing a death-sentence,
The heave'e'yo of stevedores unlading ships by the wharves, the refrain of the anchor-lifters,
The ring of alarm-bells, the cry of fire, the whir of swift-streaking engines and hose-carts with premonitory tinkles and color'd lights,
The steam-whistle, the solid roll of the train of approaching cars,
The slow march play'd at the head of the association marching two and two,
(They go to guard some corpse, the flag-tops are draped with black muslin.)

I hear the violoncello, ('tis the young man's heart's complaint,)
I hear the key'd cornet, it glides quickly in through my ears,
It shakes mad-sweet pangs through my belly and breast.

I hear the chorus, it is a grand opera,
Ah this indeed is music—this suits me.

A tenor large and fresh as the creation fills me,
The orbic flex of his mouth is pouring and filling me full.

I hear the train'd soprano (what work with hers is this?)
The orchestra whirls me wider than Uranus flies,
It wrenches such ardors from me I did not know I possess'd
 them,
It sails me, I dab with bare feet, they are lick'd by the indolent
 waves,
I am cut by bitter and angry hail, I lose my breath,
Steep'd amid honey'd morphine, my windpipe throttled in
 fakes of death,
At length let up again to feel the puzzle of puzzles,
And that we call Being.

27

To be in any form, what is that?
(Round and round we go, all of us, and ever come back
 thither,)
If nothing lay more develop'd the quahaug in its callous shell
 were enough.

Mine is no callous shell,
I have instant conductors all over me whether I pass or stop,
They seize every object and lead it harmlessly through me.

I merely stir, press, feel with my fingers, and am happy,
To touch my person to some one else's is about as much as I
 can stand.

28

Is this then a touch? quivering me to a new identity,
Flames and ether making a rush for my veins,
Treacherous tip of me reaching and crowding to help them,
My flesh and blood playing out lightning to strike what is
 hardly different from myself,

On all sides prurient provokers stiffening my limbs,
Straining the udder of my heart for its withheld drip,
Behaving licentious toward me, taking no denial,
Depriving me of my best as for a purpose,
Unbuttoning my clothes, holding me by the bare waist,
Deluding my confusion with the calm of the sunlight and
 pasture-fields,
Immodestly sliding the fellow-senses away,
They bribed to swap off with touch and go and graze at the
 edges of me,
No consideration, no regard for my draining strength or my
 anger,
Fetching the rest of the herd around to enjoy them a while,
Then all uniting to stand on a headland and worry me.

The sentries desert every other part of me,
They have left me helpless to a red marauder,
They all come to the headland to witness and assist against me.

I am given up by traitors,
I talk wildly, I have lost my wits, I and nobody else am the
 greatest traitor,
I went myself first to the headland, my own hands carried me
 there.
You villain touch! what are you doing? my breath is tight in
 its throat,
Unclench your floodgates, you are too much for me.

29

Blind loving wrestling touch, sheath'd hooded sharp-tooth'd
 touch!
Did it make you ache so, leaving me?

Parting track'd by arriving, perpetual payment of perpetual
 loan,
Rich showering rain, and recompense richer afterward.

Sprouts take and accumulate, stand by the curb prolific and
 vital,
Landscapes projected masculine, full-sized and golden.

30

All truths wait in all things,
They neither hasten their own delivery nor resist it,
They do not need the obstetric forceps of the surgeon,
The insignificant is as big to me as any,
(What is less or more than a touch?)

Logic and sermons never convince,
The damp of the night drives deeper into my soul.

(Only what proves itself to every man and woman is so,
Only what nobody denies is so.)

A minute and a drop of me settle my brain,
I believe the soggy clods shall become lovers and lamps,
And a compend of compends is the meat of a man or woman,
And a summit and flower there is the feeling they have for
each other,
And they are to branch boundlessly out of that lesson until it
becomes omnific,
And until one and all shall delight us, and we them.

31

I believe a leaf of grass is no less than the journey-work of
the stars,
And the pismire is equally perfect, and a grain of sand, and
the egg of the wren,
And the tree-toad is a chef-d'œuvre for the highest,
And the running blackberry would adorn the parlors of heaven,
And the narrowest hinge in my hand puts to scorn all
machinery,
And the cow crunching with depress'd head surpasses any
statue,
And a mouse is miracle enough to stagger sextillions of
infidels.

I find I incorporate gneiss, coal, long-threaded moss, fruits,
grains, esculent roots,

And am stucco'd with quadrupeds and birds all over,
And have distanced what is behind me for good reasons,
But call any thing back again when I desire it.

In vain the speeding or shyness,
In vain the plutonic rocks send their old heat against my
approach,
In vain the mastodon retreats beneath its own powder'd bones,
In vain objects stand leagues off and assume manifold shapes,
In vain the ocean settling in hollows and the great monsters
lying low,
In vain the buzzard houses herself with the sky,
In vain the snake slides through the creepers and logs,
In vain the elk takes to the inner passes of the woods,
In vain the razor-bill'd auk sails far north to Laborador,
I follow quickly, I ascend to the nest in the fissure of the cliff.

32

I think I could turn and live with animals, they're so placid
and self-contain'd,
I stand and look at them long and long.

They do not sweat and whine about their condition,
They do not lie awake in the dark and weep for their sins,
They do not make me sick discussing their duty to God,
Not one is dissatisfied, not one is demented with the mania of
owning things,
Not one kneels to another, nor to his kind that lived thousands
of years ago,
Not one is respectable or unhappy over the whole earth.

So they show their relations to me and I accept them,
They bring me tokens of myself, they evince them plainly in
their possession.

I wonder where they get those tokens,
Did I pass that way huge times ago and negligently drop
them?

Myself moving forward then and now and forever,
Gathering and showing more always and with velocity,
Infinite and omnigenous, and the like of these among them,
Not too exclusive toward the reachers of my remembrancers,
Picking out here one that I love, and now go with him on
brotherly terms.

A gigantic beauty of a stallion, fresh and responsive to my
caresses,
Head high in the forehead, wide between the ears,
Limbs glossy and supple, tail dusting the ground,
Eyes full of sparkling wickedness, ears finely cut, flexibly
moving.

His nostrils dilate as my heels embrace him,
His well-built limbs tremble with pleasure as we race around
and return.
I but use you a minute, then I resign you, stallion,
Why do I need your paces when I myself out-gallop them?
Even as I stand or sit passing faster than you.

33

Space and Time! now I see it is true, what I guess'd at,
What I guess'd when I loaf'd on the grass,
What I guess'd while I lay alone in my bed,
And again as I walk'd the beach under the paling stars of the
morning.

My ties and ballasts leave me, my elbows rest in sea-gaps,
I skirt sierras, my palms cover continents,
I am afoot with my vision.

By the city's quadrangular houses—in log huts, camping with
lumbermen,
Along the ruts of the turnpike, along the dry gulch and
rivulet bed,
Weeding my onion-patch or hoeing rows of carrots and
parsnips, crossing savannas, trailing in forests,

Prospecting, gold-digging, girdling the trees of a new purchase,
Scorch'd ankle-deep by the hot sand, hauling my boat down the shallow river,
Where the panther walks to and fro on a limb overhead, where the buck turns furiously at the hunter,
Where the rattlesnake suns his flabby length on a rock, where the otter is feeding on fish,
Where the alligator in his tough pimples sleeps by the bayou,
Where the black bear is searching for roots or honey, where the beaver pats the mud with his paddle-shaped tail;
Over the growing sugar, over the yellow-flower'd cotton plant, over the rice in its low moist field,
Over the sharp-peak'd farm house, with its scallop'd scum and slender shoots from the gutters,
Over the western persimmon, over the long-leav'd corn, over the delicate blue-flower flax,
Over the white and brown buckwheat, a hummer and buzzer there with the rest,
Over the dusky green of the rye as it ripples and shades in the breeze;
Scaling mountains, pulling myself cautiously up, holding on by low scragged limbs,
Walking the path worn in the grass and beat through the leaves of the brush,
Where the quail is whistling betwixt the woods and the wheat-lot,
Where the bat flies in the Seventh-month eve, where the great gold-bug drops through the dark,
Where the brook puts out of the roots of the old tree and flows to the meadow,
Where cattle stand and shake away flies with the tremulous shuddering of their hides,
Where the cheese-cloth hangs in the kitchen, where andirons straddle the hearth-slab, where cobwebs fall in festoons from the rafters;
Where trip-hammers crash, where the press is whirling its cylinders,
Wherever the human heart beats with terrible throes under its ribs,

Where the pear-shaped balloon is floating aloft, (floating in it myself and looking composedly down,)
Where the life-car is drawn on the slip-noose, where the heat hatches pale-green eggs in the dented sand,
Where the she-whale swims with her calf and never forsakes it,
Where the steam-ship trails hind-ways its long pennant of smoke,
Where the fin of the shark cuts like a black chip out of the water,
Where the half-burn'd brig is riding on unknown currents,
Where shells grow to her slimy deck, where the dead are corrupting below;
Where the dense-starr'd flag is borne at the head of the regiments,
Approaching Manhattan up by the long-stretching island,
Under Niagara, the cataract falling like a veil over my countenance,
Upon a door-step, upon the horse-block of hard wood outside,
Upon the race-course, or enjoying picnics or jigs or a good game of base-ball,
At he-festivals, with blackguard gibes, ironical license, bull-dances, drinking, laughter,
At the cider-mill tasting the sweets of the brown mash, sucking the juice through a straw,
At apple-peelings wanting kisses for all the red fruit I find,
At musters, beach-parties, friendly bees, huskings, house-raisings;
Where the mocking-bird sounds his delicious gurgles, cackles, screams, weeps,
Where the hay-rick stands in the barn-yard, where the dry stalks are scatter'd, where the brood-cow waits in the hovel,
Where the bull advances to do his masculine work, where the stud to the mare, where the cock is treading the hen,
Where the heifers browse, where geese nip their food with short jerks,
Where sun-down shadows lengthen over the limitless and lonesome prairie,
Where herds of buffalo make a crawling spread of the square miles far and near,

Where the humming-bird shimmers, where the neck of the long-lived swan is curving and winding,
Where the laughing-gull scoots by the shore, where she laughs her near-human laugh,
Where bee-hives range on a gray bench in the garden half hid by the high weeds,
Where band-neck'd partridges roost in a ring on the ground with their heads out,
Where burial coaches enter the arch'd gates of a cemetery,
Where winter wolves bark amid wastes of snow and icicled trees,
Where the yellow-crown'd heron comes to the edge of the marsh at night and feeds upon small crabs,
Where the splash of swimmers and divers cools the warm moon,
Where the katy-did works her chromatic reed on the walnut-tree over the well,
Through patches of citrons and cucumbers with silver-wired leaves,
Through the salt-lick or orange glade, or under conical firs,
Through the gymnasium, through the curtain'd saloon, through the office or public hall;
Pleas'd with the native and pleas'd with the foreign, pleas'd with the new and old,
Pleas'd with the homely woman as well as the handsome,
Pleas'd with the quakeress as she puts off her bonnet and talks melodiously,
Pleas'd with the tune of the choir of the whitewash'd church,
Pleas'd with the earnest words of the sweating Methodist preacher, impress'd seriously at the camp-meeting;
Looking in at the shop-windows of Broadway the whole forenoon, flatting the flesh of my nose on the thick plate glass,
Wandering the same afternoon with my face turn'd up to the clouds, or down a lane or along the beach,
My right and left arms round the sides of two friends, and I in the middle;
Coming home with the silent and dark-cheek'd bush-boy, (behind me he rides at the drape of the day,)

Far from the settlements studying the print of animals' feet, or
the moccasin print,
By the cot in the hospital reaching lemonade to a feverish
patient,
Nigh the coffin'd corpse when all is still, examining with a
candle;
Voyaging to every port to dicker and adventure,
Hurrying with the modern crowd as eager and fickle as any,
Hot toward one I hate, ready in my madness to knife him,
Solitary at midnight in my back yard, my thoughts gone from
me a long while,
Walking the old hills of Judæa with the beautiful gentle God
by my side,
Speeding through space, speeding through heaven and the
stars,
Speeding amid the seven satellites and the broad ring, and the
diameter of eighty thousand miles,
Speeding with tail'd meteors, throwing fire-balls like the rest,
Carrying the crescent child that carries its own full mother in
its belly,
Storming, enjoying, planning, loving, cautioning,
Backing and filling, appearing and disappearing,
I tread day and night such roads.

I visit the orchards of spheres and look at the product,
And look at quintillions ripen'd and look at quintillions green

I fly those flights of a fluid and swallowing soul,
My course runs below the soundings of plummets.

I help myself to material and immaterial,
No guard can shut me off, no law prevent me.

I anchor my ship for a little while only,
My messengers continually cruise away or bring their returns
to me.

I go hunting polar furs and the seal, leaping chasms with a
pike-pointed staff, clinging to topples of brittle and blue.

I ascend to the foretruck,
I take my place at night in the crow's-nest,
We sail the arctic sea, it is plenty light enough,
Through the clear atmosphere I stretch around on the wonderful beauty,
The enormous masses of ice pass me and I pass them, the scenery is plain in all directions,
The white-topt mountains show in the distance, I fling out my fancies toward them,
We are approaching some great battle-field in which we are soon to be engaged,
We pass the colossal outposts of the encampment, we pass with still feet and caution,
Or we are entering by the suburbs some vast and ruin'd city,
The blocks and fallen architecture more than all the living cities of the globe.

I am a free companion, I bivouac by invading watchfires,
I turn the bridegroom out of bed and stay with the bride myself,
I tighten her all night to my thighs and lips.

My voice is the wife's voice, the screech by the rail of the stairs,
They fetch my man's body up dripping and drown'd.

I understand the large hearts of heroes,
The courage of present times and all times,
How the skipper saw the crowded and rudderless wreck of the steam-ship, and Death chasing it up and down the storm,
How he knuckled tight and gave not an inch, and was faithful of days and faithful of nights,
And chalk'd in large letters on a board, *Be of good cheer, we will not desert you;*
How he follow'd with them and tack'd with them three days and would not give it up,
How he saved the drifting company at last,
How the lank loose-gown'd women look'd when boated from the side of their prepared graves,

How the silent old-faced infants and the lifted sick, and the sharp-lipp'd unshaven men;
All this I swallow, it tastes good, I like it well, it becomes mine,
I am the man, I suffer'd, I was there.

The disdain and calmness of martyrs,
The mother of old, condemn'd for a witch, burnt with dry wood, her children gazing on,
The hounded slave that flags in the race, leans by the fence, blowing, cover'd with sweat.
The twinges that sting like needles his legs and neck, the murderous buckshot and the bullets
All these I feel or am.

I am the hounded slave, I wince at the bite of the dogs,
Hell and despair are upon me, crack and again crack the marksmen,
I clutch the rails of the fence, my gore dribs, thinn'd with the ooze of my skin,
I fall on the weeds and stones,
The riders spur their unwilling horses, haul close,
Taunt my dizzy ears and beat me violently over the head with whip-stocks.

Agonies are one of my changes of garments,
I do not ask the wounded person how he feels, I myself become the wounded person,
My hurts turn livid upon me as I lean on a cane and observe.

I am the mash'd fireman with breast-bone broken,
Tumbling walls buried me in their debris,
Heat and smoke I inspired, I heard the yelling shouts of my comrades,
I heard the distant click of their picks and shovels,
They have clear'd the beams away, they tenderly lift me forth,

I lie in the night air in my red shirt, the pervading hush is for my sake,
Painless after all I lie exhausted but not so unhappy,

White and beautiful are the faces around me, the heads are bared of their fire-caps,
The kneeling crowd fades with the light of the torches.

Distant and dead resuscitate,
They show as the dial or move as the hands of me, I am the clock myself.

I am an old artillerist, I tell of my fort's bombardment,
I am there again.

Again the long roll of the drummers,
Again the attacking cannon, mortars,
Again to my listening ears the cannon responsive.

I take part, I see and hear the whole,
The cries, curses, roar, the plaudits for well-aim'd shots,
The ambulanza slowly passing trailing its red drip,
Workmen searching after damages, making indispensable repairs,
The fall of grenades through the rent roof, the fan-shaped explosion,
The whizz of limbs, heads, stone, wood, iron, high in the air.

Again gurgles the mouth of my dying general, he furiously waves with his hand,
He gasps through the clot *Mind not me—mind—the entrenchments.*

34

Now I tell what I knew in Texas in my early youth,
(I tell not the fall of Alamo,
Not one escaped to tell the fall of Alamo,
The hundred and fifty are dumb yet at Alamo,)
'Tis the tale of the murder in cold blood of four hundred and twelve young men.

Retreating they had form'd in a hollow square with their baggage for breastworks,

Nine hundred lives out of the surrounding enemy's, nine times
their number, was the price they took in advance,
Their colonel was wounded and their ammunition gone,
They treated for an honorable capitulation, receiv'd writing
and seal, gave up their arms and march'd back prisoners
of war.

They were the glory of the race of rangers,
Matchless with horse, rifle, song, supper, courtship,
Large, turbulent, generous, handsome, proud, and affectionate,
Bearded, sunburnt, drest in the free costume of hunters,
Not a single one over thirty years of age.

The second First-day morning they were brought out in squads
and massacred, it was beautiful early summer,
The work commenced about five o'clock and was over by
eight.

None obey'd the command to kneel,
Some made a mad and helpless rush, some stood stark and
straight,
A few fell at once, shot in the temple or heart, the living and
dead lay together,
The maim'd and mangled dug in the dirt, the new-comers
saw them there,
Some half-kill'd attempted to crawl away,
These were despatch'd with bayonets or batter'd with the
blunts of muskets,
A youth not seventeen years old seiz'd his assassin till two
more came to release him,
The three were all torn and cover'd with the boy's blood.

At eleven o'clock began the burning of the bodies;
That is the tale of the murder of the four hundred and twelve
young men.

35

Would you hear of an old-time sea-fight?
Would you learn who won by the light of the moon and
stars?

List to the yarn, as my grandmother's father the sailor told
it to me.

Our foe was no skulk in his ship I tell you, (said he,)
His was the surly English pluck, and there is no tougher or
truer, and never was, and never will be;
Along the lower'd eve he came horribly raking us.

We closed with him, the yards entangled, the cannon touch'd,
My captain lash'd fast with his own hands.

We had receiv'd some eighteen pound shots under the water,
On our lower-gun-deck two large pieces had burst at the first
fire, killing all around and blowing up overhead.

Fighting at sun-down, fighting at dark,
Ten o'clock at night, the full moon well up, our leaks on the
gain, and five feet of water reported,
The master-at-arms loosing the prisoners confined in the after-
hold to give them a chance for themselves.

The transit to and from the magazine is now stopt by the
sentinels,
They see so many strange faces they do not know whom to
trust.

Our frigate takes fire,
The other asks if we demand quarter?
If our colors are struck and the fighting done?

Now I laugh content, for I hear the voice of my little captain,
We have not struck, he composedly cries, *we have just begun
our part of the fighting.*

Only three guns are in use,
One is directed by the captain himself against the enemy's
main-mast,
Two well serv'd with grape and canister silence his musketry
and clear his decks.

The tops alone second the fire of this little battery, especially
the main-top,
They hold out bravely during the whole of the action.

Not a moment's cease,
The leaks gain fast on the pumps, the fire eats toward the
powder-magazine.

One of the pumps has been shot away, it is generally thought
we are sinking.

Serene stands the little captain,
He is not hurried, his voice is neither high nor low,
His eyes give more light to us than our battle-lanterns.

Toward twelve there in the beams of the moon they surrender
to us.

36

Stretch'd and still lies the midnight,
Two great hulls motionless on the breast of the darkness,
Our vessel riddled and slowly sinking, preparations to pass to
the one we have conquer'd,
The captain on the quarter-deck coldly giving his orders
through a countenance white as a sheet,
Near by the corpse of the child that serv'd in the cabin,
The dead face of an old salt with long white hair and carefully
curl'd whiskers,
The flames spite of all that can be done flickering aloft and
below,
The husky voices of the two or three officers yet fit for duty,
Formless stacks of bodies and bodies by themselves, dabs of
flesh upon the masts and spars,
Cut of cordage, dangle of rigging, slight shock of the soothe of
waves,
Black and impassive guns, litter of powder parcels, strong
scent,
A few large stars overhead, silent and mournful shining,
Delicate sniffs of sea-breeze, smells of sedgy grass and fields
by the shore, death-messages given in charge to survivors,

The hiss of the surgeon's knife, the gnawing teeth of his saw,
Wheeze, cluck, swash of falling blood, short wild scream, and
long, dull, tapering groan,
These so, these irretrievable.

37

You laggards there on guard! look to your arms!
In at the conquer'd doors they crowd! I am possess'd!
Embody all presences outlaw'd or suffering,
See myself in prison shaped like another man,
And feel the dull unintermitted pain.

For me the keepers of convicts shoulder their carbines and keep
watch,
It is I let out in the morning and barr'd at night.

Not a mutineer walks handcuff'd to jail but I am handcuff'd
to him and walk by his side,
(I am less the jolly one there, and more the silent one with
sweat on my twitching lips.)

Not a youngster is taken for larceny but I go up too, and am
tried and sentenced.

Not a cholera patient lies at the last gasp but I also lie at the
last gasp,
My face is ash-color'd, my sinews gnarl, away from me people
retreat.

Askers embody themselves in me and I am embodied in them,
I project my hat, sit shame-faced, and beg.

38

Enough! enough! enough!
Somehow I have been stunn'd. Stand back!
Give me a little time beyond my cuff'd head, slumbers, dreams,
gaping,
I discover myself on the verge of a usual mistake.

That I could forget the mockers and insults!
That I could forget the trickling tears and the blows of the bludgeons and hammers!
That I could look with a separate look on my own crucifixion and bloody crowning.

I remember now,
I resume the overstaid fraction,
The grave of rock multiplies what has been confided to it, or to any graves,
Corpses rise, gashes heal, fastenings roll from me.

I troop forth replenish'd with supreme power, one of an average unending procession,
Inland and sea-coast we go, and pass all boundary lines,
Our swift ordinances on their way over the whole earth,
The blossoms we wear in our hats the growth of thousands of years.

Eleves, I salute you! come forward!
Continue your annotations, continue your questionings.

39

The friendly and flowing savage, who is he?
Is he waiting for civilization, or past it and mastering it?

Is he some Southwesterner rais'd out-doors? is he Kanadian?
Is he from the Mississippi country? Iowa, Oregon, California?
The mountains? prairie-life, bush-life? or sailor from the sea?

Wherever he goes men and women accept and desire him,
They desire he should like them, touch them, speak to them, stay with them.

Behavior lawless as snow-flakes, words simple as grass, uncomb'd head, laughter, and naivetè,
Slow-stepping feet, common features, common modes and emanations,

They descend in new forms from the tips of his fingers,
They are wafted with the odor of his body or breath, they fly out of the glance of his eyes.

40

Flaunt of the sunshine I need not your bask—lie over!
You light surfaces only, I force surfaces and depths also.

Earth! you seem to look for something at my hands,
Say, old top-knot, what do you want?

Man or woman, I might tell how I like you, but cannot,
And might tell what it is in me and what it is in you, but cannot,
And might tell that pining I have, that pulse of my nights and days.

Behold, I do not give lectures or a little charity,
When I give I give myself.

You there, impotent, loose in the knees,
Open your scarf'd chops till I blow grit within you,
Spread your palms and lift the flaps of your pockets,
I am not to be denied, I compel, I have stores plenty and to spare,
And any thing I have I bestow.

I do not ask who you are, that is not important to me,
You can do nothing and be nothing but what I will infold you.

To cotton-field drudge or cleaner of privies I lean,
On his right cheek I put the family kiss,
And in my soul I swear I never will deny him.

On women fit for conception I start bigger and nimbler babes,
(This day I am jetting the stuff of far more arrogant republics.)

To any one dying, thither I speed and twist the knob of the door,

Turn the bed-clothes toward the foot of the bed,
Let the physician and the priest go home.

I seize the descending man and raise him with resistless will,
O despairer, here is my neck,
By God, you shall not go down! hang your whole weight
upon me.

I dilate you with tremendous breath, I buoy you up,
Every room of the house do I fill with an arm'd force,
Lovers of me, bafflers of graves.

Sleep—I and they keep guard all night,
Not doubt, not decease shall dare to lay finger upon you,
I have embraced you, and henceforth possess you to myself,
And when you rise in the morning you will find what I tell
you is so.

41

I am he bringing help for the sick as they pant on their backs,
And for strong upright men I bring yet more needed help.

I heard what was said of the universe,
Heard it and heard it of several thousand years;
It is middling well as far as it goes—but is that all?

Magnifying and applying come I,
Outbidding at the start the old cautious hucksters,
Taking myself the exact dimensions of Jehovah,
Lithographing Kronos, Zeus his son, and Hercules his grandson,
Buying drafts of Osiris, Isis, Belus, Brahma, Buddha,
In my portfolio placing Manito loose, Allah on a leaf, the crucifix engraved,
With Odin and the hideous-faced Mexitli and every idol and
image,
Taking them all for what they are worth and not a cent more,
Admitting they were alive and did the work of their days,
(They bore mites as for unfledg'd birds who have now to rise
and fly and sing for themselves,)

Accepting the rough deific sketches to fill out better in myself,
bestowing them freely on each man and woman I see,
Discovering as much or more in a framer framing a house,
Putting higher claims for him there with his roll'd-up sleeves
driving the mallet and chisel,
Not objecting to special revelations, considering a curl of
smoke or a hair on the back of my hand just as curious as
any revelation,
Lads ahold of fire-engines and hook-and-ladder ropes no less to
me than the gods of the antique wars,
Minding their voices peal through the crash of destruction,
Their brawny limbs passing safe over charr'd laths, their white
foreheads whole and unhurt out of the flames;
By the mechanic's wife with her babe at her nipple interceding
for every person born,
Three scythes at harvest whizzing in a row from three lusty
angels with shirts bagg'd out at their waists,
The snag-tooth'd hostler with red hair redeeming sins past and
to come,
Selling all he possesses, travelling on foot to fee lawyers for his
brother and sit by him while he is tried for forgery;
What was strewn in the amplest strewing the square rod about
me, and not filling the square rod then,
The bull and the bug never worshipp'd half enough,
Dung and dirt more admirable than was dream'd,
The supernatural of no account, myself waiting my time to be
one of the supremes,
The day getting ready for me when I shall do as much good
as the best, and be as prodigious;
By my life-lumps! becoming already a creator,
Putting myself here and now to the ambush'd womb of the
shadows.

42

A call in the midst of the crowd,
My own voice, orotund, sweeping and final.

Come my children,
Come my boys and girls, my women, household and intimates,

Now the performer launches his nerve, he has pass'd his prelude on the reeds within.

Easily written loose-finger'd chords—I feel the thrum of your climax and close.

My head slues round on my neck,
Music rolls, but not from the organ,
Folks are around me, but they are no household of mine.

Ever the hard unsunk ground,
Ever the eaters and drinkers, ever the upward and downward sun, ever the air and the ceaseless tides,
Ever myself and my neighbors, refreshing, wicked, real,
Ever the old inexplicable query, ever that thorn'd thumb, that breath of itches and thirsts,
Ever the vexer's *hoot! hoot!* till we find where the sly one hides and bring him forth,
Ever love, ever the sobbing liquid of life,
Ever the bandage under the chin, ever the trestles of death.

Here and there with dimes on the eyes walking,
To feed the greed of the belly the brains liberally spooning,
Tickets buying, taking, selling, but in to the feast never once going,
Many sweating, ploughing, thrashing, and then the chaff for payment receiving,
A few idly owning, and they the wheat continually claiming.

This is the city and I am one of the citizens,
Whatever interests the rest interests me, politics, wars, markets, newspapers, schools,
The mayor and councils, banks, tariffs, steamships, factories, stocks, stores, real estate and personal estate.

The little plentiful manikins skipping around in collars and tail'd coats,
I am aware who they are, (they are positively not worms or fleas,)

I acknowledge the duplicates of myself, the weakest and
shallowest is deathless with me,
What I do and say the same waits for them,
Every thought that flounders in me the same flounders in them.

I know perfectly well my own egotism,
Know my omnivorous lines and must not write any less,
And would fetch you whoever you are flush with myself.

Not words of routine this song of mine,
But abruptly to question, to leap beyond yet nearer bring;
This printed and bound book—but the printer and the printing-office boy?
The well-taken photographs—but your wife or friend close and
solid in your arms?
The black ship mail'd with iron, her mighty guns in her
turrets—but the pluck of the captain and engineers?
In the houses the dishes and fare and furniture—but the host
and hostess, and the look out of their eyes?
The sky up there—yet here or next door, or across the way?
The saints and sages in history—but you yourself?
Sermons, creeds, theology—but the fathomless human brain,
And what is reason? and what is love? and what is life?

43

I do not despise you priests, all time, the world over,
My faith is the greatest of faiths and the least of faiths,
Enclosing worship ancient and modern and all between ancient
and modern,
Believing I shall come again upon the earth after five thousand
years,
Waiting responses from oracles, honoring the gods, saluting
the sun,
Making a fetich of the first rock or stump, powowing with
sticks in the circle of obis,
Helping the lama or brahmin as he trims the lamps of the
idols,
Dancing yet through the streets in a phallic procession, rapt
and austere in the woods a gymnosophist,

Drinking mead from the skull-cup, to Shastas and Vedas admirant, minding the Koran,
Walking the Teokallis, spotted with gore from the stone and knife, beating the serpent-skin drum,
Accepting the Gospels, accepting him that was crucified, knowing assuredly that he is divine,
To the mass kneeling or the puritan's prayer rising, or sitting patiently in a pew,
Ranting and frothing in my insane crisis, or waiting dead-like till my spirit arouses me,
Looking forth on pavement and land, or outside of pavement and land,
Belonging to the winders of the circuit of circuits.

One of that centripetal and centrifugal gang I turn and talk like a man leaving charges before a journey.

Down-hearted doubters dull and excluded,
Frivolous, sullen, moping, angry, affected, dishearten'd, atheistical,
I know every one of you, I know the sea of torment, doubt, despair and unbelief.

How the flukes splash!
How they contort rapid as lightning, with spasms and spouts of blood!

Be at peace bloody flukes of doubters and sullen mopers,
I take my place among you as much as among any,
The past is the push of you, me, all, precisely the same,
And what is yet untried and afterward is for you, me, all, precisely the same.

I do not know what is untried and afterward,
But I know it will in its turn prove sufficient, and cannot fail.

Each who passes is consider'd, each who stops is consider'd, not a single one can it fail.

It cannot fail the young man who died and was buried,
Nor the young woman who died and was put by his side,

Nor the little child that peep'd in at the door, and then drew back and was never seen again,
Nor the old man who has lived without purpose, and feels it with bitterness worse than gall,
Nor him in the poor house tubercled by rum and the bad disorder,
Nor the numberless slaughter'd and wreck'd, nor the brutish koboo call'd the ordure of humanity,
Nor the sacs merely floating with open mouths for food to slip in,
Nor any thing in the earth, or down in the oldest graves of the earth,
Nor any thing in the myriads of spheres, nor the myriads of myriads that inhabit them,
Nor the present, nor the least wisp that is known.

44

It is time to explain myself—let us stand up.

What is known I strip away,
I launch all men and women forward with me into the Unknown.

The clock indicates the moment—but what does eternity indicate?

We have thus far exhausted trillions of winters and summers,
There are trillions ahead, and trillions ahead of them.

Births have brought us richness and variety,
And other births will bring us richness and variety.

I do not call one greater and one smaller,
That which fills its period and place is equal to any.

Were mankind murderous or jealous upon you, my brother, my sister?
I am sorry for you, they are not murderous or jealous upon me,

All has been gentle with me, I keep no account with
lamentation,
(What have I to do with lamentation?)

I am an acme of things accomplish'd, and I an encloser of
things to be.

My feet strike an apex of the apices of the stairs,
On every step bunches of ages, and larger bunches between the
steps,
All below duly travel'd, and still I mount and mount.

Rise after rise bow the phantoms behind me,
Afar down I see the huge first Nothing, I know I was even
there,
I waited unseen and always, and slept through the lethargic
mist,
And took my time, and took no hurt from the fetid carbon.

Long I was hugg'd close—long and long.

Immense have been the preparations for me,
Faithful and friendly the arms that have help'd me.

Cycles ferried my cradle, rowing and rowing like cheerful
boatmen,
For room to me stars kept aside in their own rings,
They sent influences to look after what was to hold me.

Before I was born out of my mother generations guided me,
My embryo has never been torpid, nothing could overlay it.

For it the nebula cohered to an orb,
The long slow strata piled to rest it on,
Vast vegetables gave it sustenance,
Monstrous sauroids transported it in their mouths and deposited
it with care.

All forces have been steadily employ'd to complete and delight
me,
Now on this spot I stand with my robust soul.

45

O span of youth! ever-push'd elasticity.
O manhood, balanced, florid and full.

My lovers suffocate me,
Crowding my lips, thick in the pores of my skin,
Jostling me through streets and public halls, coming naked to me at night,
Crying by day *Ahoy!* from the rocks of the river, swinging and chirping over my head,
Calling my name from flower-beds, vines, tangled underbrush,
Lighting on every moment of my life,
Bussing my body with soft balsamic busses,
Noiselessly passing handfuls out of their hearts and giving them to be mine.

Old age superbly rising! O welcome, ineffable grace of dying days!

Every condition promulges not only itself, it promulges what grows after and out of itself,
And the dark hush promulges as much as any.

I open my scuttle at night and see the far-sprinkled systems,
And all I see multiplied as high as I can cipher edge but the rim of the farther systems.

Wider and wider they spread, expanding, always expanding,
Outward and outward and forever outward.

My sun has his sun and round him obediently wheels,
He joins with his partners a group of superior circuit,
And greater sets follow, making specks of the greatest inside them.

There is no stoppage and never can be stoppage,
If I, you, and the worlds, and all beneath or upon their surfaces, were this moment reduced back to a pallid float, it would not avail in the long run,

We should surely bring up again where we now stand,
And surely go as much farther, and then farther and farther.

A few quadrillions of eras, a few octillions of cubic leagues, do
not hazard the span or make it impatient,
They are but parts, any thing is but a part.

See ever so far, there is limitless space outside of that,
Count ever so much, there is limitless time around that.

My rendezvous is appointed, it is certain,
The Lord will be there and wait till I come on perfect terms,
The great Camerado, the lover true for whom I pine will be
there.

46

I know I have the best of time and space, and was never meas
ured and never will be measured.

I tramp a perpetual journey, (come listen all!)
My signs are a rain-proof coat, good shoes, and a staff cut from
the woods,
No friend of mine takes his ease in my chair,
I have no chair, no church, no philosophy,
I lead no man to a dinner-table, library, exchange,
But each man and each woman of you I lead upon a knoll,
My left hand hooking you round the waist,
My right hand pointing to landscapes of continents and the
public road.

Not I, not any one else can travel that road for you,
You must travel it for yourself.

It is not far, it is within reach,
Perhaps you have been on it since you were born and did not
know,
Perhaps it is everywhere on water and on land.

Shoulder your duds dear son, and I will mine, and let us hasten forth,
Wonderful cities and free nations we shall fetch as we go.

If you tire, give me both burdens, and rest the chuff of your hand on my hip,
And in due time you shall repay the same service to me,
For after we start we never lie by again.

This day before dawn I ascended a hill and look'd at the crowded heaven,
And I said to my spirit *When we become the enfolders of those orbs, and the pleasure and knowledge of every thing in them, shall we be fill'd and satisfied then?*
And my spirit said *No, we but level that lift to pass and continue beyond.*

You are also asking me questions and I hear you,
I answer that I cannot answer, you must find out for yourself.

Sit a while dear son,
Here are biscuits to eat and here is milk to drink,
But as soon as you sleep and renew yourself in sweet clothes, I kiss you with a good-by kiss and open the gate for your egress hence.

Long enough have you dream'd contemptible dreams,
Now I wash the gum from your eyes,
You must habit yourself to the dazzle of the light and of every moment of your life.

Long have you timidly waded holding a plank by the shore,
Now I will you to be a bold swimmer,
To jump off in the midst of the sea, rise again, nod to me, shout, and laughingly dash with your hair.

47

I am the teacher of athletes,
He that by me spreads a wider breast than my own proves the width of my own,

He most honors my style who learns under it to destroy the teacher.

The boy I love, the same becomes a man not through derived power, but in his own right,
Wicked rather than virtuous out of conformity or fear,
Fond of his sweetheart, relishing well his steak,
Unrequited love or a slight cutting him worse than sharp steel cuts,
First-rate to ride, to fight, to hit the bull's eye, to sail a skiff, to sing a song or play on the banjo,
Preferring scars and the beard and faces pitted with small-pox over all latherers,
And those well-tann'd to those that keep out of the sun.

I teach straying from me, yet who can stray from me?
I follow you whoever you are from the present hour,
My words itch at your ears till you understand them.

I do not say these things for a dollar or to fill up the time while I wait for a boat,
(It is you talking just as much as myself, I act as the tongue of you,
Tied in your mouth, in mine it begins to be loosen'd.)

I swear I will never again mention love or death inside a house,
And I swear I will never translate myself at all, only to him or her who privately stays with me in the open air.

If you would understand me go to the heights or water-shore,
The nearest gnat is an explanation, and a drop or motion of waves a key,
The maul, the oar, the hand-saw, second my words.

No shutter'd room or school can commune with me,
But roughs and little children better than they.

The young mechanic is closest to me, he knows me well,
The woodman that takes his axe and jug with him shall take me with him all day,

The farm-boy ploughing in the field feels good at the sound of my voice,
In vessels that sail my words sail, I go with fishermen and seamen and love them.

The soldier camp'd or upon the march is mine,
On the night ere the pending battle many seek me, and I do not fail them,
On that solemn night (it may be their last) those that know me seek me.

My face rubs to the hunter's face when he lies down alone in his blanket,
The driver thinking of me does not mind the jolt of his wagon,
The young mother and old mother comprehend me,
The girl and the wife rest the needle a moment and forget where they are,
They and all would resume what I have told them.

48

I have said that the soul is not more than the body,
And I have said that the body is not more than the soul,
And nothing, not God, is greater to one than one's self is,
And whoever walks a furlong without sympathy walks to his own funeral drest in his shroud,
And I or you pocketless of a dime may purchase the pick of the earth,
And to glance with an eye or show a bean in its pod confounds the learning of all times,
And there is no trade or employment but the young man following it may become a hero,
And there is no object so soft but it makes a hub for the wheel'd universe,
And I say to any man or woman, Let your soul stand cool and composed before a million universes.

And I say to mankind, Be not curious about God,
For I who am curious about each am not curious about God,

(No array of terms can say how much I am at peace about God
and about death.)

I hear and behold God in every object, yet understand God not
in the least,
Nor do I understand who there can be more wonderful than
myself.

Why should I wish to see God better than this day?
I see something of God each hour of the twenty-four, and each
moment then,
In the faces of men and women I see God, and in my own
face in the glass,
I find letters from God dropt in the street, and every one is
sign'd by God's name,
And I leave them where they are, for I know that where-
soe'er I go,
Others will punctually come for ever and ever.

49

And as to you Death, and you bitter hug of mortality, it is
idle to try to alarm me.

To his work without flinching the accoucheur comes,
I see the elder-hand pressing receiving supporting,
I recline by the sills of the exquisite flexible doors,
And mark the outlet, and mark the relief and escape.

And as to you Corpse I think you are good manure, but that
does not offend me,
I smell the white roses sweet-scented and growing,
I reach to the leafy lips, I reach to the polish'd breasts of
melons.

And as to you Life I reckon you are the leavings of many
deaths,
(No doubt I have died myself ten thousand times before.)

I hear you whispering there O stars of heaven,
O suns—O grass of graves—O perpetual transfers and promotions,
If you do not say any thing how can I say any thing?

Of the turbid pool that lies in the autumn forest,
Of the moon that descends the steeps of the soughing twilight,
Toss, sparkles of day and dusk—toss on the black stems that decay in the muck,
Toss to the moaning gibberish of the dry limbs.

I ascend from the moon, I ascend from the night,
I perceive that the ghastly glimmer is noonday sunbeams reflected,
And debouch to the steady and central from the offspring great or small.

50

There is that in me—I do not know what it is—but I know it is in me.

Wrench'd and sweaty—calm and cool then my body becomes,
I sleep—I sleep long.

I do not know it—it is without name—it is a word unsaid,
It is not in any dictionary, utterance, symbol.

Something it swings on more than the earth I swing on,
To it the creation is the friend whose embracing awakes me.

Perhaps I might tell more. Outlines! I plead for my brothers and sisters.

Do you not see O my brothers and sisters?
It is not chaos or death—it is form, union, plan—it is eternal life—it is Happiness.

51

The past and present wilt—I have fill'd them, emptied them,
And proceed to fill my next fold of the future.

Listener up there! what have you to confide to me?
Look in my face while I snuff the sidle of evening,
(Talk honestly, no one else hears you, and I stay only a minute
longer.)

Do I contradict myself?
Very well then I contradict myself,
(I am large, I contain multitudes.)

I concentrate toward them that are nigh, I wait on the door-
slab.

Who has done his day's work? who will soonest be through
with his supper?
Who wishes to walk with me?

Will you speak before I am gone? will you prove already too
late?

52

The spotted hawk swoops by and accuses me, he complains of
my gab and my loitering.

I too am not a bit tamed, I too am untranslatable,
I sound my barbaric yawp over the roofs of the world.

The last scud of day holds back for me,
It flings my likeness after the rest and true as any on the
shadow'd wilds,
It coaxes me to the vapor and the dusk.

I depart as air, I shake my white locks at the runaway sun,
I effuse my flesh in eddies, and drift it in lacy jags.

I bequeath myself to the dirt to grow from the grass I love,
If you want me again look for me under your boot-soles.

You will hardly know who I am or what I mean,
But I shall be good health to you nevertheless,
And filter and fibre your blood.

Failing to fetch me at first keep encouraged,
Missing me one place search another,
I stop somewhere waiting for you.

TO THINK OF TIME
(1855, 1881)

1

TO think of time—of all that retrospection,
To think of to-day, and the ages continued henceforward.

Have you guess'd you yourself would not continue?
Have you dreaded these earth-beetles?
Have you fear'd the future would be nothing to you?

Is to-day nothing? is the beginningless past nothing?
If the future is nothing they are just as surely nothing.

To think that the sun rose in the east—that men and women
were flexible, real, alive—that every thing was alive,
To think that you and I did not see, feel, think, nor bear our
part,
To think that we are now here and bear our part.

2

Not a day passes, not a minute or second without an accouche-
ment,
Not a day passes, not a minute or second without a corpse.

The dull nights go over and the dull days also,
The soreness of lying so much in bed goes over,
The physician after long putting off gives the silent and ter-
rible look for an answer,

The children come hurried and weeping, and the brothers and sisters are sent for,
Medicines stand unused on the shelf, (the camphor-smell has long pervaded the rooms,)
The faithful hand of the living does not desert the hand of the dying,
The twitching lips press lightly on the forehead of the dying,
The breath ceases and the pulse of the heart ceases,
The corpse stretches on the bed and the living look upon it,
It is palpable as the living are palpable.

The living look upon the corpse with their eyesight,
But without eyesight lingers a different living and looks curiously on the corpse.

3

To think the thought of death merged in the thought of materials,
To think of all these wonders of city and country, and others taking great interest in them, and we taking no interest in them.

To think how eager we are in building our houses,
To think others shall be just as eager, and we quite indifferent.

(I see one building the house that serves him a few years, or seventy or eighty years at most,
I see one building the house that serves him longer than that.)

Slow-moving and black lines creep over the whole earth—they never cease—they are the burial lines,
He that was President was buried, and he that is now President shall surely be buried.

4

A reminiscence of the vulgar fate,
A frequent sample of the life and death of workmen,
Each after his kind.

Cold dash of waves at the ferry-wharf, posh and ice in the river, half-frozen mud in the streets,
A gray discouraged sky overhead, the short last daylight of December,
A hearse and stages, the funeral of an old Broadway stage-driver, the cortege mostly drivers.

Steady the trot to the cemetery, duly rattles the death-bell,
The gate is pass'd, the new-dug grave is halted at, the living alight, the hearse uncloses,
The coffin is pass'd out, lower'd and settled, the whip is laid on the coffin, the earth is swiftly shovel'd in,
The mound above is flatted with the spades—silence,
A minute—no one moves or speaks—it is done,
He is decently put away—is there any thing more?

He was a good fellow, free-mouth'd, quick-temper'd, not bad-looking,
Ready with life or death for a friend, fond of women, gambled, ate hearty, drank hearty,
Had known what it was to be flush, grew low-spirited toward the last, sicken'd, was help'd by a contribution,
Died, aged forty-one years—and that was his funeral.

Thumb extended, finger uplifted, apron, cape, gloves, strap, wet-weather clothes, whip carefully chosen,
Boss, spotter, starter, hostler, somebody loafing on you, you loafing on somebody, headway, man before and man behind,
Good day's work, bad day's work, pet stock, mean stock, first out, last out, turning-in at night,
To think that these are so much and so nigh to other drivers, and he there takes no interest in them.

GOOD-BYE, MY FANCY

GOOD-BYE, my Fancy!
Farewell, dear mate, dear love!
I'm going away, I know not where,

Or to what fortune, or whether I may ever see you again,
So Good-bye, my Fancy.

Now for my last—let me look back a moment;
The slower fainter ticking of the clock is in me,
Exit, nightfall, and soon the heart-thud stopping.
Long have we lived, joy'd, caress'd together;
Delightful!—now separation—Good-bye, my Fancy.

Yet let me not be too hasty:
Long indeed have we lived, slept, filter'd, become really
blended into one;
Then if we die we die together (yes, we'll remain one),
If we go anywhere we 'll go together to meet what happens,
May-be we 'll be better off and blither, and learn something,
May-be it is yourself now really ushering me to the true songs
(who knows?),
May-be it is you the mortal knob really undoing, turning—so
now finally,
Good-bye—and hail! my Fancy.

WHISPERS OF HEAVENLY DEATH

WHISPERS of heavenly death murmur'd I hear,
Labial gossip of night, sibilant chorals,
Footsteps gently ascending, mystical breezes wafted soft and
low,
Ripples of unseen rivers, tides of a current flowing, forever
flowing
(Or is it the plashing of tears? the measureless waters of hu
man tears?)

I see, just see skyward, great cloud-masses;
Mournfully, slowly they roll, silently swelling and mixing,
With at times a half-dimm'd sadden'd far-off star,
Appearing and disappearing.

(Some parturition rather, some solemn immortal birth;
On the frontiers to eyes impenetrable,
Some soul is passing over.)

O CAPTAIN! MY CAPTAIN!

O CAPTAIN! my Captain! our fearful trip is done,
The ship has weathered every rack, the prize we sought is won,
The port is near, the bells I hear, the people all exulting,
While follow eyes the steady keel, the vessel grim and daring;
But O heart! heart! heart!
O the bleeding drops of red,
Where on the deck my Captain lies,
Fallen cold and dead.

O Captain! my Captain! rise up and hear the bells;
Rise up—for you the flag is flung—for you the bugle trills,
For you bouquets and ribboned wreaths—for you the shores acrowding,
For you they call, the swaying mass, their eager faces turning;
Here Captain! dear father!
This arm beneath your head!
It is some dream that on the deck
You've fallen cold and dead.

My Captain does not answer, his lips are pale and still,
My father does not feel my arm, he has no pulse nor will,
The ship is anchored safe and sound, its voyage closed and done,
From fearful trip the victor ship comes in with object won;
Exult O shores, and ring O bells!
But I, with mournful tread,
Walk the deck my Captain lies,
Fallen cold and dead.

Louise Chandler Moulton

HIC JACET

SO Love is dead that has been quick so long!
Close, then, his eyes, and bear him to his rest,
With eglantine and myrtle on his breast,

And leave him there, their pleasant scents among;
And chant a sweet and melancholy song
About the charms whereof he was possessed,
And how of all things he was loveliest,
And to compare with aught were him to wrong.
Leave him beneath the still and solemn stars,
That gather and look down from their far place
With their long calm our brief woes to deride,
Until the Sun the Morning's gate unbars
And mocks, in turn, our sorrows with his face;—
And yet, had Love been Love, he had not died.

Richard Realf

INDIRECTION

FAIR are the flowers and the children, but their subtle suggestion is fairer;
Rare is the roseburst of dawn, but the secret that clasps it is rarer;
Sweet the exultance of song, but the strain that precedes it is sweeter;
And never was poem yet writ, but the meaning outmastered the metre.

Never a daisy that grows, but a mystery guideth the growing;
Never a river that flows, but a majesty sceptres the flowing;
Never a Shakespeare that soared, but a stronger than he did enfold him,
Nor ever a prophet foretells, but a mightier seer hath foretold him.

Back of the canvas that throbs the painter is hinted and hidden;
Into the statue that breathes the soul of the sculptor is bidden;
Under the joy that is felt lie the infinite issues of feeling;
Crowning the glory revealed is the glory that crowns the revealing.

Great are the symbols of being, but that which is symboled is greater;
Vast the create and beheld, but vaster the inward creator;
Back of the sound broods the silence, back of the gift stands the giving;
Back of the hand that receives thrill the sensitive nerves of receiving.

Space is as nothing to spirit, the deed is outdone by the doing;
The heart of the wooer is warm, but warmer the heart of the wooing;
And up from the pits where these shiver, and up from the heights where those shine,
Twin voices and shadows swim starward, and the essence of life is divine.

Emily Dickinson

I

I FOUND THE PHRASE

I FOUND the phrase to every thought
I ever had, but one;
And that defies me,—as a hand
Did try to chalk the sun

To races nurtured in the dark:—
How would your own begin?
Can blaze be done in cochineal,
Or noon in mazarin?

II

PARTING

MY life closed twice before its close;
It yet remains to see
If Immortality unveil
A third event to me,

So huge, so hopeless to conceive,
  As these that twice befell:
Parting is all we know of heaven,
  And all we need of hell.

III

CALLED BACK

JUST lost when I was saved!
  Just felt the world go by!
Just girt me for the onset with eternity,
When breath blew back,
And on the other side
I heard recede the disappointed tide;

Therefore, as one returned, I feel,
Odd secrets of the line to tell!
Some sailor, skirting foreign shores,
Some pale reporter from the awful doors
Before the seal!

Next time, to stay!
Next time, the things to see
By ear unheard,
Unscrutinized by eye.

Next time, to tarry,
While the ages steal,—
Slow tramp the centuries,
And the cycles wheel.

IV

CHOICE

OF all the souls that stand create
  I have elected one.
When sense from spirit files away,
And subterfuge is done;

When that which is and that which was
Apart, intrinsic, stand,
And this brief tragedy of flesh
Is shifted like a sand;

When figures show their royal front
And mists are carved away,—
Behold the atom I preferred
To all the lists of clay!

V

TO HEAR AN ORIOLE

TO hear an oriole sing
May be a common thing,
Or only a divine.

It is not of the bird
Who sings the same, unheard,
As unto crowd.

The fashion of the ear
Attireth that it hear
In dun or fair.

So whether it be rune,
Or whether it be none,
Is of within;

The "tune is in the tree,"
The sceptic showeth me;
"No, sir! In thee!"

VI

THERE'S A CERTAIN SLANT OF LIGHT

THERE'S a certain slant of light,
On winter afternoons,
That oppresses, like the weight
Of cathedral tunes.

Heavenly hurt it gives us;
We can find no scar,
But internal difference
Where the meanings are.

None may teach it anything
'Tis the seal, despair,—
An imperial affliction
Sent us of the air.

When it comes, the landscape listens,
Shadows hold their breath;
When it goes, 'tis like the distance
On the look of death.

VII

APPARENTLY WITH NO SURPRISE

APPARENTLY with no surprise
To any happy flower,
The frost beheads it at its play
In accidental power.
The blond assassin passes on,
The sun proceeds unmoved
To measure off another day
For an approving God.

VIII

THE LAST NIGHT

THE last night that she lived,
It was a common night,
Except the dying; this to us
Made nature different.

We noticed smallest things,—
Things overlooked before,
By this great light upon our minds
Italicized, as 'twere.

That others could exist
While she must finish quite,
A jealousy for her arose
So nearly infinite.

We waited while she passed;
It was a narrow time,
Too jostled were our souls to speak,
At length the notice came.

She mentioned, and forgot;
Then lightly as a reed
Bent to the water, shivered scarce,
Consented, and was dead.

And we, we placed the hair,
And drew the head erect;
And then an awful leisure was,
Our faith to regulate.

IX

THE BUSTLE IN A HOUSE

THE bustle in a house
The morning after death
Is solemnest of industries
Enacted upon earth,—

The sweeping up the heart,
And putting love away
We shall not want to use again
Until eternity.

X

I KNOW THAT HE EXISTS

I KNOW that he exists
Somewhere, in silence.
He has hid his rare life
From our gross eyes.

'Tis an instant's play,
'Tis a fond ambush,
Just to make bliss
Earn her own surprise!

But should the play
Prove piercing earnest,
Should the glee glaze
In death's stiff stare,

Would not the fun
Look too expensive?
Would not the jest
Have crawled too far?

XI

WE NEVER KNOW HOW HIGH

WE never know how high we are
Till we are called to rise;
And then, if we are true to plan,
Our statures touch the skies.

The heroism we recite
Would be a daily thing,
Did not ourselves the cubits warp
For fear to be a king.

XII

THE SOUL SELECTS

THE soul selects her own society,
Then shuts the door;
On her divine majority
Obtrude no more.

Unmoved, she notes the chariot's pausing
At her low gate;
Unmoved, an emperor is kneeling

Upon her mat.
I've known her from an ample nation
Choose one;
Then close the valves of her attention
Like stone.

XIII

A THOUGHT WENT UP MY MIND

A THOUGHT went up my mind to-day
That I have had before,
But did not finish,—some way back,
I could not fix the year,

Nor where it went, nor why it came
The second time to me,
Nor definitely what it was,
Have I the art to say.

But somewhere in my soul, I know
I've met the thing before;
It just reminded me—'twas all—
And came my way no more.

XIV

DYING

I HEARD a fly buzz when I died;
The stillness round my form
Was like the stillness in the air
Between the heaves of storm.

The eyes beside had wrung them dry,
And breaths were gathering sure
For that last onset, when the king
Be witnessed in his power.

I willed my keepsakes, signed away
What portion of me I

Could make assignable—and then
There interposed a fly,

With blue, uncertain, stumbling buzz,
Between the light and me;
And then the windows failed, and then
I could not see to see.

XV

A CLOCK STOPPED

A CLOCK stopped—not the mantel's;
Geneva's farthest skill
Can't put the puppet bowing
That just now dangled still.

An awe came on the trinket!
The figures hunched with pain,
Then quivered out of decimals
Into degreeless noon.

It will not stir for doctors,
This pendulum of snow;
The shopman importunes it,
While cool, concernless No

Nods from the gilded pointers,
Nods from the seconds slim,
Decades of arrogance between
The dial life and him.

XVI

NOT ANY SUNNY TONE

NOT any sunny tone
From any fervent zone
Finds entrance there.
Better a grave of Balm
Toward human nature's home,

And Robins near,
Than a stupendous Tomb
Proclaiming to the gloom
How dead we are.

XVII

I FELT A FUNERAL

I FELT a funeral in my brain,
And mourners, to and fro,
Kept treading, treading, till it seemed
That sense was breaking through.

And when they all were seated,
A service like a drum
Kept beating, beating, till I thought
My mind was going numb.

And then I heard them lift a box,
And creak across my soul
With those same boots of lead, again.
Then space began to toll.

As all the heavens were a bell,
And Being but an ear,
And I and silence some strange race,
Wrecked, solitary, here.

XVIII

TO MY QUICK EAR

TO my quick ear the leaves conferred;
The bushes they were bells;
I could not find a privacy
From Nature's sentinels.

In cave if I presumed to hide,
The walls began to tell;
Creation seemed a mighty crack
To make me visible.

XIX

IN THE GARDEN

A BIRD came down the walk:
He did not know I saw;
He bit an angle-worm in halves
And ate the fellow raw.

And then he drank a dew
From a convenient grass,
And then hopped sidewise to the wall
To let a beetle pass.

He glanced with rapid eyes
That hurried all abroad—
They looked like frightened beads, I thought;
He stirred his velvet head

Like one in danger; cautious,
I offered him a crumb,
And he unrolled his feathers
And rowed him softer home

Than oars divide the ocean,
Too silver for a seam,
Or butterflies, off banks of noon,
Leap, plashes, as they swim.

XX

SAFE IN THEIR ALABASTER CHAMBERS

SAFE in their alabaster chambers,
Untouched by morning and untouched by noon,
Sleep the meek members of the resurrection,
Rafter of satin, and roof of stone.

Light laughs the breeze in her castle of sunshine;
Babbles the bee in a stolid ear;
Pipe the sweet birds in ignorant cadence—
Ah, what sagacity perished here!

Grand go the years in the crescent above them;
Worlds scoop their arcs, and firmaments row,
Diadems drop and Doges surrender,
Soundless as dots on a disk of snow.

XXI

THE WIND

OF all the sounds despatched abroad,
There's not a charge to me
Like that old measure in the boughs,
That phraseless melody

The wind does, working like a hand
Whose fingers brush the sky,
Then quiver down, with tufts of tune
Permitted gods and me.

When winds go round and round in bands,
And thrum upon the door,
And birds take places overhead,
To bear them orchestra,

I crave him grace, of summer boughs,
If such an outcast be,
He never heard that fleshless chant
Rise solemn in the tree,

As if some caravan of sound
On deserts, in the sky,
Had broken rank,
Then knit, and passed
In seamless company.

XXII

THE CHARIOT

BECAUSE I could not stop for Death,
He kindly stopped for me;
The carriage held but just ourselves
And Immortality.

We slowly drove, he knew no haste,
And I had put away
My labour, and my leisure too,
For his civility.

We passed the school where children played
Their lessons scarcely done;
We passed the fields of gazing grain,
We passed the setting sun.

We paused before a house that seemed
A swelling on the ground;
The roof was scarcely visible,
The cornice but a mound.

Since then 'tis centuries; but each
Feels shorter than the day
I first surmised the horses' heads
Were toward eternity.

XXIII

I DIED FOR BEAUTY

I DIED for beauty, but was scarce
Adjusted in the tomb,
When one who died for truth was lain
In an adjoining room.

He questioned softly why I failed?
"For beauty," I replied.
"And I for truth—the two are one;
We brethren are," he said.

And so, as kinsmen met a-night,
We talked between the rooms,
Until the moss had reached our lips,
And covered up our names.

XXIV

MYSTERIES

THE murmur of a bee
A witchcraft yieldeth me.
If any ask me why,
'Twere easier to die
Than tell.

The red upon the hill
Taketh away my will;
If anybody sneer,
Take care, for God is here,
That's all.

The breaking of the day
Addeth to my degree;
If any ask me how,
Artist, who drew me so,
Must tell!

Helen Hunt Jackson

EMIGRAVIT

WITH sails full set, the ship her anchor weighs.
Strange names shine out beneath her figure head.
What glad farewells with eager eyes are said!
What cheer for him who goes, and him who stays!
Fair skies, rich lands, new homes, and untried days
Some go to seek: the rest but wait instead,
Watching the way wherein their comrades led,
Until the next stanch ship her flag doth raise.
Who knows what myriad colonies there are
Of fairest fields, and rich, undreamed-of gains
Thick planted in the distant shining plains
Which we call sky because they lie so far?
Oh, write of me, not "Died in bitter pains,"
But "Emigrated to another star!"

A DREAM

I DREAMED that I was dead and crossed heavens,—
Heavens after heavens with burning feet and swift,—
And cried: "O God, where art Thou? I left one
On earth, whose burden I would pray Thee lift."

I was so dead I wondered at no thing,—
Not even that the angels slowly turned
Their faces, speechless, as I hurried by
(Beneath my feet the golden pavements burned);

Nor, at the first, that I could not find God,
Because the heavens stretched endlessly like space.
At last a terror seized my very soul;
I seemed alone in all the crowded place.

Then, sudden, one compassionate cried out,
Though like the rest his face from me he turned,
As I were one no angel might regard
(Beneath my feet the golden pavements burned):

"No more in heaven than earth will he find God
Who does not know his loving mercy swift
But waits the moment consummate and ripe,
Each burden from each human soul to lift."

Though I was dead, I died again for shame;
Lonely, to flee from heaven again I turned;
The ranks of angels looked away from me
(Beneath my feet the golden pavements burned).

DANGER

WITH what a childish and short-sighted sense
Fear seeks for safety; reckons up the days
Of danger and escape, the hours and ways

Of death; it breathless flies the pestilence;
It walls itself in towers of defence;
By land, by sea, against the storm it lays
Down barriers; then, comforted, it says:
"This spot, this hour is safe." Oh, vain pretence!
Man born of man knows nothing when he goes;
The winds blow where they list, and will disclose
To no man which brings safety, which brings risk.
The mighty are brought low by many a thing
Too small to name. Beneath the daisy's disk
Lies hid the pebble for the fatal sling.

Edward Rowland Sill

FIVE LIVES

FIVE mites of monads dwelt in a round drop
That twinkled on a leaf by a pool in the sun.
To the naked eye they lived invisible;
Specks, for a world of whom the empty shell
Of a mustard-seed had been a hollow sky.

One was a meditative monad, called a sage;
And, shrinking all his mind within, he thought:
"Tradition, handed down for hours and hours,
Tells that our globe, this quivering crystal world,
Is slowly dying. What if, seconds hence,
When I am very old, yon shimmering dome
Come drawing down and down, till all things end?"
Then with a weazen smirk he proudly felt
No other mote of God had ever gained
Such giant grasp of universal truth.

One was a transcendental monad; thin
And long and slim in the mind; and thus he mused:
"Oh, vast, unfathomable monad-souls!
Made in the image"—a hoarse frog croaks from the pool—

"Hark! 't was some god, voicing his glorious thought
In thunder music! Yea, we hear their voice,
And we may guess their minds from ours, their work.
Some taste they have like ours, some tendency
To wriggle about, and munch a trace of scum."
He floated up on a pin-point bubble of gas
That burst, pricked by the air, and he was gone.

One was a barren-minded monad, called
A positivist; and he knew positively:
"There is no world beyond this certain drop.
Prove me another! Let the dreamers dream
Of their faint dreams, and noises from without,
And higher and lower; life is life enough."
Then swaggering half a hair's breadth, hungrily
He seized upon an atom of bug, and fed.

One was a tattered monad, called a poet;
And with shrill voice ecstatic thus he sang:
"Oh, the little female monad's lips!
Oh, the little female monad's eyes:
Ah, the little, little, female, female monad!"

The last was a strong-minded monadess,
Who dashed amid the infusoria,
Danced high and low, and wildly spun and dove
Till the dizzy others held their breath to see.

But while they led their wondrous little lives
Aeonian moments had gone wheeling by,
The burning drop had shrunk with fearful speed;
A glistening film—'t was gone; the leaf was dry.
The little ghost of an inaudible squeak
Was lost to the frog that goggled from his stone;
Who, at the huge, slow tread of a thoughtful ox
Coming to drink, stirred sideways fatly, plunged,
Launched backward twice, and all the pool was still.

John Townsend Trowbridge

MIDWINTER

THE speckled sky is dim with snow,
The light flakes falter and fall slow;
Athwart the hill-top, rapt and pale,
Silently drops a silvery veil;
And all the valley is shut in
By flickering curtains gray and thin.

But cheerily the chickadee
Singeth to me on fence and tree;
The snow sails round him as he sings,
White as the down of angels' wings.

I watch the slow flakes as they fall
On bank and brier and broken wall;
Over the orchard, waste and brown,
All noiselessly they settle down,
Tipping the apple-boughs, and each
Light quivering twig of plum and peach.

On turf and curb and bower-roof
The snow-storm spreads its ivory woof;
It paves with pearl the garden-walk;
And lovingly round tattered stalk
And shivering stem its magic weaves
A mantle fair as lily-leaves.

The hooded beehive, small and low,
Stands like a maiden in the snow;
And the old door-slab is half-hid
Under an alabaster lid.

All day it snows: the sheeted post
Gleams in the dimness like a ghost;
All day the blasted oak has stood
A muffled wizard of the wood;

Garland and airy cap adorn
The sumach and the wayside thorn,
And clustering spangles lodge and shine
In the dark tresses of the pine.

The ragged bramble, dwarfed and old,
Shrinks like a beggar in the cold;
In surplice white the cedar stands,
And blesses him with priestly hands.

Still cheerily the chickadee
Singeth to me on fence and tree:
But in my inmost ear is heard
The music of a holier bird;
And heavenly thoughts as soft and white
As snow-flakes, on my soul alight,
Clothing with love my lonely heart,
Healing with peace each bruisëd part,
Till all my being seems to be
Transfigured by their purity.

George Henry Boker

DIRGE FOR A SOLDIER

CLOSE his eyes; his work is done!
  What to him is friend or foeman,
Rise of moon, or set of sun,
  Hand of man, or kiss of woman?
    Lay him low, lay him low,
    In the clover or the snow!
    What cares he? he cannot know:
      Lay him low!

As man may, he fought his fight,
  Proved his truth by his endeavor;
Let him sleep in solemn night,
  Sleep forever and forever.

Lay him low, lay him low,
In the clover or the snow!
What cares he? he cannot know:
Lay him low!

Fold him in his country's stars,
Roll the drum and fire the volley!
What to him are all our wars,
What but death bemocking folly?
Lay him low, lay him low,
In the clover or the snow!
What cares he? he cannot know:
Lay him low!

Leave him to God's watching eye,
Trust him to the hand that made him.
Mortal love weeps idly by:
God alone has power to aid him.
Lay him low, lay him low,
In the clover or the snow!
What cares he? he cannot know:
Lay him low!

Maurice Thompson

WILD HONEY

WHERE hints of racy sap and gum
Out of the old dark forest come;

Where birds their beaks like hammers wield,
And pith is pierced and bark is peeled;

Where the green walnut's outer rind
Gives precious bitterness to the wind;

There lurks the sweet creative power,
As lurks the honey in the flower.

In winter's bud that bursts in spring,
In nut of autumn's ripening,

In acrid bulb beneath the mold,
Sleeps the elixir, strong and old,

That Rosicrucians sought in vain,—
Life that renews itself again!

What bottled perfume is so good
As fragrance of split tulip-wood?

What fabled drink of God or muse
Was rich as purple mulberry juice?

And what school-polished gem of thought
Is like the rune from Nature caught?

He is a poet strong and true
Who loves wild thyme and honey-dew;

And like a brown bee works and sings
With morning freshness on his wings,

And a gold burden on his thighs,—
The pollen-dust of centuries!

John Vance Cheney

THE HAPPIEST HEART

WHO drives the horses of the sun
Shall lord it but a day;
Better the lowly deed were done,
And kept the humble way.

The rust will find the sword of fame,
The dust will hide the crown;
Ay, none shall nail so high his name
Time will not tear it down.

The happiest heart that ever beat
Was in some quiet breast
That found the common daylight sweet,
And left to Heaven the rest.

Stephen Collins Foster

MY OLD KENTUCKY HOME

THE sun shines bright in the old Kentucky home;
'Tis summer, the darkeys are gay;
The corn-top's ripe, and the meadow's in the bloom,
While the birds make music all the day.
The young folks roll on the little cabin floor,
All merry, all happy and bright;
By-'n'-by hard times comes a-knocking at the door:—
Then my old Kentucky home, good-night!

Weep no more, my lady,
O, weep no more to-day!
We will sing one song for the old Kentucky home,
For the old Kentucky home, far away.

They hunt no more for the possum and the coon,
On the meadow, the hill, and the shore;
They sing no more by the glimmer of the moon,
On the bench by the old cabin door.
The day goes by like a shadow o'er the heart,
With sorrow, where all was delight;
The time has come when the darkeys have to part:—
Then my old Kentucky home, good-night!

The head must bow, and the back will have to bend
Wherever the darkey may go;
A few more days, and the trouble all will end,
In the field where the sugar-canes grow.
A few more days for to tote the weary load,—
No matter, 'twill never be light;
A few more days till we totter on the road:—
Then my old Kentucky home, good-night!

Weep no more, my lady,
O, weep no more to-day!
We will sing one song for the old Kentucky home,
For the old Kentucky home, far away.

Thomas Bailey Aldrich

MEMORY

MY mind lets go a thousand things,
Like dates of wars and deaths of kings,
And yet recalls the very hour—
'Twas noon by yonder village tower,
And on the last blue noon in May
The wind came briskly up this way,
Crisping the brook beside the road;
Then, pausing here, set down its load
Of pine-scents, and shook listlessly
Two petals from that wild-rose tree.

ENAMORED ARCHITECT OF AIRY RHYME

ENAMORED architect of airy rhyme,
Build as thou wilt; heed not what each man says:
Good souls, but innocent of dreamers' ways,
Will come, and marvel why thou wastest time;
Others, beholding how thy turrets climb

'Twixt theirs and heaven, will hate thee all thy days;
But most beware of those who come to praise.
O Wondersmith, O worker in sublime
And heaven-sent dreams, let art be all in all;
Build as thou wilt, unspoiled by praise or blame,
Build as thou wilt, and as thy light is given:
Then, if at last the airy structure fall,
Dissolve, and vanish—take thyself no shame.
They fail, and they alone, who have not striven.

Herman Melville

L'ENVOI
THE RETURN OF THE SIRE DE NESLE
A.D. 16—

MY towers at last! These rovings end,
Their thirst is slaked in larger dearth:
The yearning infinite recoils,
For terrible is earth.

Kaf thrusts his snouted crags through fog:
Araxes swells beyond his span,
And knowledge poured by pilgrimage
Overflows the banks of man.

But thou, my stay, thy lasting love
One lonely good, let this but be!
Weary to view the wide world's swarm,
But blest to fold but thee.

John Burroughs

WAITING

SERENE, I fold my hands and wait,
Nor care for wind, or tide, or sea;
I rave no more 'gainst time or fate,
For, lo! my own shall come to me.

I stay my haste, I make delays,
 For what avails this eager pace?
I stand amid the eternal ways,
 And what is mine shall know my face.

Asleep, awake, by night or day,
 The friends I seek are seeking me;
No wind can drive my bark astray,
 Nor change the tide of destiny.

What matter if I stand alone?
 I wait with joy the coming years;
My heart shall reap where it has sown,
 And garner up its fruit of tears.

The waters know their own and draw
 The brook that springs in yonder height;
So flows the good with equal law
 Unto the soul of pure delight.

The stars come nightly to the sky;
 The tidal wave unto the sea;
Nor time, nor space, nor deep, nor high,
 Can keep my own away from me.

Joaquin Miller

AT THE GRAVE OF WALKER

HE lies low in the levelled sand,
 Unsheltered from the tropic sun,
And now of all he knew not one
Will speak him fair in that far land.
Perhaps 'twas this that made me seek,
Disguised, his grave one winter-tide;
A weakness for the weaker side,
A siding with the helpless weak.

A palm not far held out a hand,
Hard by a long green bamboo swung,
And bent like some great bow unstrung,
And quivered like a willow wand;
Perched on its fruits that crooked hand,
Beneath a broad banana's leaf,
A bird in rainbow splendor sang
A low, sad song, of tempered grief.

No sod, no sign, no cross nor stone,
But at his side a cactus green
Upheld its lances long and keen;
It stood in sacred sands alone,
Flat-palmed and fierce with lifted spears;
One bloom of crimson crowned its head,
A drop of blood, so bright, so red,
Yet redolent as roses' tears.

In my left hand I held a shell,
All rosy lipped and pearly red;
I laid it by his lowly bed,
For he did love so passing well
The grand songs of the solemn sea.
O shell! sing well, wild, with a will,
When storms blow loud and birds be still,
The wildest sea-song known to thee!

I said some things with folded hands,
Soft whispered in the dim sea-sound,
And eyes held humbly to the ground,
And frail knees sunken in the sands.
He had done more than this for me,
And yet I could not well do more:
I turned me down the olive shore,
And set a sad face to the sea.

Sidney Lanier

OPPOSITION

Of fret, of dark, of thorn, of chill,
  Complain no more; for these, O heart.
Direct the random of the will
  As rhymes direct the rage of art.

The lute's fixt fret, that runs athwart
  The strain and purpose of the string,
For governance and nice consort
  Doth bar his wilful wavering.

The dark hath many dear avails;
  The dark distils divinest dews;
The dark is rich with nightingales,
  With dreams, and with the heavenly Muse.

Bleeding with thorns of petty strife,
  I'll ease (as lovers do) my smart
With sonnets to my lady Life
  Writ red in issues from the heart.

What grace may lie within the chill
  Of favor frozen fast in scorn!
When Good's a-freeze, we call it Ill!
  This rosy Time is glacier-born.

Of fret, of dark, of thorn, of chill,
  Complain thou not, O heart; for these
Bank-in the current of the will
  To uses, arts, and charities.

Henry Augustin Beers

ECCE IN DESERTO

THE wilderness a secret keeps
  Upon whose guess I go:
Eye hath not seen, ear hath not heard;
  And yet I know, I know,

Some day the viewless latch will lift,
  The door of air swing wide
To one lost chamber of the wood
  Where those shy mysteries hide,—

One yet unfound, receding depth,
  From which the wood-thrush sings,
Still luring in to darker shades,
  In—in to colder springs.

There is no wind abroad to-day.
  But hark!—the pine-tops' roar,
That sleep and in their dreams repeat
  The music of the shore.

What wisdom in their needles stirs?
  What song is that they sing?
Those airs that search the forest's heart,
  What rumor do they bring?

A hushed excitement fills the gloom,
  And, in the stillness, clear
The vireo's tell-tale warning rings:
  "'Tis near—'tis near—'tis near!"

As, in the fairy-tale, more loud
  The ghostly music plays
When, toward the enchanted bower, the prince
  Draws closer through the maze.

Nay—nay. I track a fleeter game,
A wilder than ye know,
To lairs beyond the inmost haunt
Of thrush or vireo.

This way it passed: the scent lies fresh;
The ferns still lightly shake.
Ever I follow hard upon,
But never overtake.

To other woods the trail leads on,
To other worlds and new,
Where they who keep the secret here
Will keep the promise too.

John Banister Tabb

CLOVER

LITTLE masters, hat in hand
Let me in your presence stand,
Till your silence solve for me
This your threefold mystery.

Tell me—for I long to know—
How, in darkness there below,
Was your fairy fabric spun,
Spread and fashioned, three in one.

Did your gossips gold and blue,
Sky and Sunshine, choose for you,
Ere your triple forms were seen,
Suited liveries of green?

Can ye,—if ye dwelt indeed
Captives of a prison seed,—
Like the Genie, once again
Get you back into the grain?

Little masters, may I stand
In your presence, hat in hand,
Waiting till you solve for me
This your threefold mystery?

Edwin Markham

THE MAN WITH THE HOE

God made man in his own image
in the image of God He made him.—Genesis.

BOWED by the weight of centuries he leans
Upon his hoe and gazes on the ground,
The emptiness of ages in his face,
And on his back the burden of the world.
Who made him dead to rapture and despair,
A thing that grieves not and that never hopes,
Stolid and stunned, a brother to the ox?
Who loosened and let down this brutal jaw?
Whose was the hand that slanted back this brow?
Whose breath blew out the light within this brain?

Is this the Thing the Lord God made and gave
To have dominion over sea and land;
To trace the stars and search the heavens for power;
To feel the passion of Eternity?
Is this the dream He dreamed who shaped the suns
And markt their ways upon the ancient deep?
Down all the caverns of Hell to their last gulf
There is no shape more terrible than this—
More tongued with censure of the world's blind greed—
More filled with signs and portents for the soul—
More packt with danger to the universe.

What gulfs between him and the seraphim!
Slave of the wheel of labor, what to him
Are Plato and the swing of Pleiades?

What the long reaches of the peaks of song,
The rift of dawn, the reddening of the rose?
Through this dread shape the suffering ages look;
Time's tragedy is in that aching stoop;
Through this dread shape humanity betrayed,
Plundered, profaned and disinherited,
Cries protest to the Powers that made the world,
A protest that is also prophecy.

O masters, lords and rulers in all lands,
Is this the handiwork you give to God,
This monstrous thing distorted and soul-quencht?
How will you ever straighten up this shape;
Touch it again with immortality;
Give back the upward looking and the light;
Rebuild in it the music and the dream;
Make right the immemorial infamies,
Perfidious wrongs, immedicable woes?

O masters, lords and rulers in all lands,
How will the future reckon with this Man?
How answer his brute question in that hour
When whirlwinds of rebellion shake all shores?
How will it be with kingdoms and with kings—
With those who shaped him to the thing he is—
When this dumb Terror shall rise to judge the world,
After the silence of the centuries?

William Vaughn Moody

A GREY DAY

GREY drizzling mists the moorlands drape,
Rain whitens the dead sea,
From headland dim to sullen cape
Grey sails creep wearily.
I know not how that merchantman
Has found the heart; but 'tis her plan
Seaward her endless course to shape.

Unreal as insects that appall
A drunkard's peevish brain,
O'er the grey deep the dories crawl,
Four-legged, with rower's twain:
Midgets and minims of the earth,
Across old ocean's vasty girth
Toiling—heroic, comical!

I wonder how that merchant's crew
Have ever found the will!
I wonder what the fishers do
To keep them toiling still!
I wonder how the heart of man
Has patience to live out its span,
Or wait until its dreams come true.

PANDORA SONG

I STOOD within the heart of God;
It seemed a place that I had known:
(I was blood-sister to the clod,
Blood-brother to the stone.)

I found my love and labor there,
My house, my raiment, meat and wine,
My ancient rage, my old despair,—
Yea, all things that were mine.

I saw the spring and summer pass,
The trees grow bare, and winter come;
All was the same as once it was
Upon my hills at home.

Then suddenly in my own heart
I felt God walk and gaze about;
He spoke; his words seemed held apart
With gladness and with doubt.

"Here is my meat and wine," He said,
"My love, my toil, my ancient care;
Here is my cloak, my book, my bed,
And here my old despair.

"Here are my seasons: winter, spring,
Summer the same, and autumn spills
The fruits I look for; everything
As on my heavenly hills."

AN ODE IN TIME OF HESITATION

I

BEFORE the solemn bronze Saint Gaudens made
To thrill the heedless passer's heart with awe,
And set here in the city's talk and trade
To the good memory of Robert Shaw,
This bright March morn I stand,
And hear the distant spring come up the land;
Knowing that what I hear is not unheard
Of this boy soldier and his Negro band,
For all their gaze is fixed so stern ahead,
For all the fatal rhythm of their tread.
The land they died to save from death and shame
Trembles and waits, hearing the spring's great name
And by her pangs these resolute ghosts are stirred.

II

Through street and mall the tides of people go
Heedless; the trees upon the Common show
No hint of green; but to my listening heart
The still earth doth impart
Assurance of her jubilant emprise,
And it is clear to my long-searching eyes
That love at last has might upon the skies.
The ice is runneled on the little pond;
A telltale patter drips from off the trees;

The air is touched with Southland spiceries,
As if but yesterday it tossed the frond
Of pendent mosses where the live-oaks grow
Beyond Virginia and the Carolines,
Or had its will among the fruits and vines
Of aromatic isles asleep beyond
Florida and the Gulf of Mexico.

III

Soon shall the Cape Ann children shout in glee,
Spying the arbutus, spring's dear recluse;
Hill lads at dawn shall hearken the wild goose
Go hanking northward over Tennessee;
West from Oswego to Sault Sainte-Marie,
And on to where the Pictured Rocks are hung,
And yonder where, gigantic, wilful, young,
Chicago sitteth at the northwest gates,
With restless violent hands and casual tongue
Moulding her mighty fates,
The Lakes shall robe them in ethereal sheen;
And like a larger sea, the vital green
Of springing wheat shall vastly be outflung
Over Dakota and the prairie states.
By desert people immemorial
On Arizonan mesas shall be done
Dim rites unto the thunder and the sun;
Nor shall the primal gods lack sacrifice
More splendid, when the white Sierras call
Unto the Rockies straightway to arise
And dance before the unveiled ark of the year.
Sounding their windy cedars as for shawms,
Unrolling rivers clear
For flutter of broad phylacteries;
While Shasta signals to Alaskan seas
That watch old sluggish glaciers downward creep
To fling their icebergs thundering from the steep,
And Mariposa through the purple calms
Gazes at far Hawaii crowned with palms

Where East and West are met,—
A rich seal on the ocean's bosom set
To say that East and West are twain,
With different loss and gain:
The Lord hath sundered them; let them be sundered yet.

IV

Alas! what sounds are these that come
Sullenly over the Pacific seas,—
Sounds of ignoble battle, striking dumb
The season's half-awakened ecstasies?
Must I be humble, then,
Now when my heart hath need of pride?
Wild love falls on me from these sculptured men;
By loving much the land for which they died
I would be justified.
My spirit was away on pinions wide
To soothe in praise of her its passionate mood
And ease it of its ache of gratitude.
Too sorely heavy is the debt they lay
On me and the companions of my day.
I would remember now
My country's goodliness, make sweet her name.
Alas! what shade art thou
Of sorrow or of blame
Liftest the lyric leafage from her brow,
And pointest a slow finger at her shame?

V

Lies! lies! It cannot be! The wars we wage
Are noble, and our battles still are won
By justice for us, ere we lift the gage.
We have not sold our loftiest heritage.
The proud republic hath not stooped to cheat
And scramble in the market-place of war;
Her forehead weareth yet its solemn star.
Here is her witness: this, her perfect son,
This delicate and proud New England soul

Who leads despisèd men, with just-unshackled feet,
Up the large ways where death and glory meet,
To show all peoples that our shame is done,
That once more we are clean and spirit-whole.

VI

Crouched in the sea-fog on the moaning sand
All night he lay, speaking some simple word
From hour to hour to the slow minds that heard,
Holding each poor life gently in his hand
And breathing on the base rejected clay
Till each dark face shone mystical and grand
Against the breaking day;
And lo, the shard the potter cast away
Was grown a fiery chalice crystal-fine,
Fulfilled of the divine
Great wine of battle wrath by God's ring-finger stirred.
Then upward, where the shadowy bastion loomed
Huge on the mountain in the wet sea light,
Whence now, and now, infernal flowerage bloomed,
Bloomed, burst, and scattered down its deadly seed,—
They swept, and died like freemen on the height,
Like freemen, and like men of noble breed;
And when the battle fell away at night
By hasty and contemptuous hands were thrust
Obscurely in a common grave with him
The fair-haired keeper of their love and trust.
Now limb doth mingle with dissolvèd limb
In nature's busy old democracy
To flush the mountain laurel when she blows
Sweet by the Southern sea,
And heart with crumbled heart climbs in the rose:—
The untaught hearts with the high heart that knew
This mountain fortress for no earthly hold
Of temporal quarrel, but the bastion old
Of spiritual wrong,
Built by an unjust nation sheer and strong,
Expugnable but by a nation's rue

And bowing down before that equal shrine
By all men held divine,
Whereof his band and he were the most holy sign.

VII

O bitter, bitter shade!
Wilt thou not put the scorn
And instant tragic question from thine eye?
Do thy dark brows yet crave
That swift and angry stave—
Unmeet for this desirous morn—
That I have striven, striven to evade?
Gazing on him, must I not deem they err
Whose careless lips in street and shop aver
As common tidings, deeds to make his cheek
Flush from the bronze, and his dead throat to speak?
Surely some elder singer would arise,
Whose harp hath leave to threaten and to mourn
Above this people when they go astray.
Is Whitman, the strong spirit, overworn?
Has Whittier put his yearning wrath away?
I will not and I dare not yet believe!
Though furtively the sunlight seems to grieve,
And the spring-laden breeze
Out of the gladdening west is sinister
With sounds of nameless battle overseas;
Though when we turn and question in suspense
If these things be indeed after these ways,
And what things are to follow after these,
Our fluent men of place and consequence
Fumble and fill their mouths with hollow phrase,
Or for the end-all of deep arguments
Intone their dull commercial liturgies—
I dare not yet believe! My ears are shut!
I will not hear the thin satiric praise
And muffled laughter of our enemies,
Bidding us never sheathe our valiant sword
Till we have changed our birthright for a gourd
Of wild pulse stolen from a barbarian's hut;

Showing how wise it is to cast away
The symbols of our spiritual sway,
That so our hands with better ease
May wield the driver's whip and grasp the jailer's keys.

VIII

Was it for this our fathers kept the law?
This crown shall crown their struggle and their ruth?
Are we the eagle nation Milton saw
Mewing its mighty youth,
Soon to possess the mountain winds of truth,
And be a swift familiar of the sun
Where aye before God's face his trumpets run?
Or have we but the talons and the maw,
And for the abject likeness of our heart
Shall some less lordly bird be set apart?
Some gross-billed wader where the swamps are fat?
Some gorger in the sun? Some prowler with the bat?

IX

Ah, no!
We have not fallen so.
We are our fathers' sons: let those who lead us know!
'T was only yesterday sick Cuba's cry
Came up the tropic wind, "Now help us, for we die!"
Then Alabama heard,
And rising, pale, to Maine and Idaho
Shouted a burning word.
Proud state with proud impassioned state conferred,
And at the lifting of a hand sprang forth,
East, west, and south, and north,
Beautiful armies. Oh, by the sweet blood and young
Shed on the awful hill slope at San Juan,
By the unforgotten names of eager boys
Who might have tasted girl's love and been stung
With the old mystic joys
And starry griefs, now the spring nights come on,

But that the heart of youth is generous,—
We charge you, ye who lead us,
Breathe on their chivalry no hint of stain!
Turn not their new-world victories to gain!
One least leaf plucked for chaffer from the bays
Of their dear praise,
One jot of their pure conquest put to hire,
The implacable republic will require;
With clamor, in the glare and gaze of noon,
Or subtly, coming as a thief at night,
But surely, very surely, slow or soon
That insult deep we deeply will requite.
Tempt not our weakness, our cupidity!
For save we let the island men go free,
Those baffled and dislaureled ghosts
Will curse us from the lamentable coasts
Where walk the frustrate dead.
The cup of trembling shall be drainèd quite,
Eaten the sour bread of astonishment,
With ashes of the hearth shall be made white
Our hair, and wailing shall be in the tent;
Then on your guiltier head
Shall our intolerable self-disdain
Wreak suddenly its anger and its pain;
For manifest in that disastrous light
We shall discern the right
And do it, tardily.—O ye who lead,
Take heed!
Blindness we may forgive, but baseness we will smite.

Stephen Crane

WAR IS KIND

DO not weep, maiden, for war is kind.
Because your lover threw wild hands toward the sky
And the affrighted steed ran on alone,
Do not weep.
War is kind.

Hoarse, booming drums of the regiment,
Little souls who thirst for fight,
These men were born to drill and die.
The unexplained glory flies above them,
Great is the battle-god, great, and his kingdom—
A field where a thousand corpses lie.

Do not weep, babe, for war is kind.
Because your father tumbled in the yellow trenches,
Raged at his breast, gulped and died,
Do not weep.
War is kind.

Swift blazing flag of the regiment,
Eagle with crest of red and gold,
These men were born to drill and die.
Point for them the virtue of slaughter,
Make plain to them the excellence of killing
And a field where a thousand corpses lie.

Mother whose heart hung humble as a button
On the bright splendid shroud of your son,
Do not weep.
War is kind.

George Cabot Lodge

DAY AND DARK

NOW the golden fields of sunset rose on rose to me-ward fall,
Down the dark reverberate beaches clear and far the sea-birds call,
Blue across the fire-stained waters, eastward thrusts the chuckling tide,
Fresh as when the immortal impulse took the lifeless world for bride.

Now the shore's thin verge of shallows keep the tense and tender light,
Now the stars hang few and faultless, diademed on the brows of night,
Now the moon's unstinted silver falls like dew along the sea
While from far a friendly casement softly fills with light for me.

So it ends! I reaped the harvest, lived the long and lavish day,
Saw the earliest sunlight shiver thro' the breakers' endless play,
Felt the noonday's warm abundance, shared the hours of large repose,
While the stately sun descended thro' the twilight's sumptuous close.

Now the night-fall—Ah! I guess the immortal secret, glimpse the goal,
Know the hours have scanted nothing, know each fragment hints the whole,
While the Soul in power and freedom dares and wills to claim its own,
Star over star, a larger, lovelier unknown heaven beyond the known!

George Santayana

ON THE DEATH OF A METAPHYSICIAN

UNHAPPY dreamer, who outwinged in flight
The pleasant region of the things I love,
And soared beyond the sunshine, and above
The golden cornfields and the dear and bright
Warmth of the hearth,—blasphemer of delight,
Was your proud bosom not at peace with Jove,
That you sought, thankless for his guarded grove,
The empty horror of absymal night?

Ah, the thin air is cold above the moon!
I stood and saw you fall, befooled in death,
As, in your numbëd spirit's fatal swoon,
You cried you were a god, or were to be;
I heard with feeble moan your boastful breath
Bubble from depths of the Icarian sea.

'AS IN THE MIDST OF BATTLE THERE IS ROOM'

AS in the midst of battle there is room
For thoughts of love, and in foul sin for mirth,
As gossips whisper of a trinket's worth
Spied by the death-bed's flickering candle-gloom;
As in the crevices of Cæsar's tomb
The sweet herbs flourish on a little earth:
So in this great disaster of our birth
We can be happy, and forget our doom.

For morning, with a ray of tenderest joy
Gilding the iron heaven, hides the truth,
And evening gently woos us to employ
Our grief in idle catches. Such is youth;
Till from that summer's trance we wake, to find
Despair before us, vanity behind.

SOLIPSISM

I COULD believe that I am here alone,
And all the world my dream;
The passion of the scene is all my own,
And things that seem but seem.

Perchance an exhalation of my sorrow
Hath raised this vaporous show,
For whence but from my soul should all things borrow
So deep a tinge of woe?

I keep the secret doubt within my breast
  To be the gods' defence,
To ease the heart by too much ruth oppressed
  And drive the horror hence.

O sorrow that the patient brute should cower
  And die, not having sinned!
O pity that the wild and fragile flower
  Should shiver in the wind!

Then were I dreaming dreams I know not of,
  For that is part of me
That feels the piercing pang of grief and love
  And doubts eternally.

But whether all to me the vision come
  Or break in many beams,
The pageant ever shifts, and being's sum
  Is but the sum of dreams.

ODES

I

WHAT god will choose me from this labouring
  nation
To worship him afar, with inward gladness,
At sunset and at sunrise, in some Persian
    Garden of roses;

Or under the full moon, in rapturous silence,
Charmed by the trickling fountain, and the moaning
Of the death-hallowed cypress, and the myrtle
    Hallowed by Venus?

O for a chamber in an eastern tower,
Spacious and empty, roofed in odorous cedar,
A silken soft divan, a woven carpet
    Rich, many-coloured;

A jug that, poised on her firm head, a negress
Fetched from the well; a window to the ocean,
Lest of the stormy world too deep seclusion
Make me forgetful!

Thence I might watch the vessel-bearing waters
Beat the slow pulses of the life eternal,
Bringing of nature's universal travail
Infinite echoes;

And there at even I might stand and listen
To thrum of distant lutes and dying voices
Chanting the ditty an Arabian captive
Sang to Darius.

So would I dream awhile, and ease a little
The soul long stifled and the straitened spirit,
Tasting new pleasures in a far-off country
Sacred to beauty.

II

My heart rebels against my generation,
That talks of freedom and is slave to riches,
And, toiling 'neath each day's ignoble burden,
Boasts of the morrow.

No space for noonday rest or midnight watches,
No purest joy of breathing under heaven!
Wretched themselves, they heap, to make them happy,
Many possessions.

But thou, O silent Mother, wise, immortal,
To whom our toil is laughter,—take, divine one,
This vanity away, and to thy lover
Give what is needful:—

III

Gathering the echoes of forgotten wisdom,
And mastered by a proud, adventurous purpose,
Columbus sought the golden shores of India
Opposite Europe.

He gave the world another world, and ruin
Brought upon blameless, river-loving nations,
Cursed Spain with barren gold, and made the Andes
Fiefs of Saint Peter;

While in the cheerless North the thrifty Saxon
Planted his corn, and, narrowing his bosom,
Made covenant with God, and by keen virtue
Trebled his riches.

What venture hast thou left us, bold Columbus?
What honour left thy brothers, brave Magellan?
Daily the children of the rich for pastime
Circle the planet.

And what good comes to us of all your dangers?
A smaller earth and smaller hope of heaven.
Ye have but cheapened gold, and, measuring ocean,
Counted the islands.

No Ponce de Leon shall drink in fountains,
On any flowering Easter, youth eternal;
No Cortes look upon another ocean;
No Alexander

Found in the Orient dim a boundless kingdom,
And, clothing his Greek strength with barbarous
splendour,
Build by the sea his throne, while Sacred Egypt
Honours his godhead.

The earth, the mother once of godlike Theseus
And mighty Heracles, at length is weary,
And now brings forth a spawn of antlike creatures,
Blackening her valleys,

Inglorious in their birth and in their living,
Curious and querulous, afraid of battle,
Rummaging earth for coals, in camps of hovels
Crouching from winter,

As if grim fate, amid our boastful prating,
Made us the image of our brutish fathers,
When from their caves they issued, crazed with terror,
Howling and hungry.

For all things come about in sacred cycles,
And life brings death, and light eternal darkness,
And now the world grows old apace; its glory
Passes for ever.

Perchance the earth will yet for many ages
Bear her dead child, her moon, around her orbit;
Strange craft may tempt the ocean streams, new forests
Cover the mountains.

If in those latter days men still remember
Our wisdom and our travail and our sorrow,
They never can be happy, with that burden
Heavy upon them,

Knowing the hideous past, the blood, the famine,
The ancestral hate, the eager faith's disaster,
All ending in their little lives, and vulgar
Circle of troubles.

But if they have forgot us, and the shifting
Of sands has buried deep our thousand cities,
Fell superstition then will seize upon them;
Protean error,

Will fill their panting heart with sickly phantoms
Of sudden blinding good and monstrous evil;
There will be miracles again, and torment,
Dungeon and fagot,—

Until the patient earth, made dry and barren,
Sheds all her herbage in a final winter,
And the gods turn their eyes to some far distant
Bright constellation.

IV

Slowly the black earth gains upon the yellow,
And the caked hill-side is ribbed soft with furrows.
Turn now again, with voice and staff, my ploughman,
Guiding thy oxen.

Lift the great ploughshare, clear the stones and brambles,
Plant it the deeper, with thy foot upon it,
Uprooting all the flowering weeds that bring not
Food to thy children.

Patience is good for man and beast, and labour
Hardens to sorrow and the frost of winter.
Turn then, again, in the brave hope of harvest,
Singing to heaven.

V

Of thee the Northman by his beachèd galley
Dreamt, as he watched the never-setting Ursa
And longed for summer and thy light, O sacred
Mediterranean.

Unseen he loved thee; for the heart within him
Knew earth had gardens where he might be blessed,
Putting away long dreams and aimless, barbarous
Hunger for battle.

The foretaste of thy languors thawed his bosom;
A great need drove him to thy caverned islands
From the gray, endless reaches of the outer
Desert of Ocean.

He saw thy pillars, saw thy sudden mountains
Wrinkled and stark, and in their crooked gorges,
'Neath peeping pine and cypress, guessed the torrent
Smothered in flowers.

Thine incense to the sun, thy gathered vapours,
He saw suspended on the flanks of Taurus,
Or veiling the snowed bosom of the virgin
Sister of Atlas.

He saw the luminous top of wide Olympus,
Fit for the happy gods; he saw the pilgrim
River, with rains of Ethiopia flooding
Populous Egypt.

And having seen, he loved thee. His racked spirit,
By thy breath tempered and the light that clothes thee,
Forgot the monstrous gods, and made of Nature
Mistress and mother.

The more should I, O fatal sea, before thee
Of alien words make echoes to thy music;
For I was born where first the rills of Tagus
Turn to the westward.

And wandering long, alas! have need of drinking
Deep of the patience of thy perfect sadness,
O thou that constant through the change of ages,
Beautiful ever,

Never wast wholly young and void of sorrows,
Nor ever canst be old, while yet the morning
Kindles thy ripples, or the golden evening
Dyes thee in purple.

Thee, willing to be tamed but still untamable,
The Roman called his own until he perished,
As now the busy English hover o'er thee,
Stalwart and noble;

But all is naught to thee, while no harsh winter
Congeals thy fountains, and the blown Sahara
Chokes not with dreadful sand thy deep and placid
Rock-guarded havens.

Thou carest not what men may tread thy margin;
Nor I, while from some heather-scented headland
I may behold thy beauty, the eternal
Solace of mortals.

Trumbull Stickney

BE STILL. THE HANGING GARDENS WERE A DREAM

BE still. The Hanging Gardens were a dream
That over Persian roses flew to kiss
The curlèd lashes of Semiramis.
Troy never was, nor green Skamander stream.
Provence and Troubadour are merest lies,
The glorious hair of Venice was a beam
Made within Titian's eye. The sunsets seem,
The world is very old and nothing is.
Be still. Thou foolish thing, thou canst not wake,
Nor thy tears wedge thy soldered lids apart,
But patter in the darkness of thy heart.
Thy brain is plagued. Thou art a frighted owl
Blind with the light of life thou'ldst not forsake,
And error loves and nourishes thy soul.

LIVE BLINDLY

LIVE blindly and upon the hour. The Lord,
Who was the Future, died full long ago.
Knowledge which is the Past is folly. Go,
Poor child, and be not to thyself abhorred.
Around thine earth sun-wingèd winds do blow
And planets roll; a meteor draws his sword;
The rainbow breaks his seven-coloured chord
And the long strips of river-silver flow:
Awake! Give thyself to the lovely hours.
Drinking their lips, catch thou the dream in flight
About their fragile hairs' aërial gold.
Thou art divine, thou livest,—as of old
Apollo springing naked to the light,
And all his island shivered into flowers.

HE SAID: "IF IN HIS IMAGE I WAS MADE"

HE said: "If in his image I was made,
I am his equal and across the land
We two should make our journey hand in hand
Like brothers dignified and unafraid."
And God that day was walking in the shade.
To whom he said: "The world is idly planned,
We cross each other, let us understand
Thou who thou art, I who I am," he said.
Darkness came down. And all that night was heard
Tremendous clamour and the broken roar
Of things in turmoil driven down before.
Then silence. Morning broke, and sang a bird.
He lay upon the earth, his bosom stirred;
But God was seen no longer any more.

ON SOME SHELLS FOUND INLAND

THESE are my murmur-laden shells that keep
A fresh voice tho' the years lie very gray.
The wave that washed their lips and tuned their lay
Is gone, gone with the faded ocean sweep,
The royal tide, gray ebb and sunken neap
And purple midday,—gone! To this hot clay
Must sing my shells, where yet the primal day,
Its roar and rhythm and splendour will not sleep.
What hand shall join them to their proper sea
If all be gone? Shall they forever feel
Glories undone and worlds that cannot be?—
'T were mercy to stamp out this agèd wrong,
Dash them to earth and crunch them with the heel
And make a dust of their seraphic song.

IN AMPEZZO

ONLY once more and not again—the larches
Shake to the wind their echo, "Not again,"—
We see, below the sky that over-arches
Heavy and blue, the plain

Between Tofana lying and Cristallo
In meadowy earths above the ringing stream:
Whence interchangeably desire may follow,
Hesitant as in dream,

At sunset, south, by lilac promontories
Under green skies to Italy, or forth
By calms of morning beyond Lavinores
Tyrolward and to north:

As now, this last of latter days, when over
The brownish field by peasants are undone
Some widths of grass, some plots of mountain clover
Under the autumn sun.

With honey-warm perfume that risen lingers
In mazes of low heat, or takes the air,
Passing delicious as a woman's fingers
Passing amid the hair;

When scythes are swishing and the mower's muscle
Spans a repeated crescent to and fro,
Or in dry stalks of corn the sickles rustle,
Tangle, detach and go,

Far thro' the wide blue day and greening meadow
Whose blots of amber beaded are with sheaves,
Whereover pallidly a cloud-shadow
Deadens the earth and leaves:

Whilst high around and near, their heads of iron
Sunken in sky whose azure overlights
Ravine and edges, stand the gray and maron
Desolate Dolomites,—

And older than decay from the small summit
Unfolds a stream of pebbly wreckage down
Under the suns of midday, like some comet
Struck into gravel stone.

Faintly across this gold and amethystine
September, images of summer fade;
And gentle dreams now freshen on the pristine
Viols, awhile unplayed,

Of many a place where lovingly we wander,
More dearly held that quickly we forsake,—
A pine by sullen coasts, an oleander
Reddening on the lake.

And there, each year with more familiar motion,
From many a bird and windy forestries,
Or along shaking fringes of the ocean
Vapours of music rise.

From many easts the morning gives her splendour;
The shadows fill with colours we forget;
Remembered tints at evening grow tender,
Tarnished with violet.

Let us away! soon sheets of winter metal
On this discoloured mountain-land will close,
While elsewhere Spring-time weaves a crimson petal,
Builds and perfumes a rose.

Away! for here the mountain sinks in gravel.
Let us forget the unhappy site with change,
And go, if only happiness be travel
After the new and strange:—

Unless 'twere better to be very single,
To follow some diviner monotone,
And in all beauties, where ourselves commingle,
Love but a love, but one,

Across this shadowy minute of our living,
What time our hearts so magically sing,
To mitigate our fever, simply giving
All in a little thing?

Just as here, past yon dumb and melancholy
Sameness of ruin, while the mountains ail,
Summer and sunset-coloured autumn slowly
Dissipate down the vale;

And all these lines along the sky that measure,
Sorapis and the rocks of Mezzodi
Crumble by foamy miles into the azure
Mediterranean sea:

Whereas to-day at sunrise, under brambles,
A league above the moss and dying pines
I picked this little—in my hand that trembles—
Parcel of columbines.

MT. LYKAION

ALONE on Lykaion since man hath been
Stand on the height two columns, where at rest
Two eagles hewn of gold sit looking East
Forever; and the sun goes up between.
Far down around the mountain's oval green
An order keeps the falling stones abreast.
Below within the chaos last and least
A river like a curl of light is seen.
Beyond the river lies the even sea,
Beyond the sea another ghost of sky,—
O God, support the sickness of my eye
Lest the far space and long antiquity
Suck out my heart, and on this awful ground
The great wind kill my little shell with sound.

Shaemas O'Sheel

THEY WENT FORTH TO BATTLE, BUT THEY ALWAYS FELL

THEY went forth to battle, but they always fell;
Their eyes were fixed above the sullen shields;
Nobly they fought and bravely, but not well,
And sank heart-wounded by a subtle spell.
They knew not fear that to the foeman yields,
They were not weak, as one who vainly wields
A futile weapon; yet the sad scrolls tell
How on the hard-fought field they always fell.

It was a secret music that they heard,
A sad sweet plea for pity and for peace;
And that which pierced the heart was but a word,
Though the white breast was red-lipped where the sword
Pressed a fierce cruel kiss, to put surcease
On its hot thirst, but drank a hot increase.

Ah, they by some strange troubling doubt were stirred,
And died for hearing what no foeman heard.

They went forth to battle, but they always fell;
  Their might was not the might of lifted spears;
Over the battle-clamor came a spell
Of troubling music, and they fought not well.
  Their wreaths are willows and their tribute, tears;
  Their names are old sad stories in men's ears;
Yet they will scatter the red hordes of Hell,
Who went to battle forth and always fell.

Adelaide Crapsey

VENDOR'S SONG

MY songs to sell, good sir!
  I pray you buy.
Here's one will win a lady's tears,
  Here's one will make her gay,
Here's one will charm your rtue love true
  Forever and a day;
Good sir, I pray you buy!

Oh, no, he will not buy.

My songs to sell, sweet maid!
  I pray you buy.
This one will teach you Lilith's lore,
  And this what Helen knew,
And this will keep your gold hair gold,
  And this your blue eyes blue;
Sweet maid, I pray you buy!

Oh, no, she will not buy.

If I'd as much money as I could tell,
I never would cry my songs to sell.
I never would cry my songs to sell.

THE LONELY DEATH

IN the cold I will rise, I will bathe
In waters of ice; myself
Will shiver, and shrive myself,
Alone in the dawn, and anoint
Forehead and feet and hands;
I will shutter the windows from light,
I will place in their sockets the four
Tall candles and set them aflame
In the grey of the dawn; and myself
Will lay myself straight in my bed,
And draw the sheet under my chin.

Edwin Arlington Robinson

BEN JONSON ENTERTAINS A MAN FROM STRATFORD

YOU are a friend then, as I make it out,
Of our man Shakespeare, who alone of us
Will put an ass's head in Fairyland
As he would add a shilling to more shillings,
All most harmonious—and out of his
Miraculous inviolable increase
Fills Ilion, Rome, or any town you like
Of olden time with timeless Englishmen;
And I must wonder what you think of him—
All you down there where your small Avon flows
By Stratford, and where you're an Alderman.
Some, for a guess, would have him riding back
To be a farrier there, or say a dyer;
Or maybe one of your adept surveyors;

Or like enough the wizard of all tanners.
Not you—no fear of that; for I discern
In you a kindling of the flame that saves—
The nimble element, the true caloric;
I see it, and was told of it, moreover,
By our discriminate friend himself, no other.
Had you been one of the sad average,
As he would have it—meaning, as I take it,
The sinew and the solvent of our Island,
You'd not be buying beer for this Terpander's
Approved and estimated friend Ben Jonson;
He'd never foist it as a part of his
Contingent entertainment of a townsman
While he goes off rehearsing, as he must,
If he shall ever be the Duke of Stratford.
And my words are no shadow on your town—
Far from it; for one town's as like another
As all are unlike London. Oh, he knows it—
And there's the Stratford in him; he denies it,
And there's the Shakespeare in him. So, God help him!
I tell him he needs Greek; but neither God
Nor Greek will help him. Nothing will help that man.
You see the fates have given him so much,
He must have all or perish—or look out
Of London, where he sees too many lords.
They're part of half what ails him: I suppose
There's nothing fouler down among the demons
Than what it is he feels when he remembers
The dust and sweat and ointment of his calling
With his lords looking on and laughing at him.
King as he is, he can't be king *de facto,*
And that's as well, because he wouldn't like it;
He'd frame a lower rating of men then
Than he has now; and after that would come
An abdication or an apoplexy.
He can't be king, not even king of Stratford—
Though half the world, if not the whole of it,
May crown him with a crown that fits no king
Save Lord Apollo's homesick emissary:

Not there on Avon, or on any stream
Where Naiads and their white arms are no more
Shall he find home again. It's all too bad.
But there's a comfort, for he'll have that House—
The best you ever saw; and he'll be there
Anon, as you're an Alderman. Good God!
He makes me lie awake o' nights and laugh.

And you have known him from his origin,
You tell me; and a most uncommon urchin
He must have been to the few seeing ones—
A trifle terrifying, I dare say,
Discovering a world with his man's eyes,
Quite as another lad might see some finches,
If he looked hard and had an eye for Nature.
But this one had his eyes and their foretelling,
And he had you to fare with, and what else?
He must have had a father and a mother—
In fact I've heard him say so—and a dog,
As a boy should, I venture; and the dog,
Most likely, was the only man who knew him.
A dog, for all I know, is what he needs
As much as anything right here to-day,
To counsel him about his disillusions,
Old aches, and parturitions of what's coming—
A dog of orders, an emeritus,
To wag his tail at him when he comes home,
And then to put his paws up on his knees
And say, "For God's sake, what's it all about?"

I don't know whether he needs a dog or not—
Or what he needs. I tell him he needs Greek;
I'll talk of rules and Aristotle with him,
And if his tongue's at home he'll say to that,
"I have your word that Aristotle knows,
And you mine that I don't know Aristotle."
He's all at odds with all the unities,
And what's yet worse it doesn't seem to matter;
He treads along through Time's old wilderness

As if the tramp of all the centuries
Had left no roads—and there are none, for him;
He doesn't see them, even with those eyes—
And that's a pity, or I say it is.
Accordingly we have him as we have him—
Going his way, the way that he goes best,
A pleasant animal with no great noise
Or nonsense anywhere to set him off—
Save only divers and inclement devils
Have made of late his heart their dwelling-place.
A flame half ready to fly out sometimes
At some annoyance may be fanned up in him,
But soon it falls, and when it falls goes out;
He knows how little room there is in there
For crude and futile animosities,
And how much for the joy of being whole,
And how much for long sorrow and old pain.
On our side there are some who may be given
To grow old wondering what he thinks of us
And some above us, who are, in his eyes,
Above himself—and that's quite right and English.
Yet here we smile, or disappoint the gods
Who made it so; the gods have always eyes
To see men scratch; and they see one down here
Who itches, manor-bitten, to the bone,
Albeit he knows himself—yes, yes, he knows—
The lord of more than England and of more
Than all the seas of England in all time
Shall ever wash. D'ye wonder that I laugh?
He sees me, and he doesn't seem to care;
And why the devil should he? I can't tell you.
I'll meet him out alone of a bright Sunday,
Trim, rather spruce, and quite the gentleman.
"What, ho, my lord!" say I. He doesn't hear me;
Wherefore I have to pause and look at him.
He's not enormous, but one looks at him.
A little on the round if you insist,
For now, God save the mark, he's growing old;
He's five and forty, and to hear him talk

These days you'd call him eighty; then you'd add
More years to that. He's old enough to be
The father of a world, and so he is.
"Ben, you're a scholar, what's the time of day?"
Says he; and there shines out of him again
An aged light that has no age or station—
The mystery that's his—a mischievous
Half-mad serenity that laughs at fame
For being won so easy, and at friends
Who laugh at him for what he wants the most,
And for his dukedom down in Warwickshire;—
By which you see we're all a little jealous. . . .
Poor Greene! I fear the colour of his name
Was even as that of his ascending soul;
And he was one where there are many others—
Some scrivening to the end against their fate,
Their puppets all in ink and all to die there;
And some with hands that once would shade an eye
That scanned Euripides and Æschylus
Will reach by this time for a pot-house mop
To slush their first and last of royalties.
Poor devils! and they all play to his hand;
For so it was in Athens and old Rome.
But that's not here or there; I've wandered off.
Greene does it, or I'm careful. Where's that boy?

Yes, he'll go back to Stratford. And we'll miss him?
Dear sir, there'll be no London here without him.
We'll all be riding, one of these fine days,
Down there to see him—and his wife won't like us;
And then we'll think of what he never said
Of women—which, if taken all in all
With what he did say, would buy many horses.
Though nowadays he's not so much for women.
"So few of them," he says, "are worth the guessing."
But there's a worm at work when he says that,
And while he says it one feels in the air
A deal of circumambient hocus-pocus.
They've had him dancing till his toes were tender,

And he can feel 'em now, come chilly rains.
There's no long cry for going into it,
However, and we don't know much about it.
But you in Stratford, like most here in London,
Have more now in the *Sonnets* than you paid for;
He's put one there with all her poison on,
To make a singing fiction of a shadow
That's in his life a fact, and always will be.
But she's no care of ours, though Time, I fear,
Will have a more reverberant ado
About her than about another one
Who seems to have decoyed him, married him,
And sent him scuttling on his way to London—
With much already learned, and more to learn,
And more to follow. Lord! how I see him now,
Pretending, maybe trying, to be like us.
Whatever he may have meant, we never had him;
He failed us, or escaped, or what you will—
And there was that about him (God knows what—
We'd flayed another had he tried it on us)
That made as many of us as had wits
More fond of all his easy distances
Than one another's noise and clap-your-shoulder.
But think you not, my friend, he'd never talk!
Talk? He was eldritch at it; and we listened—
Thereby acquiring much we knew before
About ourselves, and hitherto had held
Irrelevant, or not prime to the purpose.
And there were some, of course, and there be now,
Disordered and reduced amazedly
To resignation by the mystic seal
Of young finality the gods had laid
On everything that made him a young demon;
And one or two shot looks at him already
As he had been their executioner;
And once or twice he was, not knowing it—
Or knowing, being sorry for poor clay
And saying nothing . . . Yet, for all his engines,
You'll meet a thousand of an afternoon

Who strut and sun themselves and see around 'em
A world made out of more that has a reason
Than his, I swear, that he sees here to-day;
Though he may scarcely give a Fool an exit
But we mark how he sees in everything
A law that, given that we flout it once too often,
Brings fire and iron down on our naked heads.
To me it looks as if the power that made him,
For fear of giving all things to one creature,
Left out the first—faith, innocence, illusion,
Whatever 'tis that keeps us out o' Bedlam—
And thereby, for his too consuming vision,
Empowered him out of nature; though to see him,
You'd never guess what's going on inside him.
He'll break out some day like a keg of ale
With too much independent frenzy in it;
And all for cellaring what he knows won't keep,
And what he'd best forget—but that he can't.
You'll have it, and have more than I'm foretelling;
And there'll be such a roaring at the Globe
As never stunned the bleeding gladiators.
He'll have to change the colour of its hair
A bit, for now he calls it Cleopatra.
Black hair would never do for Cleopatra.
But you and I are not yet two old women,
And you're a man of office. What he does
Is more to you than how it is he does it—
And that's what the Lord God has never told him.
They work together, and the Devil helps 'em;
They do it of a morning, or if not,
They do it of a night; in which event
He's peevish of a morning. He seems old;
He's not the proper stomach or the sleep—
And they're two sovran agents to conserve him
Against the fiery art that has no mercy
But what's in that prodigious grand new House.
I gather something happening in his boyhood
Fulfilled him with a boy's determination
To make all Stratford 'ware of him. Well, well,

I hope at last he'll have his joy of it,
And all his pigs and sheep and bellowing beeves,
And frogs and owls and unicorns, moreover,
Be less than hell to his attendant ears.
Oh, past a doubt we'll all go down to see him.

He may be wise. With London two days off,
Down there some wind of heaven may yet revive him,
But there's no quickening breath from anywhere
Shall make of him again the young poised faun
From Warwickshire, who'd made, it seems, already
A legend of himself before I came
To blink before the last of his first lightning.
Whatever there be, there'll be no more of that;
The coming on of his old monster Time
Has made him a still man; and he has dreams
Were fair to think on once, and all found hollow.
He knows how much of what men paint themselves
Would blister in the light of what they are;
He sees how much of what was great now shares
An eminence transformed and ordinary;
He knows too much of what the world has hushed
In others, to be loud now for himself;
He knows now at what height low enemies
May reach his heart, and high friends let him fall;
But what not even such as he may know
Bedevils him the worst: his lark may sing
At heaven's gate how he will, and for as long
As joy may listen, but *he* sees no gate,
Save one whereat the spent clay waits a little
Before the churchyard has it, and the worm.
Not long ago, late in an afternoon,
I came on him unseen down Lambeth way,
And on my life I was afear'd of him:
He gloomed and mumbled like a soul from Tophet,
His hands behind him and his head bent solemn.
"What is it now," said I, "another woman?"
That made him sorry for me, and he smiled.
"No, Ben," he mused; "it's Nothing. It's all Nothing

We come, we go; and when we're done, we're done;
Spiders and flies—we're mostly one or t'other—
We come, we go; and when we're done, we're done";
"By God, you sing that song as if you knew it!"
Said I, by way of cheering him; "what ails ye?"
"I think I must have come down here to think,"
Says he to that, and pulls his little beard;
"Your fly will serve as well as anybody,
And what's his hour? He flies, and flies, and flies,
And in his fly's mind has a brave appearance;
And then your spider gets him in her net,
And eats him out, and hangs him up to dry.
That's Nature, the kind mother of us all.
And then your slattern housemaid swings her broom,
And where's your spider? And that's Nature, also.
It's Nature, and it's Nothing. It's all Nothing.
It's all a world where bugs and emperors
Go singularly back to the same dust,
Each in his time; and the old, ordered stars
That sang together, Ben, will sing the same
Old stave to-morrow."

When he talks like that,
There's nothing for a human man to do
But lead him to some grateful nook like this
Where we be now, and there to make him drink.
He'll drink, for love of me, and then be sick;
A sad sign always in a man of parts,
And always very ominous. The great
Should be as large in liquor as in love—
And our great friend is not so large in either:
One disaffects him, and the other fails him;
Whatso he drinks that has an antic in it,
He's wondering what's to pay in his insides;
And while his eyes are on the Cyprian
He's fribbling all the time with that damned House.
We laugh here at his thrift, but after all
It may be thrift that saves him from the devil;
God gave it, anyhow—and we'll suppose

He knew the compound of His handiwork.
To-day the clouds are with him, but anon
He'll out of 'em enough to shake the tree
Of life itself and bring down fruit unheard-of—
And, throwing in the bruised and whole together,
Prepare a wine to make us drunk with wonder;
And if he live, there'll be a sunset spell
Thrown over him as over a glassed lake
That yesterday was all a black wild water.

God send he live to give us, if no more,
What now's a-rampage in him, and exhibit,
With a decent half-allegiance to the ages
An earnest of at least a casual eye
Turned once on what he owes to Gutenberg,
And to the fealty of more centuries
Than are as yet a picture in our vision.
"There's time enough—I'll do it when I'm old,
And we're immortal men," he says to that;
And then he says to me, "Ben, what's 'immortal'?
Think you by any force of ordination
It may be nothing of a sort more noisy
Than a small oblivion of component ashes
That of a dream-addicted world was once
A moving atomy much like your friend here?"
Nothing will help that man. To make him laugh
I said then he was a mad mountebank—
And by the Lord I nearer made him cry.
I could have eat an eft then, on my knees,
Tails, claws, and all of him; for I had stung
The king of men, who had no sting for me,
And I had hurt him in his memories;
And I say now, as I shall say again,
I love the man this side idolatry.
He'll do it when he's old, he says. I wonder.
He may not be so ancient as all that.
For such as he the thing that is to do
Will do itself—but there's a reckoning;
The sessions that are now too much his own,

The roiling inward of a still outside,
The churning out of all those blood-fed lines,
The nights of many schemes and little sleep,
The full brain hammered hot with too much thinking,
The vexed heart over-worn with too much aching—
This weary jangling of conjoined affairs
Made out of elements that have no end,
And all confused at once, I understand,
Is not what makes a man to live forever.
O, no, not now! He'll not be going now:
There'll be time yet for God knows what explosions
Before he goes. He'll stay awhile. Just wait:
Just wait a year or two for Cleopatra,
For she's to be a balsam and a comfort;
And that's not all a jape of mine now, either.
For granted once the old way of Apollo
Sings in a man, he may then, if he's able,
Strike unafraid whatever strings he will
Upon the last and wildest of new lyres;
Nor out of his new magic, though it hymn
The shrieks of dungeoned hell, shall he create
A madness or a gloom to shut quite out
A cleaving daylight, and a last great calm
Triumphant over shipwreck and all storms.
He might have given Aristotle creeps,
But surely would have given him his *katharsis*.
He'll not be going yet. There's too much yet
Unsung within the man. But when he goes,
I'd stake ye coin o' the realm his only care
For a phantom world he sounded and found wanting
Will be a portion here, a portion there,
Of this or that thing or some other thing
That has a patent and intrinsical
Equivalence in those egregious shillings.
And yet he knows, God help him! Tell me, now,
If ever there was anything let loose
On earth by gods or devils heretofore
Like this mad, careful, proud, indifferent Shakespeare!
Where was it, if it ever was? By heaven,

'Twas never yet in Rhodes or Pergamon—
In Thebes or Nineveh, a thing like this!
No thing like this was ever out of England;
And that he knows. I wonder if he cares.
Perhaps he does. . . . O Lord, that House in Stratford!

EROS TURANNOS

SHE fears him, and will always ask
What fated her to choose him;
She meets in his engaging mask
All reasons to refuse him;
But what she meets and what she fears
Are less than are the downward years,
Drawn slowly to the foamless weirs
Of age, were she to lose him.

Between a blurred sagacity
That once had power to sound him,
And Love, that will not let him be
The Judas that she found him,
Her pride assuages her almost,
As if it were alone the cost.—
He sees that he will not be lost,
And waits and looks around him.

A sense of ocean and old trees
Envelops and allures him;
Tradition, touching all he sees,
Beguiles and reassures him;
And all her doubts of what he says
Are dimmed with what she knows of days—
Till even prejudice delays
And fades, and she secures him.

The falling leaf inaugurates
The reign of her confusion;
The pounding wave reverberates
The dirge of her illusion;

And home, where passion lived and died,
Becomes a place where she can hide,
While all the town and harbour side
  Vibrate with her seclusion.

We tell you, tapping on our brows,
  The story as it should be—
As if the story of a house
  Were told, or ever could be;
We'll have no kindly veil between
Her visions and those we have seen—
As if we guessed what hers have been,
  Or what they are or would be.

Meanwhile we do no harm; for they
  That with a god have striven,
Not hearing much of what we say,
  Take what the god has given;
Though like waves breaking it may be,
Or like a changed familiar tree,
Or like a stairway to the sea
  Where down the blind are driven.

FOR A DEAD LADY

NO more with overflowing light
  Shall fill the eyes that now are faded,
Nor shall another's fringe with night
Their woman-hidden world as they did.
No more shall quiver down the days
The flowing wonder of her ways,
Whereof no language may requite
The shifting and the many-shaded.

The grace, divine, definitive,
Clings only as a faint forestalling;
The laugh that love could not forgive
Is hushed, and answers to no calling;

The forehead and the little ears
Have gone where Saturn keeps the years;
The breast where roses could not live
Has done with rising and with falling.

The beauty, shattered by the laws
That have creation in their keeping,
No longer trembles at applause,
Or over children that are sleeping;
And we who delve in beauty's lore
Know all that we have known before
Of what inexorable cause
Makes Time so vicious in his reaping.

THE MAN AGAINST THE SKY

BETWEEN me and the sunset, like a dome
Against the glory of a world on fire,
Now burned a sudden hill,
Bleak, round, and high, by flame-lit height made higher,
With nothing on it for the flame to kill
Save one who moved and was alone up there
To loom before the chaos and the glare
As if he were the last god going home
Unto his last desire.
Dark, marvellous, and inscrutable he moved on
Till down the fiery distance he was gone,
Like one of those eternal, remote things
That range across a man's imaginings
When a sure music fills him and he knows
What he may say thereafter to few men—
The touch of ages having wrought
An echo and a glimpse of what he thought
A phantom or a legend until then;
For whether lighted over ways that save,
Or lured from all repose,
If he go on too far to find a grave,
Mostly alone he goes.

Even he, who stood where I had found him,
On high with fire all round him,
Who moved along the molten west,
And over the round hill's crest
That seemed half ready with him to go down,
Flame-bitten and flame-cleft,
As if there were to be no last thing left
Of a nameless unimaginable town—
Even he who climbed and vanished may have taken
Down to the perils of a depth not known,
From death defended, though by men forsaken,
The bread that every man must eat alone;
He may have walked while others hardly dared
Look on to see him stand where many fell;
And upward out of that as out of hell,
He may have sung and striven
To mount where more of him shall yet be given,
Bereft of all retreat,
To sevenfold heat—
As on a day when three in Dura shared
The furnace, and were spared
For glory by that king of Babylon
Who made himself so great that God, who heard,
Covered him with long feathers, like a bird.
Again, he may have gone down easily,
By comfortable altitudes, and found,
As always, underneath him solid ground
Whereon to be sufficient and to stand
Possessed already of the promised land,
Far stretched and fair to see:
A good sight, verily,
And one to make the eyes of her who bore him
Shine glad with hidden tears.
Why question of his ease of who before him,
In one place or another where they left
Their names as far behind them as their bones,
And yet by dint of slaughter, toil, and theft,
And shrewdly sharpened stones,
Carved hard the way for his ascendancy

Through deserts of lost years?
Why trouble him now who sees and hears
No more than what his innocence requires,
And therefore to no other height aspires
Than one at which he neither quails nor tires?
He may do more by seeing what he sees
Than others eager for iniquities;
He may, by seeing all things for the best,
Incite futurity to do the rest.
Or with an even likelihood,
He may have met with atrabilious eyes
The fires of time on equal terms and passed
Indifferently down, until at last
His only kind of grandeur would have been,
Apparently, in being seen.
He may have had for evil or for good
No argument; he may have had no care
For what without himself went anywhere
To failure or to glory, and least of all
For such a stale, flamboyant miracle;
He may have been the prophet of an art
Immovable to old idolatries;
He may have been a player without a part,
Annoyed that even the sun should have the skies
For such a flaming way to advertise;
He may have been a painter sick at heart
With Nature's toiling for a new surprise;
He may have been a cynic, who now, for all
Of anything divine that his effete
Negation may have tasted,
Saw truth in his own image, rather small,
Forbore to fever the ephemeral,
Found any barren height a good retreat
From any swarming street,
And in the sun saw power superbly wasted;
And when the primitive old-fashioned stars
Came out again to shine on joys and wars
More primitive, and all arrayed for doom,
He may have proved a world a sorry thing

In his imagining,
And life a lighted highway to the tomb.
Or, mounting with unfirm unsearching tread,
His hopes to chaos led,
He may have stumbled up there from the past,
And with an aching strangeness viewed the last
Abysmal conflagration of his dreams—
A flame where nothing seems
To burn but flame itself, by nothing fed;
And while it all went out,
Not even the faint anodyne of doubt
May then have eased a painful going down
From pictured heights of power and lost renown,
Revealed at length to his outlived endeavour
Remote and unapproachable forever;
And at his heart there may have gnawed
Sick memories of a dead faith foiled and flawed
And long dishonoured by the living death
Assigned alike by chance
To brutes and hierophants;
And anguish fallen on those he loved around him
May once have dealt the last blow to confound him
And so have left him as death leaves a child,
Who sees it all too near;
And he who knows no young way to forget
May struggle to the tomb unreconciled.
Whatever suns may rise and set
There may be nothing kinder for him here
Than shafts and agonies;
And under these
He may cry out and stay on horribly;
Or, seeing in death too small a thing to fear,
He may go forward like a stoic Roman
Where pangs and terrors in his pathway lie—
Or, seizing the swift logic of a woman,
Curse God and die.

Or maybe there, like many another one
Who might have stood aloft and looked ahead,

Black-drawn against wild red,
He may have built unawed by fiery gules
That in him no commotion stirred,
A living reason out of molecules
Why molecules occurred,
And one for smiling when he might have sighed
Had he seen far enough,
And in the same inevitable stuff
Discovered an odd reason too for pride
In being what he must have been by laws
Infrangible and for no kind of cause.
Deterred by no confusion or surprise
He may have seen with his mechanic eyes
A world without a meaning, and had room,
Alone amid magnificence and doom,
To build himself an airy monument
That should, or fail him in his vague intent,
Outlast an accidental universe—
To call it nothing worse—
Or, by the burrowing guile
Of Time disintegrated and effaced,
Like once-remembered mighty trees go down
To ruin, of which by man may now be traced
No part sufficient even to be rotten,
And in the book of things that are forgotten
Is entered as a thing not quite worth while.
He may have been so great
That satraps would have shivered at his frown,
And all he prized alive may rule a state
No larger than a grave that holds a clown;
He may have been a master of his fate,
And of his atoms—ready as another
In his emergence to exonerate
His father and his mother;
He may have been a captain of a host,
Self-eloquent and ripe for prodigies,
Doomed here to swell by dangerous degrees,
And then give up the ghost.

Nahum's great grasshoppers were such as these,
Sun-scattered and soon lost.

Whatever the dark road he may have taken,
This man who stood on high
And faced alone the sky,
Whatever drove or lured or guided him—
A vision answering a faith unshaken,
An easy trust assumed by easy trials,
A sick negation born of weak denials,
A crazed abhorrence of an old condition,
A blind attendance on a brief ambition—
Whatever stayed him or derided him,
His way was even as ours;
And we, with all our wounds and all our powers,
Must each await alone at his own height
Another darkness or another light;
And there, of our poor self dominion reft,
If inference and reason shun
Hell, Heaven, and Oblivion,
May thwarted will (perforce precarious,
But for our conservation better thus)
Have no misgivings left
Of doing yet what here we leave undone?
Or if unto the last of these we cleave,
Believing or protesting we believe
In such an idle and ephemeral
Florescence of the diabolical—
If, robbed of two fond old enormities,
Our being had no onward auguries,
What then were this great love of ours to say
For launching other lives to voyage again
A little farther into time and pain,
A little faster in a futile chase
For a kingdom and a power and a Race
That would have still in sight
A manifest end of ashes and eternal night?
Is this the music of the toys we shake
So loud—as if there might be no mistake

Somewhere in our indomitable will?
Are we no greater than the noise we make
Along our blind atomic pilgrimage
Whereon by crass chance billeted we go
Because our brains and bones and cartilage
Will have it so?
If this we say, then let us all be still
About our share in it, and live and die
More quietly thereby.

Where was he going, this man against the sky?
You know not, nor do I.
But this we know, if we know anything:
That we may laugh and fight and sing
And of our transcience here make offering
To an orient Word that will not be erased,
Or, save in incommunicable gleams
Too permanent for dreams,
Be found or known.
No tonic or ambitious irritant
Of increase or of want
Has made an otherwise insensate waste
Of ages overthrown
A ruthless, veiled, implacable foretaste
Of other ages that are still to be
Depleted and rewarded variously
Because a few, by fate's economy,
Shall seem to move the world the way it goes;
No soft evangel of equality,
Safe-cradled in a communal repose
That huddles into death and may at last
Be covered well with equatorial snows—
And all for what, the devil only knows—
Will aggregate an inkling to confirm
The credit of a sage or of a worm,
Or tell us why one man in five
Should have a care to stay alive
While in his heart he feels no violence
Laid on his humour and intelligence

When infant Science makes a pleasant face
And waves again that hollow toy, the Race;
No planetary trap where souls are wrought
For nothing but the sake of being caught
And sent again to nothing will attune
Itself to any key of any reason
Why man should hunger through another season
To find out why 'twere better late than soon
To go away and let the sun and moon
And all the silly stars illuminate
A place for creeping things,
And those that root and trumpet and have wings,
And herd and ruminate,
Or dive and flash and poise in rivers and seas,
Or by their loyal tails in lofty trees
Hang screeching lewd victorious derision
Of man's immortal vision.
Shall we, because Eternity records
Too vast an answer for the time-born words
We spell, whereof so many are dead that once
In our capricious lexicons
Were so alive and final, hear no more
The Word itself, the living word
That none alive has ever heard
Or ever spelt,
And few have ever felt
Without the fears and old surrenderings
And terrors that began
When Death let fall a feather from his wings
And humbled the first man?
Because the weight of our humility,
Wherefrom we gain
A little wisdom and much pain,
Falls here too sore and there too tedious,
Are we in anguish or complacency,
Not looking far enough ahead
To see by what mad couriers we are led
Along the roads of the ridiculous,
To pity ourselves and laugh at faith

And while we curse life bear it?
And if we see the soul's dead end in death,
Are we to fear it?
What folly is here that has not yet a name
Unless we say outright that we are liars?
What have we seen beyond our sunset fires
That lights again the way by which we came?
Why pay we such a price, and one we give
So clamouringly, for each racked empty day
That leads one more last human hope away,
As quiet fiends would lead past our crazed eyes
Our children to an unseen sacrifice?
If after all that we have lived and thought,
All comes to Nought—
If there be nothing after Now,
And we be nothing anyhow,
And we know that—why live?
'Twere sure but weaklings' vain distress
To suffer dungeons where so many doors
Will open on the cold eternal shores
That look sheer down
To the dark tideless floods of Nothingness
Where all who know may drown.

Anna Hempstead Branch

THE MONK IN THE KITCHEN

I

ORDER is a lovely thing;
On disarray it lays its wing,
Teaching simplicity to sing.
It has a meek and lowly grace,
Quiet as a nun's face.
Lo—I will have thee in this place!
Tranquil well of deep delight,

All things that shine through thee appear
As stones through water, sweetly clear.
Thou clarity,
That with angelic charity
Revealest beauty where thou art,
Spread thyself like a clean pool,
Then all the things that in thee are,
Shall seem more spiritual and fair,
Reflection from serener air—
Sunken shapes of many a star
In the high heavens set afar.

II

Ye stolid, homely, visible things,
Above you all brood glorious wings
Of your deep entities, set high,
Like slow moons in a hidden sky.
But you, their likenesses, are spent
Upon another element.
Truly ye are but seemings—
The shadowy cast-off gleamings
Of bright solidities. Ye seem
Soft as water, vague as dream;
Image, cast in a shifting stream.

III

What are ye?
I know not.
Brazen pan and iron pot,
Yellow brick and gray flag-stone
That my feet have trod upon—
Ye seem to me
Vessels of bright mystery.
For ye do bear a shape, and so
Though ye were made by man, I know
An inner Spirit also made,
And ye his breathings have obeyed.

IV

Shape, the strong and awful spirit,
Laid his ancient hand on you.
He waste chaos doth inherit;
He can alter and subdue.
Verily, he doth lift up
Matter, like a sacred cup,
Into deep substance he reached, and lo
Where ye were not, ye were; and so
Out of useless nothing, ye
Groaned and laughed and came to be.
And I use you, as I can,
Wonderful uses, made for man,
Iron pot and brazen pan.

V

What are ye?
I know not;
Nor what I really do
When I move and govern you.
There is no small work unto God.
He required of us greatness;
Of His least creature
A high angelic nature,
Stature superb and bright completeness,
He sets to us no humble duty.
Each act that He would have us do
Is haloed round with strangest beauty;
Terrific deeds and cosmic tasks
Of His plainest child He asks.
When I polish the brazen pan
I hear a creature laugh afar
In the gardens of a star,
And from his burning presence run
Flaming wheels of many a sun.
Whoever makes a thing more bright,
He is an angel of all light.

When I cleanse this earthen floor
My spirit leaps to see
Bright garments trailing over it,
A cleanness made by me.
Purger of all men's thoughts and ways,
With labour do I sound Thy praise,
My work is done for Thee.
Whoever makes a thing more bright,
He is an angel of all light.
Therefore let me spread abroad
The beautiful cleanness of my God.

VI

One time in the cool of dawn
Angels came and worked with me.
The air was soft with many a wing.
They laughed amid my solitude
And cast bright looks on everything.
Sweetly of me did they ask
That they might do my common task.
And all were beautiful—but One
With garments whiter than the sun
Had such a face
Of deep, remembered grace;
That when I saw I cried—"Thou art
The great Blood-Brother of my heart.
Where have I seen Thee?"—And He said,
"When we are dancing round God's throne,
How often thou art there.
Beauties from thy hands have flown
Like white doves wheeling in mid air.
Nay—thy soul remembers not?
Work on, and cleanse thy iron pot."

VII

What are we? I know not.

ERE THE GOLDEN BOWL IS BROKEN

HE gathered for His own delight
  The sparkling waters of my soul.
A thousand creatures, bubbling bright—
  He set me in a golden bowl.

From the deep cisterns of the earth
  He bade me up—the shining daughter—
And I am exquisite with mirth,
  A brightening and a sunlit water.

The wild, the free, the radiant one,
  A happy bubble I did glide.
I poised my sweetness to the sun
  And there I sleeked my silver side.

Sometimes I lifted up my head
  And globed the moonlight with my hands,
Or thin as flying wings I spread
  Angelic wildness through the sands.

Then, woven into webs of light,
  I breathed, I sighed, I laughed aloud,
And lifting up my pinions bright
  I shone in Heaven, a bird-white cloud.

Then did I dance above the mead,
  And through the crystal fields would run,
And from my scarlet splendours breed
  The golden thunders of the sun.

Beneath the whitening stars I flew
  And floated moon-like on the breeze,
Or my frail heart was piercèd through
  With sharp sweet flowers of the trees.

Of giant crags I bear the scars,
  And I have swept along the gale,
Such multitudes as are the stars,
  My myriad faces rapt and pale.

As savage creatures strong and free
  Make wild the jungle of the wood,
The starry powers that sport in me
  Habit my silver solitude.

From out my smallness, soft as dew,
  That utter fastness, stern and deep,
Terrible meanings look at you
  Like vision from the eyes of sleep.

I cannot leap—I cannot run—
  I only glimmer, soft and mild,
A limpid water in the sun,
  A sparkling and a sunlit child.

What stranger ways shall yet be mine
  When I am spilled, you cannot see.
But now you laugh to watch me shine,
  And smooth the hidden stars in me.

Lightly you stroke my silver wing—
  The folded carrier of my soul.
A soft, a shy, a silent thing,
  A water in a golden bowl.

Amy Lowell

LITTLE IVORY FIGURES PULLED WITH STRING

IS it the tinkling of mandolins which disturbs you?
Or the dropping of bitter-orange petals among the coffee-cups?
Or the slow creeping of the moonlight between the olive-trees?
  Drop! drop! the rain
  Upon the thin plates of my heart.

String your blood to chord with this music,
Stir your heels upon the cobbles to the rhythm of a dance-tune.
They have slim thighs and arms of silver;
The moon washes away their garments;
They make a pattern of fleeing feet in the branch shadows,
And the green grapes knotted about them
Burst as they press against one another.
The rain knocks upon the plates of my heart,
They are crumpled with its beating.

Would you drink only from your brains, Old Man?
See, the moonlight has reached your knees,
It falls upon your head in an accolade of silver.
Rise up on the music,
Fling against the moon drifts in a whorl of young light bodies:
Leaping grape-clusters,
Vine leaves tearing from a grey wall.
You shall run, laughing, in a braid of women,
And weave flowers with the frosty spines of thorns.
Why do you gaze into your glass,
And jar the spoons with your finger-tapping?
The rain is rigid on the plates of my heart.
The murmur of it is loud—loud.

THE BOOK OF HOURS OF SISTER CLOTILDE

THE Bell in the convent tower swung.
High overhead the great sun hung,
A navel for the curving sky.
The air was a blue clarity.
Swallows flew,
And a cock crew.

The iron clanging sank through the light air,
Rustled over with blowing branches. A flare
Of spotted green, and a snake had gone
Into the bed where the snowdrops shone
In green new-started,
Their white bells parted.

Two by two, in a long brown line,
The nuns were walking to breathe the fine
Bright April air. They must go in soon
And work at their tasks all the afternoon.
    But this time is theirs!
    They walk in pairs.

First comes the Abbess, preoccupied
And slow, as a woman often tried,
With her temper in bond. Then the oldest nun.
Then younger and younger, until the last one
    Has a laugh on her lips,
    And fairly skips.

They wind about the gravel walks
And all the long line buzzes and talks.
They step in time to the ringing bell,
With scarcely a shadow. The sun is well
    In the core of a sky
    Domed silverly.

Sister Marguérite said: "The pears will soon bud."
Sister Angélique said she must get her spud
And free the earth round the jasmine roots.
Sister Véronique said: "Oh, look at those shoots!
    There's a crocus up,
    With a purple cup."

But Sister Clotilde said nothing at all,
She looked up and down the old grey wall
To see if a lizard were basking there.
She looked across the garden to where
    A sycamore
    Flanked the garden door.

She was restless, although her little feet danced,
And quite unsatisfied, for it chanced
Her morning's work had hung in her mind
And would not take form. She could not find
    The beautifulness
    For the Virgin's dress.

Should it be of pink, or damasked blue?
Or perhaps lilac with gold shotted through?
Should it be banded with yellow and white
Roses, or sparked like a frosty night?
    Or a crimson sheen
    Over some sort of green?

But Clotilde's eyes saw nothing new
In all the garden, no single hue
So lovely or so marvellous
That its use would not seem impious.
    So on she walked,
    And the others talked.

Sister Elisabeth edged away
From what her companion had to say,
For Sister Marthe saw the world in little,
She weighed every grain and recorded each tittle.
    She did plain stitching
    And worked in the kitchen.

"Sister Radegonde knows the apple won't last,
I told her so this Friday past.
I must speak to her before Compline."
Her words were like dust motes in slanting sunshine.
    The other nun sighed,
    With her pleasure quite dried.

Suddenly Sister Berthe cried out:
"The snowdrops are blooming!" They turned about.
The little white cups bent over the ground,
And in among the light stems wound
    A crested snake,
    With his eyes awake.

His body was green with a metal brightness
Like an emerald set in a kind of whiteness,

And all down his curling length were disks,
Evil vermilion asterisks,
They paled and flooded
As wounds fresh-blooded.

His crest was amber glittered with blue,
And opaque so the sun came shining through.
It seemed a crown with fiery points.
When he quivered all down his scaly joints,
From every slot
The sparkles shot.

The nuns huddled tightly together, fear
Catching their senses. But Clotilde must peer
More closely at the beautiful snake,
She seemed entranced and eased. Could she make
Colours so rare,
The dress were there.

The Abbess shook off her lethargy.
"Sisters, we will walk on," said she.
Sidling away from the snowdrop bed,
The line curved forwards, the Abbess ahead.
Only Clotilde
Was the last to yield.

When the recreation hour was done
Each went in to her task. Alone
In the library, with its great north light,
Clotilde wrought at an exquisite
Wreath of flowers
For her Book of Hours.

She twined the little crocus blooms
With snowdrops and daffodils, the glooms
Of laurel leaves were interwoven
With Stars-of-Bethlehem, and cloven
Fritillaries,
Whose colour varies.

They framed the picture she had made,
Half-delighted and half-afraid.
In a courtyard with a lozenged floor
The Virgin watched, and through the arched door
The angel came
Like a springing flame.

His wings were dipped in violet fire,
His limbs were strung to holy desire.
He lowered his head and passed under the arch,
And the air seemed beating a solemn march.
The Virgin waited
With eyes dilated.

Her face was quiet and innocent,
And beautiful with her strange assent.
A silver thread about her head
Her halo was poised. But in the stead
Of her gown, there remained
The vellum, unstained.

Clotilde painted the flowers patiently,
Lingering over each tint and dye.
She could spend great pains, now she had seen
That curious, unimagined green.
A colour so strange
It had seemed to change.

She thought it had altered while she gazed.
At first it had been simple green; then glazed
All over with twisting flames, each spot
A molten colour, trembling and hot,
And every eye
Seemed to liquefy.

She had made a plan, and her spirits danced.
After all, she had only glanced

At that wonderful snake, and she must know
Just what hues made the creature throw
  Those splashes and sprays
  Of prismed rays.

When evening prayers were sung and said,
The nuns lit their tapers and went to bed.
And soon in the convent there was no light,
For the moon did not rise until late that night,
  Only the shine
  Of the lamp at the shrine.

Clotilde lay still in her trembling sheets.
Her heart shook her body with its beats.
She could not see till the moon should rise,
So she whispered prayers and kept her eyes
  On the window-square
  Till light should be there.

The faintest shadow of a branch
Fell on the floor. Clotilde, grown staunch
With solemn purpose, softly rose
And fluttered down between the rows
  Of sleeping nuns.
  She almost runs.

She must go out through the little side door
Lest the nuns who were always praying before
The Virgin's altar should hear her pass.
She pushed the bolts, and over the grass
  The red moon's brim
  Mounted its rim.

Her shadow crept up the convent wall
As she swiftly left it, over all
The garden lay the level glow
Of a moon coming up, very big and slow.
  The gravel glistened.
  She stopped and listened.

It was still, and the moonlight was getting clearer.
She laughed a little, but she felt queerer
Than ever before. The snowdrop bed
Was reached and she bent down her head.
    On the stripéd ground
    The snake was wound.

For a moment Clotilde paused in alarm,
Then she rolled up her sleeve and stretched out her arm
She thought she heard steps, she must be quick.
She darted her hand out, and seized the thick
    Wriggling slime,
    Only just in time.

The old gardener came muttering down the path,
And his shadow fell like a broad, black swath,
And covered Clotilde and the angry snake.
He bit her, but what difference did that make!
    The Virgin should dress
    In his loveliness.

The gardener was covering his new-set plants
For the night was chilly, and nothing daunts
Your lover of growing things. He spied
Something to do and turned aside,
    And the moonlight streamed
    On Clotilde, and gleamed.

His business finished the gardener rose.
He shook and swore, for the moonlight shows
A girl with a fire-tongued serpent, she
Grasping him, laughing, while quietly
    Her eyes are weeping.
    Is he sleeping?

He thinks it is some holy vision,
Brushes that aside and with decision

Jumps—and hits the snake with his stick,
Crushes his spine, and then with quick,
    Urgent command
    Takes her hand.

The gardener sucks the poison and spits,
Cursing and praying as befits
A poor old man half out of his wits.
"Whatever possessed you, Sister, it's
    Hatched of a devil
    And very evil.

It's one of them horrid basilisks
You read about. They say a man risks
His life to touch it, but I guess I've sucked it
Out by now. Lucky I chucked it
    Away from you.
    I guess you'll do."

"Oh, no, François, this beautiful beast
Was sent to me, to me the least
Worthy in all our convent, so I
Could finish my picture of the Most High
    And Holy Queen,
    In her dress of green.

He is dead now, but his colours won't fade
At once, and by noon I shall have made
The Virgin's robe. Oh, François, see
How kindly the moon shines down on me!
    I can't die yet,
    For the task was set."

"You won't die now, for I've sucked it away,"
Grumbled oid François, "so have your play.
If the Virgin is set on snake's colours so strong—"
"François, don't say things like that, it is wrong."
    So Clotilde vented
    Her creed. He repented.

"He can't do no more harm, Sister," said he.
"Paint as much as you like." And gingerly
He picked up the snake with his stick. Clotilde
Thanked him, and begged that he would shield
    Her secret, though itching
    To talk in the kitchen.

The gardener promised, not very pleased,
And Clotilde, with the strain of adventure eased,
Walked quickly home, while the half-high moon
Made her beautiful snake-skin sparkle, and soon
    In her bed she lay
    And waited for day.

At dawn's first saffron-spired warning
Clotilde was up. And all that morning
Except when she went to the chapel to pray,
She painted, and when the April day
    Was hot with sun,
    Clotilde had done.

Done! She drooped, though her heart beat loud
At the beauty before her, and her spirit bowed
To the Virgin her finely-touched thought had made.
A lady, in excellence arrayed,
    And wonder-souled.
    Christ's Blessed Mould!

From long fasting Clotilde felt weary and faint,
But her eyes were starred like those of a saint
Enmeshed in Heaven's beatitude.
A sudden clamour hurled its rude
    Force to break
    Her vision awake.

The door nearly leapt from its hinges, pushed
By the multitude of nuns. They hushed

When they saw Clotilde, in perfect quiet,
Smiling, a little perplexed at the riot.
    And all the hive
    Buzzed "She's alive!"

Old François had told. He had found the strain
Of silence too great, and preferred the pain
Of a conscience outraged. The news had spread,
And all were convinced Clotilde must be dead.
    For François, to spite them,
    Had not seen fit to right them.

The Abbess, unwontedly trembling and mild,
Put her arms round Clotilde and wept, "My child,
Has the Holy Mother showed you this grace,
To spare you while you imaged her face?
    How could we have guessed
    Our convent so blessed!

A miracle! But Oh! My Lamb!
To have you die! And I, who am
A hollow, living shell, the grave
Is empty of me. Holy Mary, I crave
    To be taken, Dear Mother,
    Instead of this other."

She dropped on her knees and silently prayed,
With anguished hands and tears delayed
To a painful slowness. The minutes drew
To fractions. Then the west wind blew
    The sound of a bell,
    On a gusty swell.

It came skipping over the slates of the roof,
And the bright bell-notes seemed a reproof
To grief, in the eye of so fair a day.
The Abbess, comforted, ceased to pray.
    And the sun lit the flowers
    In Clotilde's Book of Hours.

It glistened the green of the Virgin's dress
And made the red spots, in a flushed excess,
Pulse and start; and the violet wings
Of the angel were colour which shines and sings.
The book seemed a choir
Of rainbow fire.

The Abbess crossed herself, and each nun
Did the same, then one by one,
They filed to the chapel, that incensed prayers
Might plead for the life of this sister of theirs.
Clotilde, the Inspired!
She only felt tired.

The old chronicles say she did not die
Until heavy with years. And that is why
There hangs in the convent church a basket
Of osiered silver, a holy casket,
And treasured therein
A dried snake-skin.

PATTERNS

I WALK down the garden paths,
And all the daffodils
Are blowing, and the bright blue squills.
I walk down the patterned garden-paths
In my stiff, brocaded gown.
With my powdered hair and jewelled fan,
I too am a rare
Pattern. As I wander down
The garden paths,
My dress is richly figured,
And the train
Makes a pink and silver stain
On the gravel, and the thrift
Of the borders.
Just a plate of current fashion,

Tripping by in high-heeled, ribboned shoes.
Not a softness anywhere about me,
Only whalebone and brocade.
And I sink on a seat in the shade
Of a lime tree. For my passion
Wars against the stiff brocade.
The daffodils and squills
Flutter in the breeze
As they please.
And I weep;
For the lime tree is in blossom
And one small flower has dropped upon my bosom.

And the plashing of waterdrops
In the marble fountain
Comes down the garden-paths.
The dripping never stops.
Underneath my stiffened gown
Is the softness of a woman bathing in a marble basin,
A basin in the midst of hedges grown
So thick, she cannot see her lover hiding,
But she guesses he is near,
And the sliding of the water
Seems the stroking of a dear
Hand upon her.
What is Summer in a fine brocaded gown!
I should like to see it lying in a heap upon the ground.
All the pink and silver crumpled up on the ground.

I would be the pink and silver as I ran along the paths,
And he would stumble after,
Bewildered by my laughter.
I should see the sun flashing from his sword-hilt and the buckles
on his shoes.
I would choose
To lead him in a maze along the patterned paths,
A bright and laughing maze for my heavy-booted lover.
Till he caught me in the shade,

And the buttons of his waistcoat bruised my body as he clasped
 me,
Aching, melting, unafraid.
With the shadows of the leaves and the sundrops,
And the plopping of the waterdrops,
All about us in the open afternoon—
I am very like to swoon
With the weight of this brocade,
For the sun sifts through the shade.

Underneath the fallen blossom
In my bosom,
Is a letter I have hid.
It was brought to me this morning by a rider from the Duke.
"Madam, we regret to inform you that Lord Hartwell
Died in action Thursday se'nnight."
As I read it in the white, morning sunlight,
The letters squirmed like snakes.
"Any answer, Madam," said my footman.
"No," I told him.
"See that the messenger takes some refreshment.
No, no answer."
And I walked into the garden,
Up and down the patterned paths,
In my stiff, correct brocade.
The blue and yellow flowers stood up proudly in the sun,
Each one.
I stood upright too,
Held rigid to the pattern
By the stiffness of my gown.
Up and down I walked,
Up and down.

In a month he would have been my husband.
In a month, here, underneath this lime,
We would have broke the pattern;
He for me, and I for him,
He as Colonel, I as Lady,
On this shady seat.

He had a whim
That sunlight carried blessing.
And I answered, "It shall be as you have said."
Now he is dead.

In Summer and in Winter I shall walk
Up and down
The patterned garden-paths
In my stiff, brocaded gown.
The squills and daffodils
Will give place to pillared roses, and to asters, and to snow.
I shall go
Up and down,
In my gown.
Gorgeously arrayed,
Boned and stayed.
And the softness of my body will be guarded from embrace
By each button, hook, and lace.
For the man who should loose me is dead,
Fighting with the Duke in Flanders,
In a pattern called a war.
Christ! What are patterns for?

Edgar Lee Masters

(*From "Spoon River Anthology"*)

THOMAS TREVELYAN

READING in Ovid the sorrowful story of Itys,
Son of the love of Tereus and Procne, slain
For the guilty passion of Tereus for Philomela,
The flesh of him served to Tereus by Procne,
And the wrath of Tereus, the murderess pursuing
Till the gods made Philomela a nightingale,
Lute of the rising moon, and Procne a swallow!
Oh livers and artists of Hellas centuries gone,
Sealing in little thuribles dreams and wisdom,

Incense beyond all price, forever fragrant,
A breath whereof makes clear the eyes of the soul!
How I inhaled its sweetness here in Spoon River!
The thurible opening when I had lived and learned
How all of us kill the children of love, and all of us,
Knowing not what we do, devour their flesh;
And all of us change to singers, although it be
But once in our lives, or change—alas!—to swallows,
To twitter amid cold winds and falling leaves!

EDMUND POLLARD

I WOULD I had thrust my hands of flesh
Into the disk-flowers bee-infested,
Into the mirror-like core of fire
Of the light of life, the sun of delight.
For what are anthers worth or petals
Or halo-rays? Mockeries, shadows
Of the heart of the flower, the central flame!
All is yours, young passer-by;
Enter the banquet room with the thought;
Don't sidle in as if you were doubtful
Whether you're welcome—the feast is yours!
Nor take but a little, refusing more
With a bashful "Thank you," when you're hungry.
Is your soul alive? Then let it feed!
Leave no balconies where you can climb;
Nor milk-white bosoms where you can rest;
Nor golden heads with pillows to share;
Nor wine cups while the wine is sweet;
Nor ecstasies of body or soul,
You will die, no doubt, but die while living
In depths of azure, rapt and mated,
Kissing the queen-bee, Life!

BERT KESSLER

I WINGED my bird,
Though he flew toward the setting sun;
But just as the shot rang out, he soared

Up and up through the splinters of golden light,
Till he turned right over, feathers ruffled,
With some of the down of him floating near,
And fell like a plummet into the grass.
I tramped about, parting the tangles,
Till I saw a splash of blood on a stump,
And the quail lying close to the rotten roots.
I reached my hand, but saw no brier,
But something pricked and stung and numbed it.
And then, in a second, I spied the rattler—
The shutters wide in his yellow eyes,
The head of him arched, sunk back in the rings of him,
A circle of filth, the color of ashes,
Or oak leaves bleached under layers of leaves.
I stood like a stone as he shrank and uncoiled
And started to crawl beneath the stump,
When I fell limp in the grass.

PETIT, THE POET

SEEDS in a dry pod, tick, tick, tick,
Tick, tick, tick, like mites in a quarrel—
Faint iambics that the full breeze wakens—
But the pine tree makes a symphony thereof.
Triolets, villanelles, rondels, rondeaus,
Ballades by the score with the same old thought:
The snows and the roses of yesterday are vanished;
And what is love but a rose that fades?
Life all around me here in the village:
Tragedy, comedy, valor and truth,
Courage, constancy, heroism, failure—
All in the loom, and oh what patterns!
Woodlands, meadows, streams and rivers—
Blind to all of it all my life long.
Triolets, villanelles, rondels, rondeaus,
Seeds in a dry pod, tick, tick, tick,
Tick, tick, tick, what little iambics,
While Homer and Whitman roared in the pines?

Vachel Lindsay

THE EAGLE THAT IS FORGOTTEN

[John P. Altgeld. Born December 30, 1847; died March 12, 1902]

SLEEP softly . . . eagle forgotten . . . under the stone,
Time has its way with you there, and the clay has its own.
"We have buried him now," thought your foes, and in secret rejoiced.
They made a brave show of their mourning, their hatred unvoiced,
They had snarled at you, barked at you, foamed at you, day after day,
Now you were ended. They praised you, . . . and laid you away.

The others that mourned you in silence and terror and truth,
The widow bereft of her pittance, the boy without youth,
The mocked and the scorned and the wounded, the lame and the poor
That should have remembered forever, . . . remember no more.

Where are those lovers of yours, on what name do they call
The lost, that in armies wept over your funeral pall?
They call on the names of a hundred high-valiant ones,
A hundred white eagles have risen, the sons of your sons,
The zeal in their wings is a zeal that your dreaming began,
The valor that wore out your soul in the service of man.

Sleep softly, . . . eagle forgotten, . . . under the stone,
Time has its way with you there, and the clay has its own.
Sleep on, O brave hearted, O wise man, that kindled the flame—
To live in mankind is far more than to live in a name,
To live in mankind, far, far more . . . than to live in a name.

ALADDIN AND THE JINN

"BRING me soft song," said Aladdin.
"This tailor-shop sings not at all.
Chant me a word of the twilight,
Of roses that mourn in the fall.
Bring me a song like hashish
That will comfort the stale and the sad,
For I would be mending my spirit,
Forgetting these days that are bad,
Forgetting companions too shallow,
Their quarrels and arguments thin,
Forgetting the shouting Muezzin:"—
"I AM YOUR SLAVE," said the Jinn.

"Bring me old wines," said Aladdin.
"I have been a starved pauper too long.
Serve them in vessels of jade and of shell,
Serve them with fruit and with song:—
Wines of pre-Adamite Sultans
Digged from beneath the black seas:—
New-gathered dew from the heavens
Dripped down from Heaven's sweet trees,
Cups from the angels' pale tables
That will make me both handsome and wise,
For I have beheld her, the princess,
Firelight and starlight her eyes.
Pauper I am, I would woo her.
And—let me drink wine, to begin,
Though the Koran expressly forbids it."
"I AM YOUR SLAVE," said the Jinn.

"Plan me a dome," said Aladdin,
"That is drawn like the dawn of the MOON,
When the sphere seems to rest on the mountains,
Half-hidden, yet full-risen soon.
Build me a dome," said Aladdin,
"That shall cause all young lovers to sigh,
The fullness of life and of beauty,

Peace beyond peace to the eye—
A palace of foam and of opal,
Pure moonlight without and within,
Where I may enthrone my sweet lady."
"I AM YOUR SLAVE," said the Jinn.

Robert Frost

THE TELEPHONE

"WHEN I was just as far as I could walk
From here to-day,
There was an hour
All still
When leaning with my head against a flower
I heard you talk.
Don't say I didn't, for I heard you say—
You spoke from that flower on the window sill—
Do you remember what it was you said?"

"First tell me what it was you thought you heard."

"Having found the flower and driven a bee away,
I leaned my head,
And holding by the stalk,
I listened and I thought I caught the word—
What was it? Did you call me by my name?
Or did you say—
Someone said 'Come'—I heard it as I bowed."

"I may have thought as much, but not aloud."

"Well, so I came."

THE ROAD NOT TAKEN

TWO roads diverged in a yellow wood,
And sorry I could not travel both
And be one traveler, long I stood
And looked down one as far as I could
To where it bent in the undergrowth;

Then took the other, as just as fair,
And having perhaps the better claim,
Because it was grassy and wanted wear;
Though as for that the passing there
Had worn them really about the same,

And both that morning equally lay
In leaves no step had trodden black.
Oh, I kept the first for another day!
Yet knowing how way leads on to way,
I doubted if I should ever come back.

I shall be telling this with a sigh
Somewhere ages and ages hence:
Two roads diverged in a wood, and I—
I took the one less traveled by,
And that has made all the difference.

MY NOVEMBER GUEST

MY sorrow, when she's here with me,
Thinks these dark days of autumn rain
Are beautiful as days can be;
She loves the bare, the withered tree;
She walks the sodden pasture lane.

Her pleasure will not let me stay.
She talks and I am fain to list:
She's glad the birds are gone away,
She's glad her simple worsted grey
Is silver now with clinging mist.

The desolate, deserted trees,
The faded earth, the heavy sky,
The beauties she so truly sees,
She thinks I have no eye for these,
And vexes me for reason why.

Not yesterday I learned to know
  The love of bare November days
Before the coming of the snow;
But it were vain to tell her so,
  And they are better for her praise.

HOME BURIAL

HE saw her from the bottom of the stairs
Before she saw him. She was starting down,
Looking back over her shoulder at some fear.
She took a doubtful step and then undid it
To raise herself and look again. He spoke
Advancing toward her: "What is it you see
From up there always—for I want to know."
She turned and sank upon her skirts at that,
And her face changed from terrified to dull.
He said to gain time: "What is it you see?"
Mounting until she cowered under him,
"I will find out now—you must tell me, dear."
She, in her place, refused him any help
With the least stiffening of her neck and silence.
She let him look, sure that he wouldn't see,
Blind creature; and a while he didn't see.
But at last he murmured, "Oh," and again,
  "Oh."
"What is it—what?" she said.

"Just that I see."
"You don't," she challenged. "Tell me what it is."

"The wonder is I didn't see at once.
I never noticed it from here before.
I must be wonted to it—that's the reason.
The little graveyard where my people are!
So small the window frames the whole of it.
Not so much larger than a bedroom, is it?
There are three stones of slate and one of marble,

Broad-shouldered little slabs there in the sunlight
On the sidehill. We haven't to mind *those*.
But I understand: it is not the stones,
But the child's mound——"

"Don't, don't, don't, don't," she cried.

She withdrew shrinking from beneath his arm
That rested on the banister, and slid downstairs;
And turned on him with such a daunting look,
He said twice over before he knew himself:
"Can't a man speak of his own child he's lost?"

"Not you! Oh, where's my hat? Oh, I don't need it!
I must get out of here. I must get air.
I don't know rightly whether any man can."

"Amy! Don't go to someone else this time.
Listen to me. I won't come down the stairs."
He sat and fixed his chin between his fists.
"There's something I should like to ask you, dear."

"You don't know how to ask it."

"Help me, then."

Her fingers moved the latch for all reply.

"My words are nearly always an offence.
I don't know how to speak of anything
So as to please you. But I might be taught
I should suppose. I can't say I see how.
A man must partly give up being a man
With women-folk. We could have some arrangement
By which I'd bind myself to keep hands off
Anything special you're a mind to name.
Though I don't like such things 'twixt those that love.
Two that don't love can't live together without them.
But two that do can't live together with them."

She moved the latch a little. "Don't, don't go.
Don't carry it to someone else this time.
Tell me about it if it's something human.
Let me into your grief. I'm not so much
Unlike other folks as your standing there
Apart would make me out. Give me my chance.
I do think, though, you overdo it a little.
What was it brought you up to think it the thing
To take your mother-loss of a first child
So inconsolably—in the face of love.
You'd think his memory might be satisfied—"

"There you go sneering now!"

"I'm not, I'm not!
You make me angry. I'll come down to you.
God, what a woman! And it's come to this,
A man can't speak of his own child that's dead."

"You can't because you don't know how.
If you had any feelings, you that dug
With your own hand—how could you?—his little grave;
I saw you from that very window there,
Making the gravel leap and leap in air,
Leap up, like that, like that, and land so lightly
And roll down the mound beside the hole.
I thought, who is that man? I don't know you.
And I crept down the stairs and up the stairs
To look again, and still your spade kept lifting.
Then you came in. I heard your rumbling voice
Out in the kitchen, and I don't know why,
But I went near to see with my own eyes.
You could sit there with the stains on your shoes
Of the fresh earth from your own baby's grave
And talk about your everyday concerns.
You had stood the spade up against the wall
Outside there in the entry, for I saw it."

"I shall laugh the worst laugh I ever laughed.
I'm cursed. God, if I don't believe I'm cursed."

"I can repeat the very words you were saying.
'Three foggy mornings and one rainy day
Will rot the best birch fence a man can build.'
Think of it, talk like that at such a time!
What had how long it takes a birch to rot
To do with that was in the darkened parlour.
You *couldn't* care! The nearest friends can go
With any one to death, comes so far short
They might as well not try to go at all.
No, from the time when one is sick to death,
One is alone, and he dies more alone.

Friends make pretence of following to the grave,
But before one is in it, their minds are turned
And making the best of their way back to life
And living people, and things they understand.
But the world's evil. I won't have my grief so
If I can change it. Oh, I won't, I won't!"

"There, you have said it all and you feel better.
You won't go now. You're crying. Close the door.
The heart's gone out of it: why keep it up.
Amy! There's someone coming down the road!"
"*You*—oh, you think the talk is all. I must go—
Somewhere out of this house. How can I make you—
"If—you—do!" She was opening the door wider.
"Where do you mean to go? First tell me that.
I'll follow and bring you back by force. I *will!*—"

THE SOUND OF THE TREES

I WONDER about the trees.
Why do we wish to bear
Forever the noise of these
More than another noise
So close to our dwelling place?
We suffer them by the day
Till we lose all measure of pace,

And fixity in our joys,
And acquire a listening air.
They are that that talks of going
But never gets away;
And that talks no less for knowing,
As it grows wiser and older,
That now it means to stay.
My feet tug at the floor
And my head sways to my shoulder
Sometimes when I watch trees sway,
From the window or the door.
I shall set forth for somewhere,
I shall make the reckless choice
Some day when they are in voice
And tossing so as to scare
The white clouds over them on.
I shall have less to say,
But I shall be gone.

HYLA BROOK

BY June our brook's run out of song and speed.
Sought for much after that, it will be found
Either to have gone groping underground
(And taken with it all the Hyla breed
That shouted in the mist a month ago,
Like ghost of sleigh-bells in a ghost of snow)—
Or flourished and come up in jewel-weed,
Weak foliage that is blown upon and bent
Even against the way its waters went.
Its bed is left a faded paper sheet
Of dead leaves stuck together by the heat—
A brook to none but who remember long.
This as it will be seen is other far
Than with brooks taken otherwhere in song.
We love the things we love for what they are.

MOWING

THERE was never a sound beside the wood but one,
And that was my long scythe whispering to the ground.
What was it it whispered? I knew not well myself;
Perhaps it was something about the heat of the sun,
Something, perhaps, about the lack of sound—
And that was why it whispered and did not speak.
It was no dream of the gift of idle hours,
Or easy gold at the hand of fay or elf:
Anything more than the truth would have seemed too weak
To the earnest love that laid the swale in rows,
Not without feeble-pointed spikes of flowers
(Pale orchises), and scared a bright green snake.
The fact is the sweetest dream that labor knows.
My long scythe whispered and left the hay to make.

TO EARTHWARD

LOVE at the lips was touch
As sweet as I could bear;
I lived on air
And once that seemed too much;

That crossed me from sweet things,
The flow of—was it musk
From hidden grapevine springs
Down hill at dusk?

I had the swirl and ache
From sprays of honeysuckle
That when they're gathered shake
Dew on the knuckle.

I craved strong sweets, but those
Seemed strong when I was young;
The petal of the rose
It was that stung.

Now no joy but lacks salt
That is not dashed with pain
And weariness and fault;
I crave the stain

Of tears, the aftermark
Of almost too much love,
The sweet of bitter bark
And burning clove.

When stiff and sore and scarred
I take away my hand
From leaning on it hard
In grass and sand,

The hurt is not enough:
I long for weight and strength
To feel the earth as rough
To all my length.

FIRE AND ICE

SOME say the world will end in fire,
Some say in ice.
From what I've tasted of desire
I hold with those who favor fire.
But if it had to perish twice,
I think I know enough of hate
To say that for destruction ice
Is also great
And would suffice.

STOPPING BY WOODS ON A SNOWY EVENING

WHOSE woods these are I think I know.
His house is in the village though;
He will not see me stopping here
To watch his woods fill up with snow.

My little horse must think it queer
To stop without a farmhouse near
Between the woods and frozen lake
The darkest evening of the year.

He gives his harness bells a shake
To ask if there is some mistake.
The only other sound's the sweep
Of easy wind and downy flake.

The woods are lovely, dark and deep,
But I have promises to keep,
And miles to go before I sleep,
And miles to go before I sleep.

Carl Sandburg

GONE

EVERYBODY loved Chick Lorimer in our town
Far off.
Everybody loved her.
So we all love a wild girl keeping a hold
On a dream she wants.
Nobody knows now where Chick Lorimer went.
Nobody knows why she packed her trunk . . .. a few old things
And is gone,
Gone with her little chin
Thrust ahead of her
And her soft hair blowing careless
From under a wide hat,
Dancer, singer, a laughing passionate lover.

Were there ten men or a hundred hunting Chick?
Were there five men or fifty with aching hearts?
Everybody loved Chick Lorimer.
Nobody knows where she's gone.

William Ellery Leonard

THE IMAGE OF DELIGHT

O HOW came I that loved stars, moon, and flame,
And unimaginable wind and sea,
All inner shrines and temples of the free,
Legends and hopes and golden books of fame;
I that upon the mountain carved my name
With cliffs and clouds and eagles over me,
O how came I to stoop to loving thee—
I that had never stooped before to shame?

O 'twas not thee! Too eager of a white
Far beauty and a voice to answer mine,
Myself I built an image of delight,
Which all one purple day I deemed divine—
And when it vanished in the fiery night,
I lost not thee, nor any shape of thine.

Alfred Kreymborg

NUN SNOW

A Pantomime of Beads

Earth Voice

IS she
Thoughtless of life,
A lover of imminent death,
Nun Snow
Touching her strings of white beads?
Is it her unseen hands
Which urge the beads to tremble?
Does Nun Snow,
Aware of the death she must die alone,
Away from the nuns

Of the green beads,
Of the ochre and brown,
Of the purple and black—
Does she improvise
Along those soundless strings
In the worldly hope
That the answering, friendly tune,
The faithful, folk-like miracle,
Will shine in a moment or two?

Moon Voice

Or peradventure,
Are the beads merely wayward,
On an evening so soft,
And One Wind
Is so gentle a mesmerist
As he draws them and her with his hand?

Earth Voice

Was it Full Moon,
Who contrives tales of this order,
And himself loves the heroine,
Nun Snow—

Wind Voice

Do you see his beads courting hers?—
Lascivious monk!—

Earth Voice

Was it Full Moon,
Slyly innocent of guile,
Propounder of sorrowless whimseys,
Who breathed that suspicion?
Is it One Wind,
The wily, scholarly pedant—
Is it he who retorts—

Wind Voice

Like olden allegros
In olden sonatas,
All tales have two themes,
She is beautiful,
He is beautiful,
With the traditional movement,
Their beads court each other,
Revealing a cadence as fatally true
As the sum which follows a one-plus-one—
So, why inquire further?
Nay, inquire further,
Deduce it your fashion!
Nun Snow,
As you say,
Touches her strings of white beads,
Full Moon,
Let you add,
His lute of yellow strings;
And, our Night
Is square, nay,
Our Night
Is round, nay
Our night
Is a blue balcony—
And therewith close your inquisition!

Earth Voice

Who urged the beads to tremble?
They're still now!
Fallen, or cast over me!
Nun, Moon, and Wind are gone!
Are they betraying her?—

Moon Voice

Ask our Night—

Earth Voice

Did the miracle appear?—

Moon Voice

Ask our Night,
Merely a child on a balcony,
Letting down her hair and
Black beads, a glissando—
Ask her what she means,
Dropping the curtain so soon!

John Gould Fletcher

IRRADIATIONS

I

THE spattering of the rain upon pale terraces
Of afternoon is like the passing of a dream
Amid the roses shuddering 'gainst the wet green stalks
Of the streaming trees—the passing of the wind
Upon the pale lower terraces of my dream
Is like the crinkling of the wet grey robes
Of the hours that come to turn over the urn
Of the day and spill its rainy dream.
Vague movement over the puddled terraces:
Heavy gold pennons—a pomp of solemn gardens
Half hidden under the liquid veil of spring:
Far trumpets like a vague rout of faded roses
Burst 'gainst the wet green silence of distant forests:
A clash of cymbals—then the swift swaying footsteps
Of the wind that undulates along the languid terraces.
Pools of rain—the vacant terraces
Wet, chill and glistening
Towards the sunset beyond the broken doors of to-day.

II

The iridescent vibrations of midsummer light
Dancing, dancing, suddenly flickering and quivering

Like little feet or the movement of quick hands clapping,
Or the rustle of furbelows or the clash of polished gems.
The palpitant mosaic of the midday light
Colliding, sliding, leaping and lingering:
O, I could lie on my back all day,
And mark the mad ballet of the midsummer sky.

III

Over the roof-tops race the shadows of clouds;
Like horses the shadows of clouds charge down the street.

Whirlpools of purple and gold,
Winds from the mountains of cinnabar,
Lacquered mandarin moments, palanquins swaying and balancing
Amid the vermilion pavilions, against the jade balustrades.
Glint of the glittering wings of dragon-flies in the light:
Silver filaments, golden flakes settling downwards,
Rippling, quivering flutters, repulse and surrender,
The sun broidered upon the rain,
The rain rustling with the sun.

Over the roof-tops race the shadows of clouds;
Like horses the shadows of clouds charge down the street.

IV

The balancing of gaudy broad pavilions
Of summer against the insolent breeze:
The bellying of the sides of striped tents,
Swelling taut, shuddering in quick collapse,
Silent under the silence of the sky.

Earth is streaked and spotted
With great splashes and dapples of sunlight:
The sun throws an immense circle of hot light upon the world,
Rolling slowly in ponderous rhythm
Darkly, musically forward.
All is silent under the steep cone of afternoon:

The sky is imperturbably profound.
The ultimate divine union seems about to be accomplished,
All is troubled at the attainment
Of the inexhaustible infinite.

The rolling and the tossing of the sides of immense pavilions
Under the whirling wind that screams up the cloudless sky.

V

Flickering of incessant rain
On flashing pavements:
Sudden scurry of umbrellas:
Bending, recurved blossoms of the storm.

The winds came clanging and clattering
From long white highroads whipping in ribbons up summits:
They strew upon the city gusty wafts of apple-blossom,
And the rustling of innumerable translucent leaves.
Uneven tinkling, the lazy rain
Dripping from the eaves.

VI

The fountain blows its breathless spray
From me to you and back to me.

Whipped, tossed, curdled,
Crashing, quivering:
I hurl kisses like blows upon your lips.
The dance of a bee drunken with sunlight:
Irradiant ecstasies, white and gold,
Sigh and relapse.

The fountain tosses pallid spray
Far in the sorrowful, silent sky.

GREEN SYMPHONY

I

THE glittering leaves of the rhododendrons
Balance and vibrate in the cool air;
While in the sky above them
White clouds chase each other.

Like scampering rabbits,
Flashes of sunlight sweep the lawn;
They fling in passing
Patterns of shadow,
Golden and green.

With long cascades of laughter,
The mating birds dart and swoop to the turf:
'Mid their mad trillings
Glints the gay sun behind the trees.

Down there are deep blue lakes:
Orange blossom droops in the water.
In the tower of the winds,
All the bells are set adrift:
Jingling
For the dawn.

Thin fluttering streamers
Of breeze lash through the swaying boughs,
Palely expectant
The earth receives the slanting rain.

I am a glittering raindrop
Hugged close by the cool rhododendron.
I am a daisy starring
The exquisite curves of the close-cropped turf.

The glittering leaves of the rhododendron
Are shaken like blue-green blades of grass,
Flickering, cracking, falling:
Splintering in a million fragments.

The wind runs laughing up the slope
Stripping off handfuls of wet green leaves,
To fling in peoples' faces.
Wallowing on the daisy-powdered turf,
Clutching at the sunlight,
Cavorting in the shadow.

Like baroque pearls,
Like cloudy emeralds,
The clouds and the trees clash together;
Whirling and swirling,
In the tumult
Of the spring,
And the wind.

II

The trees splash the sky with their fingers,
A restless green rout of stars.

With whirling movement
They swing their boughs
About their stems:
Planes on planes of light and shadow
Pass among them,
Opening fan-like to fall.

The trees are like a sea;
Tossing,
Trembling,
Roaring,
Wallowing,
Darting their long green flickering fronds up at the sky,
Spotted with white blossom-spray.

The trees are roofs:
Hollow caverns of cool blue shadow,
Solemn arches
In the afternoons.

The whole vast horizon
In terrace beyond terrace,
Pinnacle above pinnacle,
Lifts to the sky
Serrated ranks of green on green.

They caress the roofs with their fingers,
They sprawl about the river to look into it;
Up the hill they come
Gesticulating challenge:
They cower together
In dark valleys;
They yearn out over the fields.

Enamelled domes
Tumble upon the grass,
Crashing in ruin
Quiet at last.

The trees lash the sky with their leaves,
Uneasily shaking their dark green manes.

III

Far let the voices of the mad wild birds be calling me,
I will abide in this forest of pines.

When the wind blows
Battling through the forest,
I hear it distantly,
The crash of a perpetual sea.

When the rain falls,
I watch silver spears slanting downwards
From pale river-pools of sky,
Enclosed in dark fronds.

When the sun shines,
I weave together distant branches till they enclose mighty
circles,

I sway to the movement of hooded summits,
I swim leisurely in deep blue seas of air.

I hug the smooth bark of stately red pillars
And with cones carefully scattered
I mark the progression of dark dial-shadows
Flung diagonally downwards through the afternoon.

This turf is not like turf:
It is a smooth dry carpet of velvet,
Embroidered with brown patterns of needles and cones.
These trees are not like trees:
They are innumerable feathery pagoda-umbrellas,
Stiffly ungracious to the wind,
Teetering on red-lacquered stems.

In the evening I listen to the winds' lisping,
While the conflagrations of the sunset flicker and clash behind
me,
Flamboyant crenellations of glory amid the charred ebony
boles.

In the night the fiery nightingales
Shall clash and trill through the silence:
Like the voices of mermaids crying
From the sea.

Long ago has the moon whelmed this uncompleted temple.
Stars swim like gold fish far above the black arches.

Far let the timid feet of dawn fly to catch me:
I will abide in this forest of pines:
For I have unveiled naked beauty,
And the things that she whispered to me in the darkness,
Are buried deep in my heart.

Now let the black tops of the pine-trees break like a spent
wave,
Against the grey sky:
These are tombs and memorials and temples and altars sun-
kindled for me.

WHITE SYMPHONY

I

FORLORN and white,
Whorls of purity about a golden chalice,
Immense the peonies
Flare and shatter their petals over my face.

They slowly turn paler,
They seem to be melting like blue-grey flakes of ice,
Thin greyish shivers
Fluctuating 'mid the dark green lance-thrust of the leaves.

Like snowballs tossed,
Like soft white butterflies,
The peonies poise in the twilight.
And their narcotic insinuating perfume
Draws me into them
Shivering with the coolness,
Aching with the void.
They kiss the blue chalice of my dreams
Like a gesture seen for an instant and then lost forever.

. . .

Outwards the petals
Thrust to embrace me,
Pale daggers of coldness
Run through my aching breast.

Outwards, still outwards,
Till on the brink of twilight
They swirl downwards silently,
Flurry of snow in the void.

Outwards, still outwards,
Till the blue walls are hidden,

And in the blinding white radiance
Of a whirlpool of clouds, I awake.

. . .

Like spraying rockets
My peonies shower
Their glories on the night.
Wavering perfumes,
Drift about the garden;
Shadows of the moonlight,
Drift and ripple over the dew-gemmed leaves.

Soar, crash, and sparkle,
Shoal of stars drifting
Like silver fishes,
Through the black sluggish boughs.
Towards the impossible,
Towards the inaccessible,
Towards the ultimate,
Towards the silence,
Towards the eternal,
These blossoms go.

The peonies spring like rockets in the twilight,
And out of them all I rise.

II

Downwards through the blue abyss it slides,
The white snow-water of my dreams,
Downwards crashing from slippery rock
Into the boiling chasm:
In which no eye dare look, for it is the chasm of death.
Upwards from the blue abyss it rises,
The chill water-mist of my dreams;
Upwards to greyish weeping pines,
And to skies of autumn ever about my heart,
It is blue at the beginning,
And blue-white against the grey-greenness;

It wavers in the upper air,
Catching unconscious sparkles, a rainbow-glint of sunlight,
And fading in the sad depths of the sky.

Outwards rush the strong pale clouds,
Outwards and ever outwards;
The blue-grey clouds indistinguishable one from another:
Nervous, sinewy, tossing their arms and brandishing,
Till on the blue serrations of the horizon
They drench with their black rain a great peak of changeless
snow.

. . .

As evening came on, I climbed the tower,
To gaze upon the city far beneath:
I was not weary of day; but in the evening
A white mist assembled and gathered over the earth
And blotted it from sight.
But to escape:
To chase with the golden clouds galloping over the horizon'
Arrows of the northwest wind
Singing amid them,
Ruffling up my hair!

As evening came on the distance altered,
Pale wavering reflections rose from out the city,
Like sighs or the beckoning of half-invisible hands.
Monotonously and sluggishly they crept upwards
A river that had spent itself in some chasm,
And dwindled and foamed at last at my weary feet.

Autumn! Golden fountains,
And the winds neighing
Amid the monotonous hills:
Desolation of the old gods,
Rain that lifts and rain that moves away;
In the green-black torrent
Scarlet leaves.

It was now perfectly evening:
And the tower loomed like a gaunt peak in mid-air
Above the city: its base was utterly lost.
It was slowly coming on to rain,
And the immense columns of white mist
Wavered and broke before the faint-hurled spears.

I will descend the mountains like a shepherd,
And in the folds of tumultuous misty cities,
I will put all my thoughts, all my old thoughts, safely to sleep.
For it is already autumn,
O whiteness of the pale southwestern sky!
O wavering dream that was not mine to keep!

.

.

In midnight, in mournful moonlight,
By paths I could not trace,
I walked in the white garden,
Each flower had a white face.

Their perfume intoxicated me: thus I began my dream.

I was alone; I had no one to guide me,
But the moon was like the sun:
It stooped and kissed each waxen petal,
One after one.
Green and white was that garden: diamond rain hung in the
branches,
You will not believe it!

In the morning, at the dayspring,
I wakened, shivering; lo,
The white garden that blossomed at my feet
Was a garden hidden in snow.

It was my sorrow to see that all this was a dream.

III

Blue, clogged with purple,
Mists uncoil themselves:
Sparkling to the horizon,
I see the snow alone.

In the deep blue chasm,
Boats sleep under gold thatch;
Icicle-like trees fret
Faintly rose-touched sky.

Under their heaped snow-eaves,
Leaden houses shiver.
Through thin blue crevasses,
Trickles an icy stream.

The pines groan white-laden,
The waves shiver, struck by the wind;
Beyond from treeless horizons,
Broken snow-peaks crawl to the sea.

. . .

Wearily the snow glares,
Through the grey silence, day after day,
Mocking the colourless cloudless sky
With the reflection of death.

There is no smoke through the pine tops,
No strong red boatmen in pale green reeds,
No herons to flicker an instant,
No lanterns to glow with gay ray.

No sails beat up to the harbour,
With creaking cordage and sailors' song.
Somnolent, bare-poled, indifferent,
They sleep, and the city sleeps.

Mid-winter about them casts
Its dreary fortifications:
Each day is a gaunt grey rock,
And death is the last of them all.

. . .

Over the sluggish snow,
Drifts now a pallid weak shower of bloom:
Boredom of fresh creation,
Death-weariness of old returns.

White, white blossom,
Fall of the shattered cups day on day:
Is there anything here that is not ancient,
That has not bloomed a thousand years ago?

Under the glare of the white-hot day,
Under the restless wind-rakes of the winter,
White blossom or white snow scattered,
And beneath them, dark, the graves.

Dark graves never changing,
White dream, drifting, never changing above them:
O that the white scroll of heaven might be rolled up,
And the naked red lightning thrust at the smouldering earth!

H. D.

AT BAIA

I SHOULD have thought
In a dream you would have brought
Some lovely perilous thing,
Orchids piled in a great sheath,
As who would say (in a dream)
I send you this,
Who left the blue veins
Of your throat unkissed.

Why was it that your hands
(That never took mine)
Your hands that I could see
Drift over the orchid heads
So carefully,
Your hands, so fragile, sure to lift
So gently, the fragile flower stuff—
Ah, ah, how was it

You never sent (in a dream)
The very form, the very scent,
Not heavy, not sensuous,
But perilous—perilous—
Of orchids, piled in a great sheath,
And folded underneath on a bright scroll
Some word:

Flower sent to flower;
For white hands, the lesser white,
Less lovely of flower leaf,

Or

Lover to lover, no kiss,
No touch, but forever and ever this.

"NOT HONEY"

NOT honey,
Not the plunder of the bee
From meadow or sand-flower
Or mountain bush;
From winter-flower or shoot
Born of the later heat:
Not honey, not the sweet
Stain on the lips and teeth:
Not honey, not the deep
Plunge of soft belly
And the clinging of the gold-edged
Pollen-dusted feet.

Not so—
Though rapture blind my eyes,
And hunger crisp
Dark and inert my mouth,
Not honey, not the south,
Not the tall stalk
Of red twin-lilies,
Nor light branch of fruit tree
Caught in flexible light branch.

Not honey, not the south;
Ah, flower of purple iris,
Flower of white,
Or of the iris, withering the grass—
For fleck of the sun's fire,
Gathers such heat and power,
That shadow-print is light,
Cast through the petals
Of the yellow iris flower.

Not iris—old desire—old passion—
Old forgetfulness—old pain—
Not this, nor any flower.
But if you turn again,
Seek strength of arm and throat,
Touch as the god:
Neglect the lyre-note;
Knowing that you shall feel,
About the frame,
No trembling of the string
But heat more passionate
Of bone and the white shell
And fiery tempered steel.

SONG

YOU are as gold
As the half-ripe grain
That merges to gold again,
As white as the white rain

That beats through
The half-opened flowers
Of the great flower tufts
Thick on the black limbs
Of an Illyrian apple bough.

Can honey distil such fragrance
As your bright hair—
For your face is as fair as rain,
Yet as rain that lies clear
On white honey-comb,
Lends radiance to the white wax,
So your hair on your brow
Casts light for a shadow.

THE GARDEN

I

YOU are clear,
O rose, cut in rock.

I could scrape the colour
From the petals,
Like spilt dye from a rock.

If I could break you
I could break a tree.

If I could stir
I could break a tree,
I could break you.

II

O wind, rend open the heat,
Cut apart the heat,
Slit it to tatters.

Fruit cannot drop
Through this thick air;
Fruit cannot fall into heat
That presses up and blunts
The points of pears,
And rounds grapes.

Cut the heat:
Plough through it,
Turning it on either side
Of your path.

ORCHARD

I SAW the first pear
as it fell—
the honey-seeking, golden banded,
the yellow swarm,
was not more fleet than I,
(spare us from loveliness!)
and I fell prostrate,
crying:
you have flayed us with your blossoms,
spare us the beauty
of fruit-trees!

The honey-seeking
paused not;
the air thundered their song,
and I alone was prostrate.

O rough-hewn
god of the orchard,
I bring you an offering—
do you, alone unbeautiful,
son of the god,
spare us from loveliness:

these fallen hazel-nuts,
stripped late of their green sheaths,
grapes, red-purple,
their berries
dripping with wine;
pomegranates already broken,
and shrunken figs,
and quinces untouched,
I bring you as offering.

Louis Untermeyer

LONG FEUD

WHERE, without bloodshed, can there be
A more relentless enmity
Than the long feud fought silently

Between man and the growing grass?
Man's the aggressor, for he has
Weapons to humble and harass

The impudent spears that charge upon
His sacred privacy of lawn,
He mows them down, and they are gone

Only to lie in wait, although
He builds above and digs below
Where never a root would dare to go.

His are the triumphs till the day
There's no more grass to cut away,
And, tired of labor, tired of play,

Having exhausted every whim,
He stretches out each conquering limb.
And then the small grass covers him.

T. S. Eliot

THE LOVE SONG OF J. ALFRED PRUFROCK

S'io credesse che mia risposta fosse
A persona che mai tornasse al mondo,
Questa fiamma staria senza piu scosse.
Ma perciocche giammai di questo fondo
Non torno vivo alcun s'i'odo il vero,
Senza tema d'infamia ti rispondo.

LET us go then, you and I,
When the evening is spread out against the sky
Like a patient etherized upon a table;
Let us go, through certain half-deserted streets,
The muttering retreats
Of restless nights in one-night cheap hotels
And sawdust restaurants with oyster-shells:
Streets that follow like a tedious argument
Of insidious intent
To lead you to an overwhelming question. . . .
Oh, do not ask, "What is it?"
Let us go and make our visit.
In the room the women come and go
Talking of Michelangelo.

The yellow fog that rubs its back upon the window-panes,
The yellow smoke that rubs its muzzle on the window-panes,
Licked its tongue into the corners of the evening,
Lingered upon the pools that stand in drains,
Let fall upon its back the soot that falls from chimneys,
Slipped by the terrace, made a sudden leap,
And seeing that it was a soft October night,
Curled once about the house, and fell asleep.

And indeed there will be time
For the yellow smoke that slides along the street,
Rubbing its back upon the window-panes;
There will be time, there will be time

To prepare a face to meet the faces that you meet;
There will be time to murder and create,
And time for all the works and days of hands
That lift and drop a question on your plate;
Time for you and time for me,
And time yet for a hundred indecisions,
And for a hundred visions and revisions,
Before the taking of a toast and tea.
In the room the women come and go
Talking of Michelangelo.

And indeed there will be time
To wonder, "Do I dare?" and, "Do I dare?"
Time to turn back and descend the stair,
With a bald spot in the middle of my hair—
(They will say: "How his hair is growing thin!")
My morning coat, my collar mounting firmly to the chin,
My necktie rich and modest, but asserted by a simple pin—
(They will say: "But how his arms and legs are thin!")
Do I dare
Disturb the universe?
In a minute there is time
For decisions and revisions which a minute will reverse.

For I have known them all already, known them all:
Have known the evenings, mornings, afternoons,
I have measured out my life with coffee spoons;
I know the voices dying with a dying fall
Beneath the music from a farther room.
So how should I presume?

And I have known the eyes already, known them all—
The eyes that fix you in a formulated phrase,
And when I am formulated, sprawling on a pin,
When I am pinned and wriggling on the wall,
Then how should I begin
To spit out all the butt-ends of my days and ways?
And how should I presume?

And I have known the arms already, known them all—
Arms that are braceleted and white and bare
(But in the lamplight, downed with light brown hair!
Is it perfume from a dress
That makes me so digress?
Arms that lie along a table, or wrap about a shawl.
    And should I then presume?
    And how should I begin?

. . . . .

Shall I say, I have gone at dusk through narrow streets
And watched the smoke that rises from the pipes
Of lonely men in shirt-sleeves, leaning out of windows? . . .
I should have been a pair of ragged claws
Scuttling across the floors of silent seas.

. . . . .

And the afternoon, the evening, sleeps so peacefully!
Smoothed by long fingers,
Asleep . . . tired . . . or it malingers,
Stretched on the floor, here beside you and me.
Should I, after tea and cakes and ices,
Have the strength to force the moment to its crisis?
But though I have wept and fasted, wept and prayed,
Though I have seen my head (grown slightly bald) brought in
        upon a platter,
I am no prophet—and here's no great matter;
I have seen the moment of my greatness flicker,
And I have seen the eternal Footman hold my coat, and
        snicker,
And in short, I was afraid.

And would it have been worth it, after all,
After the cups, the marmalade, the tea,
Among the porcelain, among some talk of you and me,
Would it have been worth while,
To have bitten off the matter with a smile,
To have squeezed the universe into a ball
To roll it toward some overwhelming question,

To say: "I am Lazarus, come from the dead,
Come back to tell you all, I shall tell you all"—
If one, settling a pillow by her head,
    Should say: "That was not what I meant at all;
    That is not it, at all."

And would it have been worth it, after all,
Would it have been worth while,
After the sunsets and the dooryards and the sprinkled streets,
After the novels, after the teacups, after the skirts that trail
        along the floor—
And this, and so much more?—
It is impossible to say just what I mean!
But as if a magic lantern threw the nerves in patterns on a
        screen:
Would it have been worth while
If one, settling a pillow or throwing off a shawl,
And turning toward the window, should say:
    "That is not it at all,
    That is not what I meant at all."

. . . . .

No! I am not Prince Hamlet, nor was meant to be;
Am an attendant lord, one that will do
To swell a progress, start a scene or two,
Advise the prince; no doubt, an easy tool,
Deferential, glad to be of use,
Politic, cautious, and meticulous;
Full of high sentence, but a bit obtuse;
At times, indeed, almost ridiculous—
Almost, at times, the Fool.

I grow old . . . I grow old . . .
I shall wear the bottoms of my trousers rolled.

Shall I part my hair behind? Do I dare to eat a peach?
I shall wear white flannel trousers, and walk upon the beach.
I have heard the mermaids singing, each to each.

I do not think that they will sing to me.

I have seen them riding seaward on the waves
Combing the white hair of the waves blown back
When the wind blows the water white and black.
We have lingered in the chambers of the sea
By sea-girls wreathed with seaweed red and brown
Till human voices wake us, and we drown.

SWEENEY AMONG THE NIGHTINGALES

ὤμοι πέπληγμαι καιρίαν πληγὴν ἔσω.

Why should I speak of the nightingale? The nightingale sings of adulterous wrong.

APENECK SWEENEY spreads his knees
Letting his arms hang down to laugh,
The zebra stripes along his jaw
Swelling to maculate giraffe.

The circles of the stormy moon
Slide westward to the River Plate,
Death and the Raven drift above
And Sweeney guards the hornèd gate.

Gloomy Orion and the Dog
Are veiled; and hushed the shrunken seas;
The person in the Spanish cape
Tries to sit on Sweeney's knees

Slips and pulls the table cloth
Overturns a coffee cup,
Reorganized upon the floor
She yawns and draws a stocking up;

The silent man in mocha brown
Sprawls at the window-sill and gapes;
The waiter brings in oranges,
Bananas, figs and hot-house grapes;

The silent vertebrate exhales,
Contracts and concentrates, withdraws;
Rachel *née* Rabinovitch
Tears at the grapes with murderous paws;

She and the lady in the cape
Are suspect, thought to be in league;
Therefore the man with heavy eyes
Declines the gambit, shows fatigue,

Leaves the room and reappears
Outside the window, leaning in,
Branches of wistaria
Circumscribe a golden grin;

The host with someone indistinct
Converses at the door apart,
The nightingales are singing near
The Convent of the Sacred Heart,

And sang within the bloody wood
When Agamemnon cried aloud,
And let their liquid siftings fall
To stain the stiff dishonoured shroud.

WHISPERS OF IMMORTALITY

WEBSTER was much possessed by death
And saw the skull beneath the skin;
And breastless creatures underground
Leaned backward with a lipless grin.

Daffodil bulbs instead of balls
Stared from the sockets of the eyes!
He knew that thought clings round dead limbs
Tightening its lusts and luxuries.

Donne, I suppose, was such another
Who found no substitute for sense

To seize and clutch and penetrate,
Expert beyond experience.

He knew the anguish of the marrow
The ague of the skeleton;
No contact possible to flesh
Allayed the fever of the bone.

. . . . .

Grishkin is nice; her Russian eye
Is underlined for emphasis;
Uncorseted, her friendly bust
Gives promise of pneumatic bliss.

The couched Brazilian jaguar
Compels the scampering marmoset
With subtle effluence of a cat;
Grishkin has a maisonette:

The sleek and sinuous jaguar
Does not in his arboreal gloom
Distil so rank a feline smell
As Grishkin in a drawing-room.

And even abstracter entities
Circumambulate her charm;
But our lot crawls between dry ribs
To keep its metaphysics warm.

GERONTION

Thou hast nor youth nor age
But as it were an after dinner sleep
Dreaming of both.

HERE I am, an old man in a dry month,
Being read to by a boy, waiting for rain.
I was neither at the hot gates
Nor fought in the warm rain

Nor knee deep in the salt marsh, heaving a cutlass,
Bitten by flies, fought.
My house is a decayed house,
And the Jew squats on the window sill, the owner,
Spawned in some estaminet of Antwerp,
Blistered in Brussels, patched and peeled in London.
The goat coughs at night in the field overhead;
Rocks, moss, stonecrop, iron, merds.
The woman keeps the kitchen, makes tea,
Sneezes at evening, poking the peevish gutter.

I an old man,
A dull head among windy spaces.
Signs are taken for wonders. "We would see a sign!"
The word within a word, unable to speak a word,
Swaddled with darkness. In the juvescence of the year
Came Christ the tiger.

In depraved May, dogwood and chestnut, flowering judas,
To be eaten, to be divided, to be drunk
Among whispers; by Mr. Silvero
With caressing hands, at Limoges
Who walked all night in the next room;

By Hakagawa, bowing among the Titians;
By Madame de Tornquist, in the dark room
Shifting the candles; Fraulein von Kulp
Who turned in the hall, one hand on the door. Vacant shut
tles
Weave the wind. I have no ghosts,
An old man in a draughty house
Under a windy knob.

After such knowledge, what forgiveness? Think now
History has many cunning passages, contrived corridors
And issues, deceives with whispering ambitions,
Guides us by vanities. Think now
She gives when our attention is distracted
And what she gives, gives with such supple confusions
That the giving famishes the craving. Gives too late

What's not believed in, or if still believed,
In memory only, reconsidered passion. Gives too soon
Into weak hands, what's thought can be dispensed with
Till the refusal propagates a fear. Think
Neither fear nor courage saves us. Unnatural vices
Are fathered by our heroism. Virtues
Are forced upon us by our impudent crimes.
These tears are shaken from the wrath-bearing tree.

The tiger springs in the new year. Us he devours. Think at
last
We have not reached conclusion, when I
Stiffen in a rented house. Think at last
I have not made this show purposelessly
And it is not by any concitation
Of the backward devils.
I would meet you upon this honestly.
I that was near your heart was removed therefrom
To lose beauty in terror, terror in inquisition.
I have lost my passion: why should I need to keep it
Since what is kept must be adulterated?
I have lost my sight, smell, hearing, taste and touch:
How should I use it for your closer contact?

These with a thousand small deliberations
Protract the profit, of their chilled delirium,
Excite the membrane, when the sense has cooled,
With pungent sauces, multiply variety
In a wilderness of mirrors. What will the spider do,
Suspend its operations, will the weevil
Delay? De Bailhache, Fresca, Mrs. Cammell, whirled
Beyond the circuit of the shuddering Bear
In fractured atoms. Gull against the wind, in the windy
straits
Of Belle Isle, or running on the Horn,
White feathers in the snow, the Gulf claims,
And an old man driven by the Trades
To a sleepy corner.

Tenants of the house,
Thoughts of a dry brain in a dry season.

THE HOLLOW MEN

A penny for the Old Guy.

MISTAH KURTZ—HE DEAD.

I

WE are the hollow men
We are the stuffed men
Leaning together
Headpiece filled with straw. Alas!
Our dried voices, when
We whisper together
Are quiet and meaningless
As wind in dry grass
Or rats' feet over broken glass
In our dry cellar

Shape without form, shade without colour,
Paralysed force, gesture without motion;

Those who have crossed
With direct eyes, to death's other Kingdom
Remember us—if at all—not as lost
Violent souls, but only
As the hollow men
The stuffed men.

II

Eyes I dare not meet in dreams
In death's dream kingdom
These do not appear:
There, the eyes are
Sunlight on a broken column
There, is a tree swinging
And voices are
In the wind's singing
More distant and more solemn
Than a fading star.

Let me be no nearer
In death's dream kingdom
Let me also wear
Such deliberate disguises
Rat's coat, crowskin, crossed staves
In a field
Behaving as the wind behaves
No nearer—
Not that final meeting
In the twilight kingdom

III

This is the dead land
This is cactus land
Here the stone images
Are raised, here they receive
The supplication of a dead man's hand
Under the twinkle of a fading star.

Is it like this
In death's other kingdom
Waking alone
At the hour when we are
Trembling with tenderness
Lips that would kiss
Form prayers to broken stone.

IV

The eyes are not here
There are no eyes here
In this valley of dying stars
In this hollow valley
This broken jaw of our lost kingdoms

In this last of meeting places
We grope together
And avoid speech
Gathered on this beach of the tumid river

Sightless, unless
The eyes reappear
As the perpetual star
Multifoliate rose
Of death's twilight kingdom
The hope only
Of empty men.

V

Here we go round the prickly pear
Prickly pear, prickly pear
Here we go round the prickly pear
At five o'clock in the morning.

Between the idea
And the reality
Between the motion
And the act
Falls the Shadow
For Thine is the Kingdom.

Between the conception
And the creation
Between the emotion
And the response
Falls the Shadow
Life is very long.

Between the desire
And the spasm
Between the potency
And the existence
Between the essence
And the descent
Falls the Shadow
For Thine is the Kingdom.

For Thine is
Life is
For Thine is the

This is the way the world ends
This is the way the world ends
This is the way the world ends
Not with a bang but a whimper.

LA FIGLIA CHE PIANGE

O quam te memorem virgo . . .

STAND on the highest pavement of the stair—
Lean on a garden urn—
Weave, weave the sunlight in your hair—
Clasp your flowers to you with a pained surprise—
Fling them to the ground and turn
With a fugitive resentment in your eyes:
But weave, weave the sunlight in your hair.

So I would have had him leave,
So I would have had her stand and grieve,
So he would have left
As the soul leaves the body torn and bruised,
As the mind deserts the body it has used.

I should find
Some way incomparably light and deft,
Some way we both should understand,
Simple and faithless as a smile and shake of the hand.

She turned away, but with the autumn weather
Compelled my imagination many days,
Many days and many hours:
Her hair over her arms and her arms full of flowers,
And I wonder how they should have been together!
I should have lost a gesture and a pose.
Sometimes these cognitions still amaze
The troubled midnight and the noon's repose.

Wallace Stevens

TO THE ONE OF FICTIVE MUSIC

SISTER and mother and diviner love,
And of the sisterhood of the living dead
Most near, most clear, and of the clearest bloom,
And of the fragrant mothers the most dear
And queen, and of diviner love the day
And flame and summer and sweet fire, no thread
Of cloudy silver sprinkles in your gown
Its venom of renown, and on your head
No crown is simpler than the simple hair.

Now, of the music summoned by the birth
That separates us from the wind and sea,
Yet leaves us in them, until earth becomes,
By being so much of the things we are,
Gross effigy and simulacrum, none
Gives motion to perfection more serene
Than yours, out of our imperfections wrought,
Most rare, or ever of more kindred air
In the laborious weaving that you wear.

For so retentive of themselves are men
That music is intensest which proclaims
The near, the clear, and vaunts the clearest bloom,
And of all vigils musing the obscure,
That apprehends the most which sees and names,
As in your name, an image that is sure,
Among the arrant spices of the sun,
O bough and bush and scented vine, in whom
We give ourselves our likest issuance.

Yet not too like, yet not so like to be
Too near, too clear, saving a little to endow
Our feigning with the strange unlike, whence springs
The difference that heavenly pity brings.
For this, musician, in your girdle fixed

Bear other perfumes. On your pale head wear
A band entwining, set with fatal stones.
Unreal, give back to us what once you gave:
The imagination that we spurned and crave.

PETER QUINCE AT THE CLAVIER

I

JUST as my fingers on these keys
Make music, so the self-same sounds
On my spirit make a music too.

Music is feeling then, not sound;
And thus it is that what I feel,
Here in this room, desiring you,

Thinking of your blue-shadowed silk,
Is music. It is like the strain
Waked in the elders by Susanna:

Of a green evening, clear and warm,
She bathed in her still garden, while
The red-eyed elders, watching, felt

The basses of their being throb
In witching chords, and their thin blood
Pulse pizzicati of Hosanna.

II

In the green evening, clear and warm,
Susanna lay.
She searched
The touch of springs,
And found
Concealed imaginings.
She sighed
For so much melody.

Upon the bank she stood
In the cool
Of spent emotions.
She felt, among the leaves,
The dew
Of old devotions.

She walked upon the grass,
Still quavering.
The winds were like her maids,
On timid feet,
Fetching her woven scarves,
Yet wavering.

A breath upon her hand
Muted the night.
She turned—
A cymbal clashed,
And roaring horns.

III

Soon, with a noise like tambourines,
Came her attendant Byzantines.

They wondered why Susanna cried
Against the elders by her side:

And as they whispered, the refrain
Was like a willow swept by rain.

Anon their lamps' uplifted flame
Revealed Susanna and her shame.

And then the simpering Byzantines,
Fled, with a noise like tambourines.

IV

Beauty is momentary in the mind—
The fitful tracing of a portal;
But in the flesh it is immortal.

The body dies; the body's beauty lives.
So evenings die, in their green going,
A wave, interminably flowing.

So gardens die, their meek breath scenting
The cowl of Winter, done repenting.
So maidens die to the auroral
Celebration of a maiden's choral.

Susanna's music touched the bawdy strings
Of those white elders; but, escaping,
Left only Death's ironic scraping.
Now in its immortality, it plays
On the clear viol of her memory,
And makes a constant sacrament of praise.

SUNDAY MORNING

I

COMPLACENCIES of the peignoir, and late
Coffee and oranges in a sunny chair,
And the green freedom of a cockatoo
Upon a rug, mingle to dissipate
The holy hush of ancient sacrifice.
She dreams a little, and she feels the dark
Encroachment of that old catastrophe,
As a calm darkens among water-lights.
The pungent oranges and bright green wings
Seem things in some procession of the dead,
Winding across wide water, without sound.
The day is like wide water, without sound,
Stilled for the passing of her dreaming feet
Over the seas, to silent Palestine,
Dominion of the blood and sepulchre.

II

She hears, upon that water without sound,
A voice that cries: "The tomb in Palestine

Is not the porch of spirits lingering;
It is the grave of Jesus, where He lay."
We live in an old chaos of the sun,
Or old dependency of day and night,
Or island solitude, unsponsored, free,
Of that wide water, inescapable.
Deer walk upon our mountains, and the quail
Whistle about us their spontaneous cries;
Sweet berries ripen in the wilderness;
And in the isolation of the sky,
At evening, casual flocks of pigeons make
Ambiguous undulations as they sink,
Downward to darkness, on extended wings.

III

She says: "I am content when wakened birds,
Before they fly, test the reality
Of misty fields, by their sweet questionings;
But when the birds are gone, and their warm fields
Return no more, where, then, is paradise?"
There is not any haunt of prophecy,
Nor any old chimera of the grave,
Neither the golden underground, nor isle
Melodious, where spirits gat them home,
Nor visionary South, nor cloudy palm
Remote on heaven's hill, that has endured
As April's green endures; or will endure
Like her remembrance of awakened birds,
Or her desire for June and evening, tipped
By the consummation of the swallow's wings.

IV

She says, "But in contentment I still feel
The need of some imperishable bliss."
Death is the mother of beauty; hence from her,
Alone, shall come fulfilment to our dreams
And our desires. Although she strews the leaves

Of sure obliteration on our paths—
The path sick sorrow took, the many paths
Where triumph rang its brassy phrase, or love
Whispered a little out of tenderness—
She makes the willow shiver in the sun
For maidens who were wont to sit and gaze
Upon the grass, relinquished to their feet.
She causes boys to bring sweet-smelling pears
And plums in ponderous piles. The maidens taste
And stray impassioned in the littering leaves.

V

Supple and turbulent, a ring of men
Shall chant in orgy on a summer morn
Their boisterous devotion to the sun—
Not as a god, but as a god might be,
Naked among them, like a savage source.
Their chant shall be a chant of paradise,
Out of their blood, returning to the sky;
And in their chant shall enter, voice by voice,
The windy lake wherein their lord delights,
The trees, like seraphim, and echoing hills,
That choir among themselves long afterward.
They shall know well the heavenly fellowship
Of men that perish and of summer morn—
And whence they came and whither they shall go,
The dew upon their feet shall manifest.

LE MONOCLE DE MON ONCLE

I

"MOTHER of heaven, regina of the clouds,
O sceptre of the sun, crown of the moon,
There is not nothing, no, no, never nothing,
Like the clashed edges of two words that kill."
And so I mocked her in magnificent measure.

Or was it that I mocked myself alone?
I wish that I might be a thinking stone.
The sea of spuming thoughts foists up again
The radiant bubble that she was. And then
A deep up-pouring from some saltier well
Within me, bursts its watery syllable.

II

A red bird flies across the golden floor.
It is a red bird that seeks out his choir
Among the choirs of wind and wet and wing.
A torrent will fall from him when he finds.
Shall I uncrumple this much-crumpled thing?
I am a man of fortune greeting heirs;
For it has come that thus I greet the Spring.
These choirs of welcome choir for me farewell.
No Spring can follow past meridian.
Yet you persist with anecdotal bliss
To make believe a starry *connaissance*.

III

Is it for nothing, then, that old Chinese
Sat titivating by their mountain pools
Or in the Yangtse studied out their beards?
I shall not play the flat historic scale.
You know how Utamaro's beauties sought
The end of love in their all-speaking braids.
You know the mountainous coiffures of Bath.
Alas! Have all the barbers lived in vain
That not one curl in Nature has survived?
Why, without pity on these studious ghosts,
Do you come dripping in your hair from sleep?

IV

This luscious and impeccable fruit of life
Falls, it appears, of its own weight to earth.
When you were Eve, its acrid juice was sweet,

Untasted, in its heavenly, orchard air—
An apple serves as well as any skull
To be the book in which to read a round,
And is as excellent, in that it is composed
Of what, like skulls, comes rotting back to ground.
But it excels in this that as the fruit
Of love, it is a book too mad to read
Before one merely reads to pass the time.

V

In the high West there burns a furious star.
It is for fiery boys that star was set
And for sweet-smelling virgins close to them.
The measure of the intensity of love
Is measure, also, of the verve of earth.
For me, the firefly's quick, electric stroke
Ticks tediously the time of one more year.
And you? Remember how the crickets came
Out of their mother grass, like little kin. . .
In the pale nights, when your first imagery
Found inklings of your bond to all that dust.

VI

If men at forty will be painting lakes
The ephemeral blues must merge for them in one,
The basic slate, the universal hue.
There is a substance in us that prevails.
But in our amours amorists discern
Such fluctuations that their scrivening
Is breathless to attend each quirky turn.
When amorists grow bald, then amours shrink
Into the compass and curriculum
Of introspective exiles, lecturing.
It is a theme for Hyacinth alone.

VII

The mules that angels ride come slowly down
The blazing passes, from beyond the sun.
Descensions of their tinkling bells arrive.
These muleteers are dainty of their way.
Meantime centurions guffaw and beat
Their shrilling tankards on the table-boards.
This parable, in sense, amounts to this:
The honey of heaven may or may not come,
But that of earth both comes and goes at once.
Suppose these couriers brought amid their train
A damsel heightened by eternal bloom. . . .

VIII

Like a dull scholar, I behold, in love,
An ancient aspect touching a new mind.
It comes, it blooms, it bears its fruit and dies.
This trivial trope reveals a way of truth.
Our bloom is gone. We are the fruit thereof.
Two golden gourds distended on our vines,
We hang like warty squashes, streaked and rayed.
Into the Autumn weather, splashed with frost,
Distorted by hale fatness, turned grotesque.
The laughing sky will see the two of us
Washed into rinds by rotting winter rains.

IX

In verses wild with motion, full of din,
Loudened by cries, by clashes, quick and sure
As the deadly thought of men accomplishing
Their curious fates in war, come, celebrate
The faith of forty, ward of Cupido.
Most venerable heart, the lustiest conceit
Is not too lusty for your broadening.
I quiz all sounds, all thoughts, all everything
For the music and manner of the paladins
To make oblation fit. Where shall I find
Bravura adequate to this great hymn?

X

The fops of fancy in their poems leave
Memorabilia of the mystic sprouts,
Spontaneously watering their gritty soils.
I am a yeoman, as such fellows go.
I know no magic trees, no balmy boughs,
No silver-ruddy, gold-vermilion fruits.
But, after all, I know a tree that bears
A semblance to the thing I have in mind.
It stands gigantic, with a certain tip
To which all birds come sometime in their time.
But when they go that tip still tips the tree.

XI

If sex were all, then every trembling hand
Could make us speak, like dolls, the wished-for words.
But note the unconscionable treachery of fate,
That makes us weep, laugh, grunt and groan, and shout
Doleful heroics, pinching gestures forth
From madness or delight, without regard
To that first foremost law. Anguishing hour!
Last night, we sat beside a pool of pink,
Clippered with lilacs, scudding the bright chromes,
Keen to the point of starlight, while a frog
Boomed from his very belly, odious chords.

XII

A blue pigeon it is, that circles the blue sky,
On side-long wing, around and round and round.
A white pigeon it is, that flutters to the ground,
Grown tired of flight. Like a dark rabbi, I
Observed, when young, the nature of mankind,
In lordly study. Every day, I found
Man proved a gobbet in my mincing world.
Like a rose rabbi, later, I pursued,
And still pursue, the origin and course
Of love, but until now I never knew
That fluttering things have so distinct a shade.

TATTOO

THE light is like a spider.
It crawls over the water.
It crawls over the edges of the snow.
It crawls under your eyelids
And spreads its webs there—
Its two webs.

The webs of your eyes
Are fastened
To the flesh and bones of you
As to rafters or grass.

There are filaments of your eyes
On the surface of the water
And in the edges of the snow.

THE BIRD WITH THE COPPERY, KEEN CLAWS

ABOVE the forest of the parakeets,
A parakeet of parakeets prevails,
A pip of life amid a mort of tails.

(The rudiments of tropics are around,
Aloe of ivory, pear of rusty rind.)
His lids are white because his eyes are blind.

He is not paradise of parakeets,
Of his gold ether, golden alguazil.
Except because he broods there and is still,

Panache upon panache, his tails deploy
Upward and outward, in green-vented forms,
His tip a drop of water full of storms.

But though the turbulent tinges undulate
As his pure intellect applies its laws,
He moves not on his coppery, keen claws.

He munches a dry shell while he exerts
His will, yet never ceases, perfect cock,
To flare, in the sun-pallor of his rock.

OF HEAVEN CONSIDERED AS A TOMB

WHAT word have you, interpreters, of men
Who in the tomb of heaven walk by night,
The darkened ghosts of our old comedy?
Do they believe they range the gusty cold,
With lanterns borne aloft to light the way,
Freemen of death, about and still about
To find whatever it is they seek? Or does
That burial, pillared up each day as porte
And spiritous passage into nothingness,
Foretell each night the one abysmal night,
When the host shall no more wander, nor the light
Of the steadfast lanterns creep across the dark?
Make hue among the dark comedians,
Halloo them in the topmost distances
For answer from their icy Elysée.

OF THE MANNER OF ADDRESSING CLOUDS

LOOMY grammarians in golden gowns,
Meekly you keep the mortal rendezvous,
Eliciting the still sustaining pomps
Of speech which are like music so profound
They seem an exaltation without sound.
Funest philosophers and ponderers,
Their evocations are the speech of clouds.
So speech of your processionals returns
In the casual evocations of your tread
Across the stale, mysterious seasons. These
Are the music of meet resignation; these
The responsive, still sustaining pomps for you
To magnify, if in that drifting waste
You are to be accompanied by more
Than mute bare splendors of the sun and moon.

Edna St. Vincent Millay

ELEGY BEFORE DEATH

THERE will be rose and rhododendron
When you are dead and under ground;
Still will be heard from white syringas
Heavy with bees, a sunny sound;

Still will the tamaracks be raining
After the rain has ceased, and still
Will there be robins in the stubble,
Brown sheep upon the warm green hill.

Spring will not ail nor autumn falter;
Nothing will know that you are gone,
Saving alone some sullen plough-land
None but yourself set foot upon;

Saving the may-weed and the pig-weed
Nothing will know that you are dead,—
These, and perhaps a useless wagon
Standing beside some tumbled shed.

Oh, there will pass with your great passing
Little of beauty not your own,—
Only the light from common water,
Only the grace from simple stone.

WHAT LIPS MY LIPS HAVE KISSED

WHAT lips my lips have kissed, and where, and why
I have forgotten, and what arms have lain
Under my head till morning; but the rain
Is full of ghosts to-night, that tap and sigh
Upon the glass and listen for reply;
And in my heart there stirs a quiet pain
For unremembered lads that not again
Will turn to me at midnight with a cry.

Thus in the winter stands the lonely tree,
Nor knows what birds have vanished one by one,
Yet knows its boughs more silent than before:
I cannot say what loves have come and gone;
I only know that summer sang in me
A little while, that in me sings no more.

John Hall Wheelock

EARTH

GRASSHOPPER, your fairy song
And my poem alike belong
To the dark and silent earth
From which all poetry has birth;
All we say and all we sing
Is but as the murmuring
Of that drowsy heart of hers
When from her deep dream she stirs:
If we sorrow, or rejoice,
You and I are but her voice.

Deftly does the dust express
In mind her hidden loveliness,
And from her cool silence stream
The cricket's cry and Dante's dream;
For the earth that breeds the trees
Breeds cities too, and symphonies.

Equally her beauty flows
Into a savior, or a rose—
Looks down in dream, and from above
Smiles at herself in Jesus' love.
Christ's love and Homer's art
Are but the workings of her heart;
Through Leonardo's hand she seeks
Herself, and through Beethoven speaks

In holy thunderings around
The awful message of the ground.

The serene and humble mold
Does in herself all selves enfold—
Kingdoms, destinies, and creeds,
Great dreams, and dauntless deeds,
Science that metes the firmament,
The high, inflexible intent
Of one for many sacrificed—
Plato's brain, the heart of Christ;
All love, all legend, and all lore
Are in the dust forevermore.

Even as the growing grass,
Up from the soil religions pass,
And the field that bears the rye
Bears parables and prophecy.
Out of the earth the poem grows
Like the lily, or the rose;
And all man is, or yet may be,
Is but herself in agony
Toiling up the steep ascent
Toward the complete accomplishment
When all dust shall be, the whole
Universe, one conscious soul.

Yea, the quiet and cool sod
Bears in her breast the dream of God.
If you would know what earth is, scan
The intricate, proud heart of man,
Which is the earth articulate,
And learn how holy and how great,
How limitless and how profound
Is the nature of the ground—
How without terror or demur
We may entrust ourselves to her
When we are wearied out and lay
Our faces in the common clay.

For she is pity, she is love,
All wisdom, she, all thoughts that move
About her everlasting breast
Till she gathers them to rest:
All tenderness of all the ages,
Seraphic secrets of the sages,
Vision and hope of all the seers,
All prayer, all anguish, and all tears
Are but the dust that from her dream
Awakes, and knows herself supreme—
Are but earth, when she reveals
All that her secret heart conceals
Down in the dark and silent loam,
Which is ourselves, asleep, at home.

Yea, and this, my poem, too,
Is part of her as dust and dew,
Wherein herself she doth declare
Through my lips, and say her prayer.

Cale Young Rice

CHANSON OF THE BELLS OF OSENÈY

Thirteenth Century

THE bells of Osenèy
(Hautclère, Doucement, Austyn)
Chant sweetly every day,
And sadly, for our sin.
The bells of Osenèy
(John, Gabriel, Marie)
Chant lowly,
Chant slowly,
Chant wistfully and holy
Of Christ, our Paladin.

Hautclère chants to the East
(His tongue is silvery high),
And Austyn like a priest
Sends west a weighty cry.
But Doucement set between
(Like an appeasive nun)
Chants cheerly,
Chants clearly,
As if Christ heard her nearly,
A plea to every sky.

A plea that John takes up
(He is the evangelist)
Till Gabriel's angel cup
Pours sound to sun or mist.
And last of all Marie
(The virgin-voice of God)
Peals purely,
Demurely,
And with a tone so surely
Divine, that all must hear.

The bells of Oseney
(Doucement, Austyn, Hautclère)
Pour ever day by day
Their peals on the rapt air;
And with their mellow mates
(John, Gabriel, Marie)
Tell slowly,
Tell lowly,
Of Christ the High and Holy,
Who makes the whole world fair.

Elinor Wylie

THE EAGLE AND THE MOLE

AVOID the reeking herd,
Shun the polluted flock,
Live like that stoic bird,
The eagle of the rock.

The huddled warmth of crowds
Begets and fosters hate;
He keeps, above the clouds,
His cliff inviolate.

When flocks are folded warm,
And herds to shelter run,
He sails above the storm,
He stares into the sun.

If in the eagle's track
Your sinews cannot leap,
Avoid the lathered pack,
Turn from the steaming sheep.

If you would keep your soul
From spotted sight or sound,
Live like the velvet mole;
Go burrow underground.

And there hold intercourse
With roots of trees and stones,
With rivers at their source,
And disembodied bones.

ESCAPE

WHEN foxes eat the last gold grape,
And the last white antelope is killed,
I shall stop fighting and escape
Into a little house I'll build.

But first I'll shrink to fairy size,
With a whisper no one understands,
Making blind moons of all your eyes,
And muddy roads of all your hands.

And you may grope for me in vain
In hollows under the mangrove root,
Or where, in apple-scented rain,
The silver wasp-nests hang like fruit.

CONFESSION OF FAITH

I LACK the braver mind
That dares to find
The lover friend, and kind.

I fear him to the bone;
I lie alone
By the beloved one,

And, breathless for suspense,
Erect defense
Against love's violence

Whose silences portend
A bloody end
For lover never friend.

But, in default of faith,
In futile breath,
I dream no ill of Death.

ADDRESS TO MY SOUL

MY soul, be not disturbed
By planetary war;
Remain securely orbed
In this contracted star.

Fear not, pathetic flame;
Your sustenance is doubt:
Glassed in translucent dream
They cannot snuff you out.

Wear water, or a mask
Of unapparent cloud;
Be brave and never ask
A more defunctive shroud.

The universal points
Are shrunk into a flower;
Between its delicate joints
Chaos keeps no power.

The pure integral form,
Austere and silver-dark,
Is balanced on the storm
In its predestined arc.

Small as a sphere of rain
It slides along the groove
Whose path is furrowed plain
Among the suns that move.

The shapes of April buds
Outlive the phantom year:
Upon the void at odds
The dewdrop falls severe.

Five-petalled flame, be cold:
Be firm, dissolving star:
Accept the stricter mould
That makes you singular.

TRUE VINE

THERE is a serpent in perfection tarnished,
The thin shell pierced, the purity grown fainter,
The virgin silver shield no longer burnished,
The pearly fruit with ruin for its centre.

The thing that sits expectant in our bosoms
Contriving heaven out of very little
Demands such delicate immaculate blossoms
As no malicious verity makes brittle.

This wild fastidious hope is quick to languish;
Its smooth diaphanous escape is swifter
Than the pack of truth; no mortal can distinguish
Its trace upon the durable hereafter.

Not so the obdurate and savage lovely
Whose roots are set profoundly upon trouble;
This flower grows so fiercely and so bravely
It does not even know that it is noble.

This is the vine to love, whose balsams flourish
Upon a living soil corrupt and faulty,
Whose leaves have drunk the skies, and stooped to nourish
The earth again with honey sweet and salty.

Ezra Pound

ENVOI (1919)

GO, dumb-born book,
Tell her that sang me once that song of Lawes:
Hadst thou but song
As thou hast subjects known,
Then were there cause in thee that should condone
Even my faults that heavy upon me lie,
And build her glories their longevity.

Tell her that sheds
Such treasure in the air,
Recking naught else but that her graces give
Life to the moment,
I would bid them live

As roses might, in magic amber laid,
Red overwrought with orange and all made
One substance and one colour
Braving time.

Tell her that goes
With song upon her lips
But sings not out the song, nor knows
The maker of it, some other mouth,
May be as fair as hers,
Might, in new ages, gain her worshippers,
When our two dusts with Waller's shall be laid,
Siftings on siftings in oblivion,
Till change hath broken down
All things save Beauty alone.

THE TREE

I STOOD still and was a tree amid the wood,
Knowing the truth of things unseen before;
Of Daphne and the laurel bough
And that god-feasting couple old
That grew elm-oak amid the wold.
'Twas not until the gods had been
Kindly entreated, and been brought within
Unto the hearth of their heart's home
That they might do this wonder thing;
Nathless I have been a tree amid the wood
And many a new thing understood
That was rank folly to my head before.

THE TOMB AT AKR ÇAAR

I AM thy soul, Nikoptis. I have watched
These five millennia, and thy dead eyes
Moved not, nor ever answer my desire,
And thy light limbs, wherethrough I leapt aflame,
Burn not with me nor any saffron thing.

See, the light grass sprang up to pillow thee,
And kissed thee with a myriad grassy tongues;
But not thou me.
I have read out the gold upon the wall,
And wearied out my thought upon the signs.
And there is no new thing in all this place.

I have been kind. See, I have left the jars sealed,
Lest thou shouldst wake and whimper for thy wine.
And all thy robes I have kept smooth on thee.
O thou unmindful! How should I forget!
—Even the river many days ago,
The river? thou wast over young.
And three souls came upon Thee—
And I came.
And I flowed in upon thee, beat them off;
I have been intimate with thee, known thy ways.
Have I not touched thy palms and finger-tips,
Flowed in, and through thee and about thy heels?
How 'came I in'? Was I not thee and Thee?

And no sun comes to rest me in this place,
And I am torn against the jagged dark,
And no light beats upon me, and you say
No word, day after day.

Oh! I could get me out, despite the marks
And all their crafty work upon the door,
Out through the glass-green fields. . . .

. . . . .

Yet it is quiet here:

I do not go."

PORTRAIT D'UNE FEMME

YOUR mind and you are our Sargasso Sea,
London has swept about you this score years
And bright ships left you this or that in fee:

Ideas, old gossip, oddments of all things,
Strange spars of knowledge and dimmed wares of price.
Great minds have sought you—lacking someone else.
You have been second always. Tragical?
No. You preferred it to the usual thing:
One dull man, dulling and uxorious,
One average mind—with one thought less, each year.
Oh, you are patient, I have seen you sit
Hours, where something might have floated up.
And now you pay one. Yes, you richly pay.
You are a person of some interest, one comes to you
And takes strange gain away:
Trophies fished up; some curious suggestion;
Fact that leads nowhere; and a tale or two,
Pregnant with mandrakes, or with something else
That might prove useful and yet never proves,
That never fits a corner or shows use,
Or finds its hour upon the loom of days:
The tarnished, gaudy, wonderful old work;
Idols and ambergris and rare inlays,
These are your riches, your great store; and yet
For all this sea-hoard of deciduous things,
Strange woods half sodden, and new brighter stuff:
In the slow float of differing light and deep,
No! there is nothing! In the whole and all,
Nothing that's quite your own.
Yet this is you.

APPARUIT

GOLDEN rose the house, in the portal I saw
thee, a marvel, carven in subtle stuff, a
portent. Life died down in the lamp and flickered,
caught at the wonder.

Crimson, frosty with dew, the roses bend where
thou afar, moving in the glamorous sun,
drinkst in life of earth, of the air, the tissue
golden about thee.

Green the ways, the breath of the fields is thine there,
open lies the land, yet the steely going
darkly hast thou dared and the dreaded æther
parted before thee.

Swift at courage thou in the shell of gold, cast-
ing a-loose the cloak of the body, camest
straight, then shone thine oriel and the stunned light
faded about thee.

Half the graven shoulder, the throat aflash with
strands of light inwoven about it, loveliest of all things, frail alabaster, ah me!
swift in departing.

Clothed in goldish weft, delicately perfect,
gone as wind! The cloth of the magical hands:
Thou a slight thing, thou in access of cunning
dar'dst to assume this?

A VIRGINAL

"NO, no! Go from me. I have left her lately.
I will not spoil my sheath with lesser brightness.
For my surrounding air hath a new lightness;
Slight are her arms, yet they have bound me straitly
And left me cloaked as with a gauze of æther;
As with sweet leaves; as with subtle clearness.
Oh, I have picked up magic in her nearness
To sheathe me half in half the things that sheathe her.
No, no! Go from me. I have still the flavour,
Soft as spring wind that's come from birchen bowers.
Green come the shoots, aye April in the branches,
As winter's wound with her sleight hand she staunches,
Hath of the trees a likeness of the savour:
As white their bark, so white this lady's hours."

THE RETURN

SEE, they return; ah, see the tentative
Movements, and the slow feet,
The trouble in the pace and the uncertain
Wavering!

See, they return, one, and by one,
With fear, as half-awakened;
As if the snow should hesitate
And murmur in the wind,
and half turned back;
These were the "Wing'd-with-Awe,"
Inviolable.

Gods of the wingèd shoe!
With them the silver hounds,
sniffing the trace of air!

Haie! Haie!
These were the swift to harry;
These the keen-scented;
These were the souls of blood.

Slow on the leash,
pallid the leash-men!

E. E. Cummings

SONGS

ALWAYS before your voice my soul
half-beautiful and wholly droll
is as some smooth and awkward foal,
whereof young moons begin
the newness of his skin,

so of my stupid sincere youth
the exquisite failure uncouth
discovers a trembling and smooth
Unstrength, against the strong
silences of your song;

or as a single lamb whose sheen
of full unsheared fleece is mean
beside its lovelier friends, between
your thoughts more white than wool
My thought is sorrowful:

but my heart smote in trembling thirds
of anguish quivers to your words,
As to a flight of thirty birds
shakes with a thickening fright
the sudden fooled light.

it is the autumn of a year:
When through the thin air stooped with fear,
across the harvest whitely peer
empty of surprise
death's faultless eyes

(whose hand my folded soul shall know
while on faint hills do frailly go
The peaceful terrors of the snow,
and before your dead face
which sleeps, a dream shall pass)

and these my days their sounds and flowers
Fall in a pride of petaled hours,
like flowers at the feet of mowers
whose bodies strong with love
through meadows hugely move.

yet what am i that such and such
mysteries very simply touch
me, whose heart-wholeness overmuch

Expects of your hair pale,
a terror musical?

while in an earthless hour my fond
soul seriously yearns beyond
this fern of sunset frond on frond
opening in a rare
Slowness of gloried air . . .

The flute of morning stilled in noon—
noon the implacable bassoon—
now Twilight seeks the thrill of moon,
washed with a wild and thin
despair of violin.

Archibald MacLeish

L'AN TRENTIESME DE MON ÂGE

AND I have come upon this place
By lost ways, by a nod, by words,
By faces, by an old man's face
At Morlaix lifted to the birds,

By hands upon the tablecloth
At Aldebori's, by the thin
Child's hands that opened to the moth
And let the flutter of the moonlight in,

By hands, by voices, by the voice
Of Mrs. Husman on the stair,
By Margaret's "If we had the choice
To choose or not"—through her thick hair,

By voices, by the creak and fall
Of footsteps on the upper floor,
By silence waiting in the hall
Between the doorbell and the door,

By words, by voices, a lost way—
And here above the chimney stack
The unknown constellations sway—
And by what way shall I go back?

THE TOO-LATE BORN

We too, we too, descending once again
The hills of our own land, we too have heard
Far off—Ah, que ce cor a longue haleine—
The horn of Roland in the passages of Spain,
The first, the second blast, the failing third,
And with the third turned back and climbed once more
The steep road southward, and heard faint the sound
Of swords, of horses, the disastrous war,
And crossed the dark defile at last, and found
At Roncevaux upon the darkening plain
The dead against the dead and on the silent ground
The silent slain—

EINSTEIN

Standing between the sun and moon
preserves
A certain secrecy. Or seems to keep
Something inviolate if only that
His father was an ape.
Sweet music makes
All of his walls sound hollow and he heard
Sighs in the panelling and underfoot
Melancholy voices. So there is a door
Behind the seamless arras and within
A living something:—but no door that will
Admit the sunlight nor no windows where
The mirror moon can penetrate his bones
With cold deflection. He is small and tight
And solidly contracted into space

Opaque and perpendicular which blots
Earth with its shadow. And he terminates
In shoes which bearing up against the sphere
Attract his concentration,
for he ends
If there why then no farther, as, beyond
Extensively the universe itself,
Or chronologically the two dates
Original and ultimate of time,

Einstein upon a public bench Wednesday the ninth contemplates finity

Nor could Jehovah and the million stars
Staring within their solitudes of light,
Nor all night's constellations be contained
Between his boundaries,
nor could the sun
Receive him nor his groping roots run down
Into the loam and steaming sink of time
Where coils the middle serpent and the ooze
Breeds maggots.
But it seems assured he ends
Precisely at his shoes in proof whereof
He can revolve in orbits opposite
The orbit of the earth and so refuse
All planetary converse. And he wears
Clothes that distinguish him from what is not
His own circumference, as first a coat
Shaped to his back or modelled in reverse
Of the surrounding cosmos and below
Trousers preserving his detachment from
The revolutions of the stars.

Einstein descends the Hartmannsweilerstrasse

His hands
And face go naked and alone converse
With what encloses him, as rough and smooth
And sound and silence and the intervals
Of rippling ether and the swarming motes
Clouding a privy: move to them and make
Shadows that mirror them within his skull
In perpendiculars and curves and planes
And bodiless significances blurred

As figures undersea and images
Patterned from eddies of the air.

Einstein ultimately before a mirror accepts the hypothesis of exterior reality

Which are
Perhaps not shadows but the thing itself
And may be understood.

Decorticate
The petals of the enfolding world and leave
A world in reason which is in himself
And has his own dimensions. Here do trees
Adorn the hillsides and hillsides enrich
The hazy marches of the sky and skies
Kindle and char to ashes in the wind,
And winds blow toward him from the verge,
 and suns
Rise on his dawn and on his dusk go down
And moons prolong his shadow. And he moves
Here as within a garden in a close
And where he moves the bubble of the world
Takes centre and there circle round his head
Like golden flies in summer the gold stars.

Disintegrates.

For suddenly he feels
The planet plunge beneath him, and a flare
Falls from the upper darkness to the dark
And awful shadows loom across the sky
That have no life from him and suns go out
And livid as a drowned man's face the moon
Floats to the lapsing surface of the night
And sinks discolored under.

Einstein unsuccessfully after lunch attempts to enter, essaying synthesis with what's not he, the Bernese Oberland

So he knows
Less than a world and must communicate
Beyond his knowledge.

Outstretched on the earth
He plunges both his arms into the swirl
Of what surrounds him but the yielding grass

Excludes his finger tips and the soft soil
Will not endure confusion with his hands,
Nor will the air receive him nor the light
Dissolve their difference but recoiling turns
Back from his touch. By which denial he can
Crawl on the earth and sense the opposing sun
But not make answer to them.
Put out leaves
And let the old remembering wind think through
A green intelligence, or under sea
Float out long filaments of amber in
The numb and wordless revery of tides.

In autumn the black branches dripping rain
Bruise his uncovered bones and in the spring
His swollen tips are gorged with aching blood
That bursts the laurel.
But although they seize
His sense he has no name for them, no word
To give them meaning and no utterance
For what they say. Feel the new summer's sun
Crawl up the warmed relaxing hide of earth
And weep for his lost youth, his childhood home
And a wide water on an inland shore!
Or to the night's mute asking in the blood
Give back a girl's name and three notes together!

Einstein dissolved in violins invades the molecular structure of F. P. Paepke's Sommergarten. Is repulsed

He cannot think the smell of after rain
Nor close his thought around the long smooth lag
And falter of a wind, nor bring to mind
Dusk and the whippoorwill.

But violins
Split out of trees and strung to tone can sing
Strange nameless words that image to the ear
What has no waiting image in the brain.

She plays in darkness and the droning wood
Dissolves to reverberations of a world
Beating in waves against him, till his sense
Trembles to rhythm and his naked brain
Feels without utterance in form the flesh
Of dumb and incommunicable earth,
And knows at once, and without knowledge
how,
The stroke of the blunt rain, and blind receives
The sun.
When he a moment occupies
The hollow of himself and like an air
Pervades all other.
But the violin
Presses its dry insistence through the dream
That swims above it, shivering its speech
Back to a rhythm that becomes again
Music and vaguely ravels into sound.

To Einstein asking at the gate of stone none opens

So then there is no speech that can resolve
Their texture to clear thought and enter them.

The Virgin of Chartres whose bleaching bones
still wear
The sapphires of her glory knew a word—
That now is three round letters like the three
Round empty staring punctures in a skull.
And there were words in Rome once and one
time
Words at Eleusis.
Now there are no words
Nor names to name them and they will not
speak
But grope against his groping touch and throw
The long unmeaning shadows of themselves
Across his shadow and resist his sense.

Einstein hearing behind the wall of the Grand Hôtel du Nord the stars discovers the Back Stair

Why then if they resist destroy them. Dumb
Yet speak them in their elements. Whole,

Break them to reason.
He lies upon his bed
Exerting on Arcturus and the moon
Forces proportional inversely to
The squares of their remoteness, and conceives
The universe.
Atomic.
He can count
Ocean in atoms and weigh out the air
In multiples of one and subdivide
Light to its numbers.
If they will not speak
Let them be silent in their particles.
Let them be dead and he will lie among
Their dust and cipher them,—undo the signs
Of their unreal identities and free
The pure and single factor of all sums,—
Solve them to unity.
Democritus
Scooped handfuls out of stones and like the sea
Let earth run through his fingers. Well, he too,
He can achieve obliquity and learn
The cold distortion of the winter's sun
That breaks the surfaces of summer.

Einstein on the terrasse of The Acacias forces the secret door

Stands
Facing the world upon a windy slope
And with his mind relaxes the stiff forms
Of all he sees so that the heavy hills
Impend like rushing water and the earth
Hangs on the steep and momentary crest
Of overflowing ruin.
Overflow!
Sweep over into movement and dissolve
All differences in the indifferent flux!
Crumble to eddyings of dust and drown
In change the thing that changes!
There begins
A vague unquiet in the fallow ground,

A seething in the grass, a bubbling swirl
Over the surface of the fields that spreads
Around him gathering until the green
Boils and beneath the frothy loam the rocks
Ferment and simmer and like thinning smoke
The trees melt into nothing.
Still he stands
Watching the vortex widen and involve
In swirling dissolution the whole earth
And circle through the skies till swaying time
Collapses crumpling into dark the stars
And motion ceases and the sifting world
Opens beneath.
When he shall feel infuse
His flesh with the rent body of all else
And spin within his opening brain the motes
Of suns and worlds and spaces.

Einstein enters

Like a foam
His flesh is withered and his shrivelling
And ashy bones are scattered on the dark.
But still the dark denies him. Still withstands
The dust his penetration and flings back
Himself to answer him.
Which seems to keep
Something inviolate. A living something.

YOU, ANDREW MARVELL

AND here face down beneath the sun,
And here upon earth's noonward height,
To feel the always coming on,
The always rising of the night.

To feel creep up the curving east
The earthly chill of dusk and slow
Upon those under lands the vast
And ever-climbing shadow grow,

And strange at Ecbatan the trees
Take leaf by leaf the evening, strange,
The flooding dark about their knees,
The mountains over Persia change,

And now at Kermanshah the gate,
Dark, empty, and the withered grass,
And through the twilight now the late
Few travellers in the westward pass.

And Baghdad darken and the bridge
Across the silent river gone,
And through Arabia the edge
Of evening widen and steal on,

And deepen on Palmyra's street
The wheel rut in the ruined stone,
And Lebanon fade out and Crete
High through the clouds and overblown,

And over Sicily the air
Still flashing with the landward gulls,
And loom and slowly disappear
The sails above the shadowy hulls,

And Spain go under and the shore
Of Africa, the gilded sand,
And evening vanish and no more
The low pale light across that land,

Nor now the long light on the sea—

And here face downward in the sun
To feel how swift, how secretly,
The shadow of the night comes on. . . .

John Crowe Ransom

BLUE GIRLS

TWIRLING your blue skirts, travelling the sward
Under the towers of your seminary,
Go listen to your teachers old and contrary
Without believing a word.

Tie the white fillets then about your lustrous hair
And think no more of what will come to pass
Than bluebirds that go walking on the grass
And chattering on the air.

Practise your beauty, blue girls, before it fail;
And I will cry with my loud lips and publish
Beauty which all our power shall never establish,
It is so frail.

For I could tell you a story which is true:
I know a lady with a terrible tongue,
Blear eyes fallen from blue,
All her perfections tarnished—and yet it is not long
Since she was lovelier than any of you.

ANTIQUE HARVESTERS

(*Scene: Of the Mississippi the bank sinister, and of the Ohio the bank sinister.*)

TAWNY are the leaves turned, but they still hold.
It is the harvest; what shall this land produce?
A meager hill of kernels, a runnel of juice.
Declension looks from our land, it is old.
Therefore let us assemble, dry, grey, spare,
And mild as yellow air.

"I hear the creak of a raven's funeral wing."
The young men would be joying in the song
Of passionate birds; their memories are not long.
What is it thus rehearsed in sable? "Nothing."
Trust not but the old endure, and shall be older
Than the scornful beholder.

We pluck the spindling ears and gather the corn.
One spot has special yield? "On this spot stood
Heroes and drenched it with their only blood."
And talk meets talk, as echoes from the horn
Of the hunter—echoes are the old men's arts,
Ample are the chambers of their hearts.

Here come the hunters, keepers of a rite.
The horn, the hounds, the lank mares coursing by
Under quaint archetypes of chivalry;
And the fox, lovely ritualist, in flight
Offering his unearthly ghost to quarry;
And the fields, themselves to harry.

Resume, harvesters. The treasure is full bronze
Which you will garner for the Lady, and the moon
Could tinge it no yellower than does this noon;
But the grey will quench it shortly—the fields, men,
stones.
Pluck fast, dreamers; prove as you rumble slowly
Not less than men, not wholly.

Bare the arm too, dainty youths, bend the knees
Under bronze burdens. And by an autumn tone
As by a grey, as by a green, you will have known
Your famous Lady's image; for so have these.
And if one say that easily will your hands
More prosper in other lands,

Angry as wasp-music be your cry then:
"Forsake the Proud Lady, of the heart of fire,
The look of snow, to the praise of a dwindled choir,

Song of degenerate specters that were men?
The sons of the fathers shall keep her, worthy of
What these have done in love."

True, it is said of our Lady, she ageth.
But see, if you peep shrewdly, she hath not stooped;
Take no thought of her servitors that have drooped,
For we are nothing; and if one talk of death—
Why, the ribs of the earth subsist frail as a breath
If but God wearieth.

CAPTAIN CARPENTER

CAPTAIN CARPENTER rose up in his prime
Put on his pistols and went riding out
But had got wellnigh nowhere at that time
Till he fell in with ladies in a rout.

It was a pretty lady and all her train
That played with him so sweetly but before
An hour she'd taken a sword with all her main
And twined him of his nose for evermore.

Captain Carpenter mounted up one day
And rode straightway into a stranger rogue
That looked unchristian but be that as may
The Captain did not wait upon prologue.

But drew upon him out of his great heart
The other swung against him with a club
And cracked his two legs at the shinny part
And let him roll and stick like any tub.

Captain Carpenter rode many a time
From male and female took he sundry harms
He met the wife of Satan crying "I'm
The she-wolf bids you shall bear no more arms."

Their strokes and counters whistled in the wind
I wish he had delivered half his blows
But where she should have made off like a hind
The bitch bit off his arms at the elbows.

And Captain Carpenter parted with his ears
To a black devil that used him in this wise
O jesus ere his threescore and ten years
Another had plucked out his sweet blue eyes.

Captain Carpenter got up on his roan
And sallied from the gate in hell's despite
I heard him asking in the grimmest tone
If any enemy yet there was to fight?

"To any adversary it is fame
If he risk to be wounded by my tongue
Or burnt in two beneath my red heart's flame
Such are the perils he is cast among.

"But if he can he has a pretty choice
From an anatomy with little to lose
Whether he cut my tongue and take my voice
Or whether it be my round red heart he choose."

It was the neatest knave that ever was seen
Stepping in perfume from his lady's bower
Who at this word put in his merry mien
And fell on Captain Carpenter like a tower.

I would not knock old fellows in the dust
But there lay Captain Carpenter on his back
His weapons were the old heart in his bust
And a blade shook between rotten teeth alack.

The rogue in scarlet and grey soon knew his mind
He wished to get his trophy and depart
With gentle apology and touch refined
He pierced him and produced the Captain's heart.

God's mercy rest on Captain Carpenter now
I thought him Sirs an honest gentleman
Citizen husband soldier and scholar enow
Let jangling kites eat of him if they can.

But God's deep curses follow after those
That shore him of his goodly nose and ears
His legs and strong arms at the two elbows
And eyes that had not watered seventy years.

The curse of hell upon the sleek upstart
Who got the Captain finally on his back
And took the red red vitals of his heart
And made the kites to whet their beaks clack clack.

Marianne Moore

THE FISH

WADE
through black jade
Of the crow-blue mussel shells, one
keeps
adjusting the ash heaps;
opening and shutting itself like

an
injured fan.
The barnacles which encrust the
side
of the wave, cannot hide
there for the submerged shafts of the

sun,
split like spun
glass, move themselves with spotlight swift-
ness
into the crevices—
in and out, illuminating

the
turquoise sea
  of bodies. The water drives a
    wedge
    of iron through the iron edge
  of the cliff, whereupon the stars,

pink
rice grains, ink
  bespattered jelly-fish, crabs like
    green
    lilies and submarine
  toadstools, slide each on the other.

All
external
  marks of abuse are present on
    this
    defiant edifice—
  all the physical features of

ac-
cident—lack
  of cornice, dynamite grooves, burns
    and
    hatchet strokes, these things stand
  out on it; the chasm side is

dead.
Repeated
  evidence has proved that it can
    live
    on what cannot revive
  its youth. The sea grows old in it.

MY APISH COUSINS

WINKED too much and were afraid of snakes. The
    zebras, supreme in
their abnormality; the elephants with their fog-colored skin
  and strictly practical appendages

were there, the small cats; and the parrakeet—
trivial and humdrum on examination, destroying
bark and portions of the food it could not eat.

I recall their magnificence, now not more magnificent
than it is dim. It is difficult to recall the ornament,
speech, and precise manner of what one might
call the minor acquaintances twenty
years back; but I shall not forget him—that Gilgamesh
among
the hairy carnivora—that cat with the

wedge-shaped, slate-gray marks on its forelegs and the resolute tail,
astringently remarking: "They have imposed on us with their
pale
half-fledged protestations, trembling about
in inarticulate frenzy, saying
it is not for us to understand art; finding it
all so difficult, examining the thing

as if it were inconceivably arcanic, as symmetrically frigid as if it had been carved out of chrysoprase
or marble—strict with tension, malignant
in its power over us and deeper
than the sea when it proffers flattery in exchange for
hemp,
rye, flax, horses, platinum, timber, and fur."

PEDANTIC LITERALIST

PRINCE RUPERT'S drop, paper muslin ghost,
White torch—"with power to say unkind
Things with kindness, and the most
Irritating things in the midst of love and
Tears," you invite destruction.

You are like the meditative man
With the perfunctory heart; its
Carved cordiality ran
To and fro at first like an inlaid and royal
Immutable production;

Then afterward "neglected to be
Painful, deluding him with
Loitering formality,"
"Doing its duty as if it did it not,"
Presenting an obstruction

To the motive that it served. What stood
Erect in you has withered. A
Little "palm tree of turned wood"
Informs your once spontaneous core in its
Immutable production.

POETRY

I TOO, dislike it: there are things that are important beyond all this fiddle.
Reading it, however, with a perfect contempt for it, one discovers that there is in
it after all, a place for the genuine.
Hands that can grasp, eyes
that can dilate, hair that can rise
if it must, these things are important not because a

high sounding interpretation can be put upon them but because they are
useful; when they become so derivative as to become unintelligible,
the same thing may be said for all of us, that we
do not admire what
we cannot understand: the bat,
holding on upside down or in quest of something to

eat, elephants pushing, a wild horse taking a roll, a tireless wolf under
a tree, the immovable critic twitching his skin like a horse that feels a flea, the base-
ball fan, the statistician—
nor is it valid
to discriminate against "business documents and

school-books"; all these phenomena are important. One must make a distinction
however: when dragged into prominence by half poets, the result is not poetry,
nor till the poets among us can be
"literalists of
the imagination"—above
insolence and triviality and can present

for inspection, imaginary gardens with real toads in them, shall we have
it. In the meantime, if you demand on one hand,
the raw material of poetry in
all its rawness and
that which is on the other hand
genuine, then you are interested in poetry.

A TALISMAN

UNDER a splintered mast,
Torn from the ship and cast
Near her hull,

A stumbling shepherd found
Embedded in the ground,
A seagull

Of lapislazuli,
A scarab of the sea,
With wings spread—

Curling its coral feet,
Parting its beak to greet
Men long dead.

INDEX

A

B

C

G

H

I

L